D0547137

Social Machines

The Coming Collision of Artificial Intelligence, Social Networking, and Humanity

James Hendler
Alice M. Mulvehill

Apress®

Social Machines: The Coming Collision of Artificial Intelligence, Social Networking, and Humanity

James Hendler
Albany, New York, USA

Alice M. Mulvehill
Pittsburgh, Pennsylvania, USA

ISBN-13 (pbk): 978-1-4842-1157-1
DOI 10.1007/978-1-4842-1156-4

ISBN-13 (electronic): 978-1-4842-1156-4

Library of Congress Control Number: 2016950738

Copyright © 2016 by James Hendler and Alice M. Mulvehill

This work is subject to copyright. All rights are reserved by the Publisher, whether the whole or part of the material is concerned, specifically the rights of translation, reprinting, reuse of illustrations, recitation, broadcasting, reproduction on microfilms or in any other physical way, and transmission or information storage and retrieval, electronic adaptation, computer software, or by similar or dissimilar methodology now known or hereafter developed.

Trademarked names, logos, and images may appear in this book. Rather than use a trademark symbol with every occurrence of a trademarked name, logo, or image we use the names, logos, and images only in an editorial fashion and to the benefit of the trademark owner, with no intention of infringement of the trademark.

The use in this publication of trade names, trademarks, service marks, and similar terms, even if they are not identified as such, is not to be taken as an expression of opinion as to whether or not they are subject to proprietary rights.

While the advice and information in this book are believed to be true and accurate at the date of publication, neither the authors nor the editors nor the publisher can accept any legal responsibility for any errors or omissions that may be made. The publisher makes no warranty, express or implied, with respect to the material contained herein.

Managing Director: Welmoed Spahr
Lead Editor: Robert Hutchinson
Technical Reviewer: Lee Spector
Editorial Board: Steve Anglin, Pramila Balan, Laura Berendson, Aaron Black, Louise Corrigan,
    Jonathan Gennick, Robert Hutchinson, Celestin Suresh John, Nikhil Karkal,
    James Markham, Susan McDermott, Matthew Moodie, Natalie Pao, Gwenan Spearing
Coordinating Editor: Melissa Maldonado
Copy Editor: Mary Behr
Compositor: SPi Global
Indexer: SPi Global
Artist: SPi Global

Distributed to the book trade worldwide by Springer Science+Business Media New York, 233 Spring Street, 6th Floor, New York, NY 10013. Phone 1-800-SPRINGER, fax (201) 348-4505, e-mail orders-ny@springer-sbm.com, or visit www.springeronline.com. Apress Media, LLC is a California LLC and the sole member (owner) is Springer Science + Business Media Finance Inc (SSBM Finance Inc). SSBM Finance Inc is a **Delaware** corporation.

For information on translations, please e-mail rights@apress.com, or visit www.apress.com.

Apress and friends of ED books may be purchased in bulk for academic, corporate, or promotional use. eBook versions and licenses are also available for most titles. For more information, reference our Special Bulk Sales–eBook Licensing web page at www.apress.com/bulk-sales.

Any source code or other supplementary materials referenced by the author in this text are available to readers at www.apress.com/9781484211571. For detailed information about how to locate your book's source code, go to www.apress.com/source-code/. Readers can also access source code at SpringerLink in the Supplementary Material section for each chapter.

Printed on acid-free paper

Jim: To Marjorie Hendler, Terry Horowit, and Sharone Horowit-Hendler.

Alice: To Robert, Irwin, and Ray.

*Together: To Michael Dean, a much-missed colleague
and friend to us both.*

Contents at a Glance

Contents

About the Authors

James Hendler is the Director of the Institute for Data Exploration and Applications and the Tetherless World Professor of Computer, Web, and Cognitive Sciences at RPI. He also serves as a Director of the UK's charitable Web Science Trust. Hendler has authored over 350 books, technical papers, and articles in the areas of Semantic Web, artificial intelligence, agent-based computing, and high performance processing. One of the originators of the "Semantic Web," Hendler was the recipient of a 1995 Fulbright Foundation Fellowship, is a former member of the US Air Force Science Advisory Board, and is a Fellow of the American Association for Artificial Intelligence, the British Computer Society, the IEEE, and the AAAS. He is also the former Chief Scientist of the Information Systems Office at the US Defense Advanced Research Projects Agency (DARPA) and was awarded a US Air Force Exceptional Civilian Service Medal in 2002. He is also the first computer scientist to serve on the Board of Reviewing editors for *Science*. In 2010, Hendler was named one of the 20 most innovative professors in America by *Playboy* magazine and was selected as an "Internet Web Expert" by the US government. In 2012, he was one of the inaugural recipients of the Strata Conference "Big Data" awards for his work on large-scale open government data, and he is a columnist and associate editor of the *Big Data* journal. In 2013, he was appointed as the Open Data Advisor to New York State and in 2015 was appointed a member of the US Homeland Security Science and Technology Advisory Committee, and in 2016 became a member of the US National Academy Board on Research Data and Information.

Alice M. Mulvehill is a research scientist and provides consulting through her company, Memory Based Research, LLC. She was previously a lead scientist at Raytheon/BBN Technologies where she led the development of several advanced decision support systems for the Air Force and DARPA. Prior to joining BBN she worked for The MITRE Corporation as a researcher, specializing in knowledge acquisition, knowledge representation, case-based reasoning, and planning. While at MITRE she was part of early research teams that explored the use of Artificial Intelligence techniques for the development of planning and scheduling systems. She was a participant in the DARPA/Rome Lab Planning Initiative and participated in the development of operationally-oriented AI-based systems for DARPA, the Air Force, and NASA. She has authored or co-authored numerous technical papers in the areas of knowledge acquisition and representation, model development, and adaptation; case-based reasoning; Semantic Web technology; and applications of these technologies to support logistics, planning, and prediction. She is a senior member of the Association for Artificial Intelligence and a member of IEEE and ACM. She currently provides consulting services to support the research and development of advanced information system technology and has an adjunct position at the University of Pittsburgh's School of Nursing, where she provides guest lectures on technology. Mulvehill took her PhD in Information Science from the University of Pittsburgh.

About the Technical Reviewer

Lee Spector is a Professor of Computer Science at the School of Cognitive Science at Hampshire College in Amherst, Massachusetts, and an adjunct professor at the College of Information and Computer Sciences at the University of Massachusetts, Amherst. He received a B.A. in Philosophy from Oberlin College in 1984 and a Ph.D. from the Department of Computer Science at the University of Maryland in 1992. His areas of teaching and research include genetic and evolutionary computation, quantum computation, and a variety of intersections between computer science, cognitive science, evolutionary biology, and the arts. He is the Editor-in-Chief of the journal *Genetic Programming and Evolvable Machines* (published by Springer) and a member of the editorial board of *Evolutionary Computation* (published by MIT Press). He is also a member of the ACM SIGEVO executive committee, and he was named a Fellow of the International Society for Genetic and Evolutionary Computation.

Acknowledgments

This book represents many years of each of us working with many wonderful people who have been mentors, colleagues, students, friends, and so much more. To try to list everyone would be impossible, but there are a few people we'd each like to thank specifically for either directly supporting the writing of this book or for helping us to develop the knowledge that was required to put it together.

From Jim: I would like to thank Dr. Shirley Ann Jackson, who took the chance on bringing me to Rensselaer Polytechnic Institute (RPI) in 2007, freeing me to explore many new directions in AI and related fields. Through the RPI connection, I have met many members of the IBM Watson team, people working on Deep Learning and Cognitive Computing, and particularly Dr. John Kelly, whose book *Smart Machines: IBM's Watson and the Era of Cognitive Computing* (Columbia Business School Publishing, 2013) will be a wonderful companion volume to those who like this one. RPI also allowed me to create the "Tetherless World Research Constellation," with my great colleagues, Deborah McGuinness and Peter Fox. More recently, the Rensselaer Institute for Data Exploration and Applications has let me interact with VP of Research Jon Dordick and other Institute Wide Research Initiative leaders Chris Carothers, Robert Hull, Hui Su, and Deepak Vashishth (as well as all the Deans, department heads, program directors, faculty, and staff). I also want to thank many RPI staff but particularly Jacqueline Carley, Michele Murray, Melissa Anderson, and Tanya Rautine, without whom I'd be too busy doing paperwork to ever have found time to get this book done. I also want to thank Michele Owens, who gave me lots of great advice about writing a non-fiction book, and Andrew Hugill, for explaining the 'pataphysical aspect of much of this work. For two decades, I was at the University of Maryland, and I thank the many colleagues there who encouraged me as I rose through the academic ranks.

I also want to thank many colleagues who gave me inspiration in writing this book with respect to AI and social machines, these include: Guru Banavar, Sir Tim Berners-Lee, Selmer Bringsjord Noshir Contractor, David DeRoure, Ed Feigenbaum, Joan Feigenbaum, Jennifer Golbeck, Dame Wendy Hall, Subbarao Kambhampati, Jon Kleinberg, Beth Noveck, Sir Nigel Shadbolt, Elena Simperl, Ben Shneiderman, Frank van Harmelen, Luis von Ahn, Daniel Weitzner, and others I am sure I am forgetting (my apologies).

The Babylonian Talmud contains the following words of wisdom: "I learned much from my teachers, more from my colleagues, but from my students most of all" (Ta'anith 7a). That is totally true, and to list all the teachers and colleagues I should mention would take up too many pages. There's also not enough room to thank all my students[1], but I can't

---

[1] See my home page, www.cs.rpi.edu/~hendler, which lists the many PhD and masters students I have learned so much from!

imagine a better set of people to have worked so closely with over all these years. Finding funding for all the students has required support from many agencies and companies, with particular thanks to IBM, Lockheed Martin, BBN, Microsoft Research, Fujitsu Labs of America, Elsevier, GlobalFoundries, and The MITRE Corporation, who have directly funded my research over the years.

From Alice: I would like to thank the many people who have journeyed with me along my AI research path. First, I would like to acknowledge the members of the AI group that I was part of while at the The MITRE Corporation in Bedford, MA. We learned a lot from each other while having fun exploring the many new languages and tools of the day. I specifically want to thank Steve Christey who worked tirelessly with me to implement several systems. I would like to also thank my colleagues from BBN Technologies, especially Ted Kral and Ed Campbell who mentored and helped me to explore new domains. Although many of the people from BBN that I worked with both supported and influenced my work, without the excellent engineering and programming skills of Dave Rager, Clint Hyde, Mary Kennedy, and Brett Benyo many of my ideas would never have seen the light of day. I want to thank my many DARPA, NASA, and AFRL program managers for funding and belief in me. Lastly, I want to thank the many domain experts, you know who you are, who let me into their heads and helped me sufficiently understand their needs and computational styles so that my team could create sophisticated, yet useful AI systems.

Together: We would both like to thank many people who have supported our work over the years. A special thanks to David Brown who introduced us to each other and suggested we work together, and to Steve Cross, Nort Fowler, Don Roberts, and many others of the (D)Arpa/Rome Labs planning initiative, and our friends at Air Force Research Labs, and particularly Rick Metzger, who has worked with us both on many projects. Thanks also to our many colleagues, and funders, at the Army Research Laboratories, Office of Naval Research, Air Force Office of Scientific Research, National Science Foundation, NASA, NGA, NSA, DARPA, and IARPA.

We also thank the many people at Apress Media LLC who helped us in preparing the manuscript, especially Mark Powers, and our agent, Carole Jelen.

Finally, Jim adds this one: My best friend growing up, Jack Pressman, passed away way too early and isn't here to help me celebrate completion of this manuscript. Over two decades ago I told him if I ever got a book done I'd acknowledge our calculus teacher, Mr. Kurt Ritterman of Stuyvesant High School, so here's to him as well.

CHAPTER 1

■ ■ ■

Introduction: Why This Book?

It is often said that the expression "May you live in interesting times!" is an ancient Chinese curse. In reality this story is probably apocryphal, but the notion behind it is not: times of great change can produce great opportunities, but also significant personal stress or major societal upheaval. Many things can cause change, but technological innovation is often a facilitator. And one challenge for people during times of change is understanding the realities of these technologies. It is a tough challenge to separate out the hype generated by those who stand to gain financially and otherwise from the truth of what is actually being achieved. News media and social networking sites offer little help; the reporters are often no more versed in the technologies than the people for whom they are writing. The optimists among them see reasons for hope. The pessimists, reasons for fear. And the truth, when it is finally found, usually lies in a more nuanced space, somewhere between the two.

We are currently living in interesting times. While there are many reasons for this, this is definitely one of those eras where rapid technological advances are propelling the change. The past 50 years have increasingly seen the advance of computers into more and more of our lives, but the past decade or so has been exceptional. Computers have moved from our workspaces to our homes and now to our day-to-day lives. They have entered our social spaces to where they now can be found in our cars, our phones, and our houses. Personal assistant programs that used to require typing sentences into our desktop can now be invoked by name. Whether at home or away, inside or out, we have Siri, Alexa, and soon a new friend named Viv, who are becoming increasingly useful, but also increasingly ubiquitous. Getting Amazon's Alexa to turn off your bedroom lights no longer requires anything other than that you ask.

Propelling much of this increasing incursion of machines into our social lives are two interwoven technologies. The first is that of social networking; machines let us interact with friends, acquaintances, and even strangers through applications like Facebook, Twitter, Snapchat, RenRen, Weibo, and dozens of others. In the US, it is now said that upwards of 40% of those getting married met their spouses through an online dating site. Where restaurants used to ask patrons to turn off their computers, nowadays tablet devices are being built into the dining tables of even posh eateries to make it easier for their patrons to avoid going connectionless. Our social lives are increasingly connected, and that doesn't look like a trend that is going away anytime soon.

© James Hendler and Alice M. Mulvehill 2016
J. Hendler and A. M. Mulvehill, *Social Machines*, DOI 10.1007/978-1-4842-1156-4_1

However, for all their ubiquity, social networks still are primarily about allowing people to interact with each other. But that is changing; because of new breakthroughs in the field of artificial intelligence (AI), more and more the "person" on the other end of the connection is a computer. This includes technologies that allow computers to react to what people say, and to answer in increasingly natural and useful ways. Powered by AI, the IBM program Watson beat two of the world's best players at the famous television gameshow Jeopardy!. Powered by AI, a computer, programmed by a team from Google, recently beat one of the world's best players at the game of Go. Self-driving cars have gone from science fiction to daily reality, with over 30 automakers competing to see whose vehicles will be the first to be successfully sold without a steering wheel.

And indeed, the challenge in this time of change, as in so many others, is understanding these technologies and the realities of how they are impacting the world in which we live. It is *indeed* currently a challenge to separate out the hype generated by many companies big and small. News media sites *indeed* offer little help, as reporters struggle to understand the technologies. Optimists see reasons for hope; perhaps these new AI technologies will make life better for all of us; Pessimists, reasons for fear: is the robot apocalypse about to start?

The next decades are going to see major changes in society wrought by the increasingly connected nature of our social existence and the AI technology that is accelerating that change at a rapid rate. In this book, we hope to help you to understand enough about the AI technology underlying this disruption to navigate through these changing times. Those of you who tend towards the optimistic will learn enough to understand what is realistically promised. Those of you who tend towards the pessimist will see what some of the real challenges are. And indeed, the truth, for at least the foreseeable future, lies in a more nuanced space somewhere between the two, a space this book intends to help you find.

Who Are the Authors?

The idea of social networking long predates the computational systems currently in use. In the real world, meeting people through school, work, and community is a powerful way to bring together people, sometimes from disparate backgrounds, to share concepts and form relationships. Our collaboration on this book is due to such real world social networking. Our paths initially crossed in the early 1990s while we were both involved in a project sponsored by the US Department of Defense's research programs. We were working on a project called the (D)ARPA/Rome Laboratory Planning Initiative (ARPI)[1] and were asked by our sponsors to integrate the work that we were each independently doing.

We have continued to cross paths many times since then due to our mutual research interests in artificial intelligence and related topics such as networking, semantic markup, analysis, decision support technology, and big data. While we are both interested in building sophisticated, useful, and smart machines, our approaches and specialties are different, yet complementary; one is more focused on algorithms, mathematical

---

[1]Tate, Austin (Editor); "Advanced Planning Technology: Technological Achievements of the ARPA/ Rome Laboratory Planning Initiative", May 29-31, 1996, Edinburgh, Scotland. Published by The AAAI Press, Menlo Park, California.

formalisms, and big data, and the other is more focused on how AI and other technologies can work together to support humans. Where Jim's focus has been on building new technologies, Alice's has been on making sure those technologies can help real people solve the problems that confront them. Where Alice is also a talented artist, as you will see from many of her watercolors that grace the pages of this book, Jim's hobby is catching up on his e-mail and tinkering with the latest gadget his students have brought into the lab.

Yet despite, or maybe because of, our differences in perspective, we both felt it was time to write this book. This is because we each see an accelerating pace of societal change caused by the very technologies we have been working with for so long. The term *social machines* has been used to describe many things, and we will discuss them throughout the book, but most importantly, it represents the concept at the nexus of the increasing convergence of artificial intelligence, social networking, and human cognition. As the pace accelerates, these technologies, and their applications, come more and more into contact with each other and with us. Looking for a term that could convey the speed and impact of the changes we are living through, we hit upon the one that graces the title of this book: *collision*.

We see this potential clash between AI, social networking, and humanity because we have been part of the research that is forcing the collision. We hope that our different perspectives will provide the reader with a better understanding of what social machines in the future will look like, where they have come from, what some of the remaining problems are, and why we can't ignore the fact that this collision is already happening and that it will have profound impacts on our humanity.

Why Read This Book?

This book is intended to educate the reader about how tools and products, developed from the perspective of the science of AI, have been, are, and will continue to influence each of us as individuals. We will explore these technologies and how, through them, we interact with our environment (which now includes more and more of these intelligent computing devices), and how we interact with others (both the human and the artificial) within larger societal networks. We will describe how AI technologies are becoming more available and more capable because of improvements in hardware, software, and the infrastructure that these tools use for communication. This infrastructure is the World Wide Web, which has had a major impact on personal and social interactions. It has also enhanced communications between us and many different types of computing technologies, in effect creating an online society or social machine.

Using a computer or smartphone application to communicate and network with friends, family, colleagues, or the world in general is now a common practice. The current availability of many different types of computers and smartphones, and the ease of operation that is now provided, has resulted in our world being much more networked and "online." This ability to easily communicate with others in our society regardless of time, geographical location, and social or economic status is the basis of the social machine. Computer technology currently helps many of us to schedule meetings, share personal experiences and pictures, learn, play, and participate in discussions with people all over the world, and even with people that we don't personally know. In fact, many of us find it hard to go a day, let alone an hour, without checking our e-mail, texts, tweets, Facebook updates, and so on. We are already a wired society, and this computerized interface between us and the things in our lives, like our homes and cars, will continue to increase as the technology is enhanced and utilized.

As we look to the future, we see that our dependency on computer technology to support the many facets of our lives will also continue to increase. We are already accepting and even relying on technology that, just 10 years ago, we would never have readily used. As our trust in technology has increased, our tendency to use technology to help us travel, manage our finances, analyze medical results, navigate our cars, and schedule our lives has also increased. Many of these technologies are powered by AI, and as our dependency on technology evolves, we expect that more AI-based technologies will become available and incorporated into our lives. We are already starting to see AI-based, cognitive computing technology available for personal assistance and that is a trend that is going to continue at an accelerating pace.

While most people seem willing to embrace the benefits offered by our wired technology, many are not aware of how the technologies work, and of some of the potential problems that are not yet resolved. It is hard to understand why it is difficult for a computer to understand the context of a question or why it is important to ensure the privacy of an individual's personal data during online transactions. Most people do not understand what AI is and many are not even aware that they are already using AI-based tools. People who aren't computer professionals often have a view of AI that is based on what they have read in popular fiction and/or seen in movies, where the AI is often portrayed as a threat. Almost daily, there are news articles and online discussions that describe some of the pros and cons of AI. This has been true since the inception of the field. As late as the 1990s, writers like philosophers Hubert Dreyfus[2] and John Searle[3] and the physicist Roger Penrose[4] argued that AI was impossible and that researchers should stop wasting their time.

However, research has marched on, and in the past few years the criticisms of artificial intelligence have changed drastically. Critics have gone from worrying that we were wasting our time to worrying that we will succeed, and possibly succeed too well. While many researchers see the potential for AI to enrich our lives, many other people are being led to believe that the use of AI technology will lead to a future where humans are slaves to the machine. A popular question that comes up over and over again is whether AI is an existential threat to humanity. A May, 2016 discussion thread on the social question-answering website Quora asked this question, and drew hundreds of answers that were read by thousands of people[5]. Where the physicist Roger Penrose asked if AI was possible, less than 20 years later his most famous student, Stephen Hawking, stated in a 2014 interview with the BBC that "the development of full artificial intelligence could spell the end of the human race!"[6] In two decades, critics have gone from arguing we shouldn't pursue AI because it is impossible to arguing that we shouldn't do AI because it isn't!

As we hinted at earlier, we are convinced that the truth lies somewhere in between. While it is easy to argue philosophy, the truth is much more complicated. AI can do, and

---

[2]Dreyfus, H., "What Computers Still Can't Do", MIT Press, 1972.
[3]Searle, J., "The Chinese Room Argument", April 9, 2014, Stanford Encyclopedia of Philosophy, http://plato.stanford.edu/entries/chinese-room/.
[4]Penrose, R., "The Emperor's New Mind", Oxford New University Press, 1989.
[5]www.quora.com/Is-A-I-an-existential-threat-to-humanity
[6]www.bbc.com/news/technology-30290540

does, some amazing things that can benefit mankind. The growing partnership of humans and computers working together has huge potential for good. It also, however, will inevitably cause social disruption and without people understanding its limits, the potential for harm is also high. Decisions will need to be made in the coming years that will have significant impact on our lives, and thus being aware of the trade-offs inherent in this technology space is important to understanding the world in which we will increasingly be living.

In short, we believe that being AI knowledgeable is crucial to future online life. Thus, one of the main purposes of this book is to help you better understand AI, social networking, and some related technologies so that you can better understand, and more importantly, help to shape the social machines of the future. In this book, we will discuss how AI technology has evolved, what it can do, and what its limits are. We will describe how humans can benefit from using machines and how machines can benefit from interactions with humans. We also describe how the integration between AI and other technologies, particularly social networking, has become a mainstay in our daily lives and provide examples of how this cross-fertilization of technologies has the potential to benefit humanity. We will also look at the potential harm that, uncontrolled and unchallenged, it could do. By understanding the technology, we hope you, the reader, will be better able to make the decisions as to which paths to take and how we will get there.

A Brief History of AI

Numerous books have been written about the field of AI, including the provocatively named *AI: The Tumultuous History of the Search for Artificial Intelligence* by Daniel Crevier.[7] In this section, we offer an abbreviated history that focuses primarily on the themes that we will be revisiting throughout the book, in order to give the reader an idea of the roots from which they derive. (Note that to save space, we omit many of the people and discoveries in the AI field.)

Artificial intelligence is a branch of computer science that researches and develops theories, algorithms, and methodologies about the design and construction of "intelligent reasoning systems." The term *artificial intelligence* to describe the emerging research discipline is often credited to a meeting that was held in 1956 at Dartmouth College in Hanover, New Hampshire.[8] (Terms such as *machine intelligence, thinking machines*, and other such descriptions go back further, and particularly in the UK, the field was already becoming controversial by the time of the US meeting). At this summer-long workshop, discussions focused on several aspects of AI problems, including a number of questions that will be discussed in this book:

- Whether automatic computers of enough power to emulate the human brain could be developed (hardware aspects)

- Whether artificial neural networks based on the architecture of the human brain might be designed

---

[7]Crevier, Daniel. *AI: The tumultuous history of the search for artificial intelligence*. Basic Books, Inc., 1993.
[8]McCarthy, J., Minsky, M., Rochester, N., and Shannon, C., "A Proposal for the Dartmouth Summer Research Project on Artificial Intelligence", August 31, 1955, in *AI Magazine*, Vol. 27, No. 4, 2006.

- How a computer could be programmed to use a human language

- How a computer could play games like checkers, chess, and Go

- Whether a computer might be able to learn concepts, form abstractions, improve its performance, generate plans, deal with randomness, or be creative

Many of the participants at the meeting, both organizers and students, are now considered the founders of the field, and went on to direct and influence the development of a variety of AI-based systems and algorithms.

Early research in AI was often partitioned by two dominant philosophical approaches. One approach (often attributed to Allen Newell and Herbert Simon[9]) advocated that AI programs should be able to solve problems in ways that mimicked human problem solving. The other main approach (with primary proponent John McCarthy[10]) argued that the computer's approach and the algorithms it uses do not need to replicate human cognitive mechanisms, as evidenced in many of the early AI programs that could play checkers, chess, and other games. McCarthy argued in particular for the use of formal logics as the basis of building intelligent systems.

The AI researchers who were trying to build computer programs that could solve problems like humans investigated how humans process sensory, perceptual, and cognitive data. Learning methods that are employed by humans, like pattern recognition, were used to program computers to analyze visual scenes (Oliver Selfridge[11], Marvin Minsky[12]) and to classify objects and learn concepts (Earl Hunt[13]). Human neurological methods were used as the basis for learning theories (Donald Hebb[14]), to build classifiers (John Holland[15]), and to develop general machine learning methods (Geoff Hinton[16]). The way that humans use language was used to develop natural language understanding theories and programs like Terry Winograd's SHRDLU[17] or Roger Schank's MARGIE.

Human problem-solving techniques and cognitive psychology research was also the basis for the development of early automated general problem solving tools and expert systems (Ed Feigenbaum[18]). Other approaches investigated the relationship of an artificial reasoning entity to a larger self-organizing system that, like the human brain,

---

[9]Simon, H. A., and Newell, A., "Human Problem Solving: The State of the Theory in 1970"; Carnegie Mellon University, Pittsburgh, PA.

[10]www-formal.stanford.edu/jmc/whatisai/, Stanford University, 2007.

[11]Selfridge, O. G., "Pandemonium: A paradigm for Learning", National Physical Laboratory, Symposium, No. 10, 1958.

[12]Minsky, Marvin and Papert, Seymour; *Perceptrons. An Introduction to Computational Geometry.* M.I.T. Press, Cambridge, Mass., 1969.

[13]Hunt, Earl; "Concept Formation", Encyclopedia Britannica, www.britannica.com/topic/concept-formation.

[14]Hebb, Donald; *The Organization of Behavior*, Wiley and Sons, NY, 1949.

[15]Holland, John, "Complex Adaptive Systems", *Daedalus*; Winter 1992; 121, 1; Research Library, page 17.

[16]Hinton, G. E. (2014); "Where do features come from?", *Cognitive Science*, Vol. 38(6), pp 1078-1101.

[17]Winograd, T., SHRDLU, 1968 (described at http://hci.stanford.edu/winograd/shrdlu/).

[18]http://amturing.acm.org/award_winners/feigenbaum_4167235.cfm, 1994.

could adapt to its environment by using feedback based on seminal earlier work by John Von Neumann[19] or cybernetic control, inspired by the 1940s work of Norbert Wiener[20]. Some of this research was used in early robots, including a famous project led by Nils Nilsson that created a robot named Shakey[21] that could use limited information about its environment, coupled with AI planning technology, to coordinate movement and perform simple tasks.

Building a cognitive computational machine that can interact with a person in multiple contexts and efficiently support problem solving is challenging and requires the expertise of researchers from many different disciplines. For example, the social machines described in this book are the result of the integration of ideas and constructs from AI, engineering, cognitive science, social science, language processing, mathematics, etc.

While the current field of AI is diverse, the following six areas have been and continue to be the primary foci of the discipline:

- Vision

- Robotics

- Natural Language

- Machine Learning

- Automated Planning Systems and Automated Programming

- Rule-Based Expert Systems

Much of the research in each of these main AI focus areas initially met with failure, although, as with most new technologies, results learned from the failures led to new approaches. In fact, many of these failures resulted from the fact that some the early AI theories and ideas were ahead of the computational technologies that were available at the time. A number of approaches that were considered failures because they were too difficult to successfully implement when they were first proposed are now being realized because of substantial changes in software, hardware, and communication technology. In fact, many of the increasingly successful programs that grew out of these early false starts will be the very approaches we discuss in later chapters.

Social Machines

Many early AI systems were developed to support a single user or to replace a user doing a task that was repetitive, boring, or complex but solvable (that is, one that was straightforward, but could take a human a long time to solve). Others were exploring whether AI could be used to support a group of users who were collaboratively solving a problem. As computers and communication technology, and particularly the Internet and later the World Wide Web, became more available and reliable, people increasingly used computers to communicate and share information. In some cases, the computer

---

[19]Von Neumann, J., *The Computer and the Brain*, Yale University Press, 1958.
[20]Wiener, N., *Cybernetics: or Control and Communication in the Animal and the Machine*, Boston, MA: Technology Press, 1948.
[21]http://www.ai.sri.com/shakey/; https://en.wikipedia.org/wiki/Shakey_the_robot

functioned simply as a means for people to communicate; in others, the computer became an essential part of that communication, facilitating people's information sharing. Around 1999, Tim Berners-Lee, the inventor of the World Wide Web, wrote that we were seeing the early days of the growth of "social machines," where computers would perform administrative tasks and provide support to enable people who would do the creative work.[22] Others used the term differently, to refer to social networking sites like the modern Facebook and Twitter, which allow social interactions at scale, but are only possible because of the advances in computing that allowed the large scale of interactions that they support.

We will use the phrase *social machines* in this book in two ways. First, we refer to the increasing ability that Artificial Intelligence provides to enable computers to interact in ways that have traditionally been considered the social space of humans only. This includes personal assistants on our phones, AI-based devices that monitor homes or other spaces to increase safety, and other applications like systems that use AI techniques to help medical personnel to improve the care they deliver. This will be our primary use of the term for Chapters 2 through 6. In Chapter 7, we will more closely explore the definition used by Berners-Lee and modern systems where humans and computers working together are creating systems of amazing power and complexity.

Social machines of the future will continue to provide people, individually and collectively, with the ability to immerse themselves in accumulated knowledge. However, the constant interactions of humankind, not just as passive recipients of information created by others but also as contributors to a global information space, will become a capability that is far beyond that of today's Web. In looking to this future, we think not primarily in terms of the cyber-infrastructure of high-speed supercomputers and their networked interconnections, but of the even more powerful human interactions these underlying systems enable, such as personalized support through cognitive support technology and other smart devices.

AI technologies are enabled by and enable smart devices. They are fast becoming active participants in the social machine. They help people solve big problems on a personal level (me, my health, daily existence), at the community level (crime, traffic), and those facing mankind (clean air, clean water, global warming). Many problems cannot be solved solely by the work of a single individual (including me in my context) or by the magic of machines. Some problems require the creativity of (multiple) humans (crowdsourcing) scaled with the power of (multiple) machines.

In this book, we describe how this future generation of social machines can take AI researchers and others into the design of new algorithms and interfaces, into new approaches for distributed inference and query, and into developing new kinds of social machinery, including policy-aware systems of privacy, trust, and accountability.

Risks and Challenges

As mentioned earlier, while these powerful technologies have exciting new uses, they also come with new risks and challenges. AI computing technologies are gaining successes and are fast becoming integral to our lives. However, every day articles in newspapers,

---

[22]Berners-Lee, Tim, and Fischetti, Mark. *Weaving the Web: The original design and ultimate destiny of the World Wide Web by its inventor*. HarperInformation, 2000.

blogs, magazines, and professional journals raise questions about if and how AI technologies should evolve. Some of these articles describe the ever increasing number of products and tools that are being developed and rapidly becoming available to support humans in a variety of daily needs and personal tasks. Some articles and discussions present a frightening view of how AI will change the way we live, our society, and maybe even end our lives. For us to understand the threats, we need to understand the AI systems and how they work.

In the not so distant future, AI tools will help us to make all types of decisions. Personal AI assistants will become increasingly common. However, in order for these assistants to better serve us, they need to understand our individual preferences and options. Most AI tools will likely learn about us by observing our behaviors, especially the behaviors that we exhibit in our online lives. As our personal AI tools learn about us, so too can other AI-based tools that might belong to commercial, government, or even adversarial entities. In order to have a better future online life and to be able to trust that our AI tools will do things that benefit us, each of us, as well as the developers, distributors, and/or managers of AI, tools need to have mechanisms in place to protect our privacy and reduce the chance that we could suffer because of information that some adversarial entity could obtain.

And this is the most important reason we had for writing this book. As exciting as this technology is, with great potential for good, it also has this potential to disrupt society as we know it today. If we are to steer the technologies between the benefits it can bring and the challenges it can create, our society needs to seriously think about and build a set of standards and policies that guide the development of these technologies. Rather than being afraid of this coming collision, we believe that people need to become more knowledgeable about what AI can, and more importantly, cannot (currently) do if we are going to make smart decisions, as individuals and as a society, as to when, where, and why we should use, or limit, these powerful technologies.

What Lies Ahead for the Reader

In this book, we look at what things people are good at and what their limitations are; we also do the same for machines. In the following chapters, we explore many topics that will help the reader better understand how AI and social networking have and will continue to affect humanity.

In Chapter 2, we use healthcare as an example to help the reader better understand the kinds of technologies that are being used now and in the not too distant future. We describe how healthcare is changing because of improvements in hardware, software, and advanced computing technologies like AI. Our discussion explores how sensor-enable devices like Fitbits are helping people manage their own health. We also describe how cognitive technologies like Watson, IBM's premier AI system, and others like it, are helping doctors fight cancer and diagnose complex diseases. We explore how web technology is being used to help patients better understand their illnesses together. Although we do highlight some potential problems, like loss of patient privacy, we save these particular challenges for a later chapter, focusing here on the improvements in health that are coming in the next few years. We also talk about how the blurring of the role between medical practitioners and computing technology will influence the future of our healthcare and the health of an aging population.

In Chapter 3, we provide a more fundamental background in how AI systems work. To do this, we focus on how AI has been used to play games, an area where it has largely excelled. We pull back the curtain to reveal how AI algorithms are used by machines to play different types of games including checkers, chess, tic-tac-toe, backgammon, poker, and the more complicated game of Go, which has only recently been successfully tackled by AI systems. We also provide a glimpse into how AI researchers have been able to incorporate observations about human strategies into their computer programs. The chapter also describes differences between the way machines play games and the way humans play those same games, with the goal of illuminating some of the differences between the artificial nature of AI systems and the more natural intelligence with which we humans are blessed.

In Chapter 4, we explore why people may need AI. We describe some human limitations, including issues with problem solving, particularly during emotional or stressful situations, and limitations such as memory loss and social isolation that often occur in advanced age. Then, in Chapter 5, we look at the limitations of machines. We talk about why it is hard for computers to accurately understand human language or to understand what they see. We also explore new capabilities in perception and why, despite recent successes, computers still lag behind humans when it comes to "understanding" that which we perceive. Taken together, these two chapters show the strengths and limitations of humans and computers compared to each other.

In Chapter 6, we discuss how, given the different capabilities of humans and machines, AI can help humans in many ways (and *vice versa*). We present background on how interfaces are designed to support human-computer interaction, and discuss future AI and other augmentation devices that show how interface technology must change in order for humans to have a more symbiotic relationship with the machines. We also discuss the future of personalized AI assistants and describe how they will need to be trained and how they might be used. We also foreshadow the later Chapter 8 with a caution about some of the problems that still need to be resolved in AI technology in order for these types of tools to become reliable assistants.

In Chapter 7, we describe Metcalfe's law of how networks work as multipliers, and particularly how this applies for humans aided by machines. Examples are presented that showcase how various aspects of crowdsourcing have been used to create online knowledge (Wikipedia) and to support humanitarian needs, such as providing quick disaster relief when natural disasters occur or dealing with social problems in the offline world. This chapter also includes examples of citizen science, showcasing how humans can help machines learn more. The chapter includes more detailed explanations about two modern AI technologies, deep learning and Watson, and describes how these technologies are still dependent on humans for much of their power. We also speculate about the potential power of the combined networks of humans and machines, and how the future of social machines technologies may evolve.

In Chapter 8, we look at some of the dangers that unregulated usage of these new technologies can create. We describe the need for better methods to protect human data privacy, ethical issues with using smart autonomous devices like autonomous drones, and how the social machine can be a two-sided sword, providing benefits for many, yet potentially enabling people with nefarious intentions. New kinds of governments and governance for our online communities are also discussed.

Finally, in Chapter 9, we summarize what we have discussed and describe some of the trends that are emerging and the decisions that you will now be able to make in a more informed way, having read all of the above.

What This Book Is Not About

Robots.

For many people, when they think about artificial intelligence they immediately think (some fondly, some in fear) about mechanical humans who may someday live among us. That may or may not be, but without the cognitive aspects of AI to guide the robots' behaviors, they are like a human without a brain. The social aspects we describe for machines are also relevant to robots; the technologies discussed in Chapter 6 are crucial for robots to interact with humans in non-artificial ways. Without being powered by the technologies we discuss, robots would lurch around without aim, randomly interacting with people and things—not a pretty concept. We absolutely agree that the technologies underlying the bodies and mechanics of robots are truly fascinating, and there are many books that can help you learn more about them,[23] but our focus is on the coming revolution in cognitive AI: the part that thinks, not the part that moves.

---

[23]For example, our publisher has an entire series that includes many excellent books on the topic; go to www.apress.com/robots-and-electronics/robots.

CHAPTER 2

▓ ▓ ▓

Who Will Be Your Next Doctor?

As we've just explored, a revolution in artificial intelligence has been occurring, powered by factors including massive amounts of data, faster machines with much more storage and processing capability, and web-based information collection. This is leading to new capabilities that are starting to impact information technologies across the board. We see new capabilities in the search engines and social networks that enable people in many different situations, whether professional or personal, to better use current applications. We also see emerging applications in areas like health, mobility (traffic and driving), business, and almost anything that is aimed at helping human beings be more productive, healthier and, in some cases, even happier. Speech input is becoming more prevalent, moving from the much-maligned voice-based telephone assistant ("please say your ten-digit identification number so I can check your records") to the speech recognizers that are currently available on your cell phone or in your car to help you to search for local restaurants or find the nearest ATM to make a withdrawal. Looking ahead, we see continued growth of technologies like these, and new ways in which they may be able to have a more profound influence on our lives.

In this chapter, we're going to explore an area where technology is having, and will continue to have, a major impact on our lives. This area is healthcare.

Going to the Doctor

Let's consider an example most of us are very familiar with: going to a doctor. Currently, our doctors tend to use computers primarily for record-keeping, diagnostic testing, billing, and prescribing care. But this is rapidly changing. In a 2004 directive by then-President Bush, a goal was set to have interoperable electronic healthcare records in place by 2014. In 2009, the Health Information Technology for Economic and Clinical Health (HITECH) Act was signed into law to promote the adoption and meaningful use of health technology. According to statistics provided in a 2013 *Wall Street Journal* article[1], there has been a monumental increase in the number of medical applications available to health professionals as well as

---

[1]Landro, Laura, "The Doctor's Team Will See You Now", *Wall Street Journal*, February 17, 2014.

© James Hendler and Alice M. Mulvehill 2016
J. Hendler and A. M. Mulvehill, *Social Machines*, DOI 10.1007/978-1-4842-1156-4_2

to the individual. The article reports that the number of unique mobile devices (worldwide) that access medical applications increased from one million in 2011 to close to four million in 2013 (and this number has certainly increased significantly since then).

Since the introduction of the HITECH Act, more healthcare companies are designing methods to access data that is collected by personal health applications like those of a Fitbit or other web- or phone-based health applications for use by the individual or for integration with larger healthcare applications for use by medical professionals. In addition, more and more people are going to the Web for information to help them evaluate a medical condition and to decide whether to see a doctor. As a result, we are seeing a trend by healthcare organizations to provide nursing staff and patients with recommendations about what web sites can be trusted, or to provide their own web services to help the patient better understand a diagnosis or test result. As these trends continue, where do they take us?

Let's consider what is involved in visiting a doctor. When you walk into a doctor's office, the administrative staff either enters data into a patient record form (if you are a new patient) or they look up and confirm the information they already have about you, including your name, date of birth, and insurance information. Once you have been checked into the office, you are examined by a nurse, who collects some basic health information, such as weight, blood pressure, and so on. When the doctor sees you, she looks at the information in the database and then provides a more thorough investigation of your health. In general, the doctor who is examining you is not only picking up on the symptoms you describe, she is also making some evaluations based on how you look, how you sound, what she hears when you say "ahhhh," and much more. This is because doctors have learned medicine in a number of ways. Although they've had a lot of book learning and memorized a lot of facts (not so easy for humans), they've also spent many hours looking at cases, working as interns and residents, and practicing medicine. As a result of their formal education and incremental experience, they have honed their intuition about patients and patient care. This is actually an amazing example of how good humans are at learning from experience and how human memory works.

But doctors face an impossible challenge: every year new medical knowledge grows. According to some of the best estimates, there were well over a million papers published in scientific journals in 2014, with the biggest percentage being in the medical and life science areas. Many doctors, especially specialists, keep up to date with the literature and attend conferences. However, when puzzled by symptoms and test results that don't lead to an obvious diagnosis, what's the probability that he or she has read the one paper in that huge stack that will give them the understanding they need, and what's the chance that they remember reading the crucial fact in that particular paper?

This is where the emerging computer technologies tied to AI could have a profound effect. First, computers are indeed able to both store and process those many papers. Because of advances in AI technology, they are getting better and better at extracting information from texts, achieving some level of "understanding" of their content, and linking information from diverse sources, including your electronic healthcare record, medical literature, and discussions in health-related blogs and forums. How can these advanced computer capabilities support a doctor in a timely way and be used to help the doctor evaluate the symptoms of a unique individual? If you are using wearable or personal applications to collect data, how much of your personalized data might you need to share with these applications to enable the sophisticated AI reasoning agents of this technology to operate?

Could an Intelligent Computer Be Your Next Doctor?

Let's look at an actual (but simplified) example of a patient receiving healthcare today, and then consider how the patient's care might be provided in a future where the next generation of artificially intelligent tools are employed.

Consider this case: a previously healthy young patient, who had recently been given a diagnosis of anemia, subsequently developed a seemingly straightforward skin infection. Then, in the span of a few weeks, his clinical condition deteriorated rapidly with systematic shutdown of one organ after another, culminating in an untimely death. This occurred despite state-of-the-art critical care services including multiple consultants, repeated laboratory testing, aggressive radiologic examinations, and invasive diagnostic procedures. In addition, the patient received care at one of the best hospitals in America. To this day, it is still unclear exactly what happened medically.

Instead of exploring the specific details of this medical situation, let's look at how this sort of case is handled currently and what AI technologies might offer in the near future.

The Situation Today

In many situations, including the medical one described here, a number of separate stakeholders are involved, often with very different goals. In the case of this patient, multiple medical specialists are trying to figure out what is wrong, each focusing on the signs and symptoms related to their area of specialization. Depending on the facility and the country this is occurring in, these specialists may be working separately and communicating directly with the patient's family, each other, or with a coordinating physician; or the specialists may meet periodically to consult and compare notes. Even in this latter case, which is happily becoming more common nowadays under the name of *team-based care*, time is at a premium. Additionally, while doctors often have access to the special tools and technologies of their specialties, their fact finding is generally carried out and recorded separately. If all of the specialists are part of the same healthcare facility, and if that facility has a computerized electric healthcare system in place that each of the specialists can access, then the doctors will be able to share published test results and notes. Otherwise, collaboration, when it occurs, will tend to be based primarily on discussion, instead of shared information or visualizations.

In many cases, one or more of these doctors might hit on the correct diagnosis or treatment, and the patient could be cured; but this is not always the case, as in the situation with this young patient. Could better computer tools that exploit AI technology help make a difference?

The Not Too Distant Future

Let's consider one aspect of this patient's condition: a skin infection. Skin infections are often considered a "secondary diagnosis." Therefore, it is natural that this dermatological issue would be given less attention than the patient's anemia and his escalating organ problems. However, in recent years there has been increasing evidence that secondary skin infections are correlated with a number of medical conditions. In fact, in the past decade, the number of medical papers that have discussed skin infection has skyrocketed. *Pubmed* is a US government-sponsored resource that collects citations and pointers to millions of articles in the fields of biomedicine, life science, healthcare, and related areas. Searching *Pubmed* using the search term "skin infections" in 2016 returns over 1,500 papers (going back to as early as 1905) that specifically mention "skin infection." However, well over half of these results have been published since 2005. As if this isn't enough, medical papers on skin infection may not use that term, and instead use terms referring to

- specific aspects of skin infections described by common terms such as "carbuncles" or "boils"

- particular kinds of skin infections known by their medical names such as "erysipelas" or "sporotrichosis"

- other information that is associated with the diagnosis or treatment of these conditions, such as specific types of examinations or tests

If we include all of these other terms in a *Pubmed* search, the number of returned hits grows into the tens of thousands of papers, again with the great bulk published in recent years. It is possible that one of these papers would have given our patient's doctors the information needed to make a timely diagnosis followed by an effective treatment. However, the current search tools that are generally available on the Internet are not very useful to doctors looking for this kind of information. Searches with these general search tools tend to retrieve pages for non-specialists, such as WebMD or the medical pages in Wikipedia.

Doctors are encouraged to use specialized medical search tools like *Pubmed*, which will find papers aimed specifically at the medical community and can respond to more complex searches. For example, if we add "anemia" to our initial *Pubmed* search for "skin infections," the number of returned documents drops to below 100 papers. However, even this number is high, and the search engines just identify the papers. It would be prohibitively time-consuming for a medical professional to read all the recent papers that might be relevant to the current case, not to mention all the other cases they are treating at the same time.

Cognitive Computing Technology

In the near future, we will see an increase in the development of systems that employ cognitive computing technology to help medical professionals, such as doctors, search for and utilize online data sources. The term *cognitive computing* has been used in different ways by different communities over time. Under one definition, *cognitive computing systems* are computer programs built by researchers trying to imitate how people reason to solve problems. A cognitive computing system of this profile, when looking at our medical problem, would want to know how the doctors are thinking about it, and then use that knowledge to solve problems.

But another meaning of the term *cognitive computing* has recently become more popular following the 2011 demonstration by IBM of a computer named Watson beating two of the world's best human players on a special edition of the game show Jeopardy! In contrast to earlier expert systems (discussed in the introduction), which tried to encode the knowledge needed to solve hard problems, Watson uses a wide variety of web sources to try to reason about the many, many things that the game show could ask about. (We will revisit Watson later in this book and look at how it works and why it could play the game so well).

Recent work in cognitive computing takes the ideas of Watson, advances in cognitive science, and some of the ideas from expert systems (also referred to as *decision support systems*) to create systems that, in the words of IBM, "learn and interact naturally with people to extend what either humans or machines could do on their own." This approach is being explored in a number of areas, and not just by IBM. One area getting a lot of attention is healthcare. Clinical decision support systems (a modern name for an expert system) have been developed to support healthcare since the early 1970s. An early example is INTERNIST-I, which was a rule-based expert system designed at the University of Pittsburgh in 1974 for the diagnosis of complex problems in general internal medicine.[2] It uses patient observations that are entered by a doctor to deduce a list of compatible disease states (based on a tree-structured database that links diseases with symptoms). Another example of a clinical decision support system is called DXplain[3]. This system was initially developed by the Laboratory of Computer Science at the Massachusetts General Hospital in 1984. DXplain uses a set of clinical findings (signs, symptoms, laboratory data) to produce a ranked list of diagnoses that might explain (or be associated with) clinical manifestations. DXplain provides justification for why each of these diseases might be considered, suggests what further clinical information would be useful to collect for each disease, and lists what clinical manifestations, if any, would be unusual or atypical for each of the specific diseases. The DXplain knowledge base includes 2,400 diseases and 5,000 symptoms in its KB. This system is still in use today. In addition, AI is being used in medicine in a variety of ways[4], and AI-based tools are currently being developed to help doctors collect data, and to analyze the potentially massive amount of data that is expected to be collected by a variety of real-time monitoring devices that are rapidly becoming available to support the individual, the home, and healthcare environments[5].

Rather than being dependent on a fixed knowledge base or constrained to general search, a doctor in the not too distant future will be able to use a cognitive computing system to input the description of the patient's signs and symptoms, much as they do today, and the computer will try to correlate the patient data with the information that is available in many data sources, including knowledge bases, blogs, chats, doctor's notes, and those thousands of papers discussed earlier. As it finds potentially relevant passages, it will rate them in terms of how likely they are to be of value to the doctor for a particular case, and will make the doctor aware of the most relevant findings.

Researchers today are working on a future doctor's information system, which has this kind of technology integrated. Once the patient information is entered, the doctor would be shown several ranked diagnosis possibilities, along with the rationale for each

---

[2]Miller, R., Pople, J., and Myers, J., "INTERNIST-1, An Experimental Computer Based Diagnostic Consultant for General Internal Medicine," *New England Journal of Medicine*, Vol 307, 1982 pp. 468–476.

[3]www.mghlcs.org/projects/dxplain/

[4]Ramesh, AN, Kambhampati, C., Monson, JRT, and Drew, PJ, "Artificial Intelligence in Medicine", *Annals of the Royal College of Surgeons of England*, 2004, 86.

[5]Daniel, Neill, "Using Artificial Intelligence to improve Hospital Inpatient Care", *IEEE Intelligent Systems*, 2 (2013): 92–95.

diagnosis. The top few diagnoses may be similar to what was learned in medical school or to results that are available from clinical decision support tools. For example, anemia and skin infections of certain types co-occur often in the case of an iron deficiency. If the doctor and the machine are in agreement, the doctor could check accepted findings. As the doctor enters more information, the computer may be able to use this information to discover literature that the doctor may not have seen, and suggest questions for the doctor to ask the patient. For example, the computer might suggest that the doctor ask the patient if they are having headaches. If the answer is negative, the computer might determine that this situation is slightly unusual for iron deficiency, but isn't that rare. If the patient mentions to the doctor that he's been bruising more easily than usual, the doctor might conclude that this isn't that rare for anemia, and might continue to believe that the symptoms are most likely associated with an iron deficiency.

The computer, on the other hand, when provided with the additional patient information, may discover that bruising is also a common symptom of a more dangerous but comparatively rare form of the disease leukemia called erythroleukemia. While anemia, skin infection, and bruising are all things that occur in this rarer disease, headaches typically are not a symptom. As a result, the computer will start to raise the probability of the rarer disease, and perhaps slightly lower the probability estimate of the more common iron deficiency problem. The computer might also recommend to the doctor that additional, specific tests be performed on the patient in order to gather more evidence to support the diagnosis.

As more symptoms are reported, and perhaps medical test results come in, the computer may detect that there is more evidence for the leukemia, yet perhaps no change in evidence for iron deficiency. This could cause the computer system to start to search the medical literature for papers that might include more information on the rarer disease. Let's assume that it discovers the paper titled "E-cadherin is a specific marker for erythroid differentiation and has utility, in combination with CD117 and CD34, for enumerating myeloblasts in hematopoietic neoplasms" in the *American Journal of Clinical Pathology* that is relatively new. In this paper, it is noted that a specific protein is associated with this disease. If at this point in the treatment a screening had been done and that protein found, the system would raise the erythroleukemia to the top of the list and perhaps send an alert to the doctor about the change. The doctor would be able to examine how the cognitive computing system arrived at this conclusion by clicking on a "why" button. The system can explain its evidence because it keeps track of all of the papers and data sources that it used to arrive at the conclusion. The rationale presented to the doctor might include the following excerpt from the paper:

Of 84 cases of AML, including cases with megakaryocytic, erythroid, monocytic, and granulocytic differentiation, all five acute erythroleukemia cases were positive, as well as one case of megakaryoblastic leukemia that showed coexpression of glycophorin A. In addition, we demonstrate that a panel of three markers, E-cadherin, CD117, and CD34, is effective in identifying lineage-specific myeloblasts in cases of MDS where left-shifted erythroid hyperplasia may complicate morphologic assessment of myeloblasts.

The system will also inform the doctor that this is information that has been reported recently. In order to validate the recommendation from the computer, the doctor may recommend additional tests or refer the patient to someone more knowledgeable about erythroleukemia. With the help of the cognitive computing system, the real cause of the patient's symptoms might be noticed much earlier and perhaps result in a different outcome for this patient.

Alternatively, let's assume that the computer finds multiple papers that don't seem to agree: some support the iron deficiency diagnosis and others the erythroleukemia diagnosis. In cases like this, the system might decide to highlight the disparities between the signs and symptoms of the candidate diagnoses, offer the available evidence for each, and recommend that a particular test be performed to support a definitive diagnosis.

In the case of conflicting evidence, the human doctor's knowledge and judgment again becomes important. For example, suppose that the recommended test was expensive, invasive, or had a potentially serious side effect. In this case, the doctor might choose to pursue the hypothesis of iron deficiency, prescribing an iron supplement that is readily available in drug stores. However, knowing that the serious disease was still a possibility (thanks to the cognitive system), the doctor might schedule a return visit sooner or warn the patient to come back right away if certain other symptoms occur. The computer's ability to find specific and detailed knowledge in the medical literature combined with the doctor's more general knowledge, experience, and judgment will offer a powerful combination for the future of patient care. The doctor alone might have missed a potentially deadly disease until it was too late. The computer alone may have recommended expensive or invasive tests. The two working together, however, could result in the best of both worlds: the patient is spared the tests and emotional trauma in the case where it is the more common disease, but possibly spared the worst outcome if the erythroleukemia is diagnosed early thanks to artificial intelligence programs that allowed for the computer's intervention.

From Individual to Network

Researchers are now exploring the idea of incorporating cognitive computing technologies into a *diagnostic theatre* where medical personnel can request information from the computer and see it jointly in a collaborative environment. Figure 2-1 shows the kind of immersive environment envisioned for this kind of work. In this figure, a group of medical personnel are examining some high-definition images associated with a patient. The board offers them the ability to navigate and explore what they are finding.

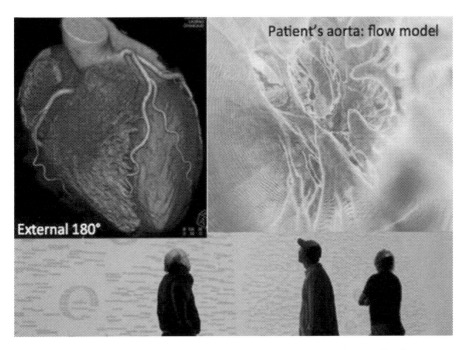

Figure 2-1. *A simulated view of a future immersive environments where medical professionals, aided by cognitive computing, will be able to collaboratively explore a patient's situation. (Shared by permission of Rensselaer Polytechnic Institute Cognitive and Immersive Systems Laboratory.)*

One drawback of this kind of technology is that it requires the medical team to be together in one place at one time. Another approach being explored offers similar capabilities through web-based technology where doctors who are located in different places can basically use a form of telecommunication to collaborate across the Web and share images, records, etc. New technologies are also exploring how these doctors could do this kind of collaboration asynchronously (where they each observe the situation at different times), even helping to overcome language barriers using machine translation technologies, another AI technology with increasing capabilities.

In short, we are not too far from the day AI technology will become a key part of getting computers to help these teams or communities be more effective at solving the problems that face us in our everyday life, and when intelligent computers will become an integral part of the team of specialists that provide healthcare to individuals.

Other AI Systems in Healthcare

In addition to using cognitive computing technologies to enhance the clinical decision support systems used by doctors and nurses to support patient diagnosis and care, AI technology will also impact the way that patient health data is collected and analyzed. One area where AI is making a difference is the area of image analysis.

For many diseases, a critical diagnostic procedure, often requiring specialized training, is to look at images taken by X-ray, ultrasound, CT scan, or MRI. For example, Figure 2-2 is an image from a mammogram, the screening test used to look for cancer. Humans are currently better than computers at determining both whether a tumor is present in such an image and the extent of the cancer.[6]

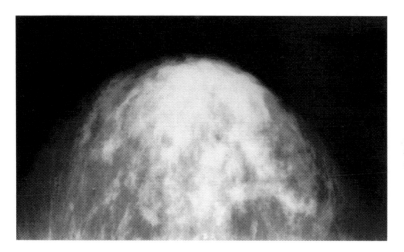

Figure 2-2. *An example of a mammogram image that a medical practitioner must use to determine whether there is evidence of a potential cancer. (Reused with permission of the National Cancer Institute.)*

However, in complex photos, or in those coming from more complex devices like MRIs, even humans have problems identifying the key features. For example, it can be hard to tell tumors from non-cancerous tissue, and it can be especially difficult to determine whether a tumor is benign or malignant. Therefore, an important aspect of research in medical informatics is to develop specialized software to assist in such analysis (which can involve the use of AI techniques; for examples, see www.med-ai. com/index.shtml). For example, AI techniques are currently being used to help doctors interactively identify and classify tumors. If a doctor identifies an area of interest in an image, the AI system can use various techniques to search available images for similar images, and provide the doctor with information about how treatment was provided in the cases with similar images.

Social Media and Trend Analytics

Many companies, large and small, are exploring whether they can use people's online behaviors and communications to predict real-world situations. For example,

[6]Parmeggiani, D1, Avenia, N., Sanguinetti, A., Ruggiero, R., Docimo, G., Siciliano, M., Ambrosino, P., Madonna, I., Peltrini, R., Parmeggiani, U., "Artificial intelligence against breast cancer (A.N.N.E.S-B.C.-Project)", *Ann Ital Chir,* 2012 Jan-Feb; 83 (1):1-5.

since 2008, Google has been exploring whether the searches coming in from users around the world can enable the tracking of, or even prediction of, disease occurrence. The search company demonstrated the successful tracking of two diseases: flu and dengue fever[7]. Figure 2-3 shows the Flu Trends site, which was able to predict the incidence of flu based on a set of keywords people used in searches during a local flu outbreak. On the Flu Trends site, the incidence of flu by country, state, and cities was provided, making it possible for a medical practitioner (or a patient) to more accurately guess if someone's symptoms are due to the flu or to some other cause. While the site no longer publishes current estimates of flu and dengue fever based on search patterns, it does continue to offer historic estimates produced by Google Flu Trends and Google Dengue Trends.

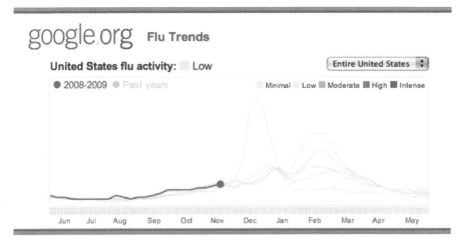

Figure 2-3. *Google Flu Trends (www.google.org/flutrends) shows how the tracking of keyword searches throughout the year allows Google to track and report on flu trends*

While Google has said it has no plans to extend this particular technique beyond these two diseases, many other companies are using social media feeds, such as Facebook, Twitter, and their overseas equivalents, to understand trends in everything from buying behaviors to health. AI technology is being used in many ways by these companies to extract and understand the data. For example, some companies use *natural language processing* techniques to interpret social media content, while other companies are exploring how the *sentiment analysis* of social media can be used to understand what people are posting.[8] The current results indicate that using either NLP or sentiment analysis helps differentiate between "I feel well" and "I feel crummy," which becomes a big differentiator in tracking health trends.

---

[7]Eysenbach, Gunther, MD, "Infodemiology: Tracking Flu-Related Searches on the Web for Syndromic Surveillance", *AMIA Annual Symposium Proceedings, 2006*; 2006: 244–248.
[8]Agarwal, A., Xie, B., Vovsha, I., Rambow, O., Passonneau, R., "Sentiment analysis of Twitter data", *Proceedings of LSM'11*, Association for Computational Linguistics, Stroudsburg, PA, 2011, pp 30–38.

Unfortunately, analyzing social media feeds is much harder than it may seem. Suppose someone was to tweet "My doctor told me to take aspirin. Boy do I feel better #not." Although the #not hashtag makes it clear that "feel better" is actually sarcastic, if we remove the hashtag, we don't know if the writer is being serious or sarcastic.

Current systems solve this problem by coupling machine learning techniques with language analysis techniques. However, in order to perform well, these techniques require a large number of examples to be "tagged" by people, meaning that people explicitly need to indicate features like sentiment and sarcasm. Once the computer has this additional annotated information, current research results indicate that the computer can then more accurately correlate large data sets to find out which words predict which features, and use the results to analyze new data sets.

Beyond sentiment analysis, AI systems are using a combination of training (leveraging models manually input by humans, annotated data, etc.) and various automated learning techniques to look at other language features. One example is to determine which tweets or status updates best indicate potential health problems that are occurring in a particular geographical area. An even more sophisticated use being explored is to try to identify patients with particular problems and see, for specific geographical areas, what medications or treatments are working best. Often, local conditions as simple as the weather or as complex as the particular allergens in the air can have a big impact on the treatment of disease, and a doctor who is made aware of special cases will have an advantage over one who does not have access to this information.

As important as language technologies may be for healthcare, getting computer systems to understand language even at this simple level is hard. While there are several initiatives to develop and standardize medical vocabularies that will enable AI and natural language technology in the future to more fully interpret text, moving to full scale interpretation and understanding is a major challenge for artificial intelligence, and an important one for us to explore. We will discuss some of the challenges machines face in dealing with human language in Chapter 5.

Web-Based (Healthcare) Applications

Web-based healthcare applications that use AI technology are being developed to help users make better health-related decisions. Some of these applications help patients find others with the same or similar conditions and other applications help people make better use of the wide range of medical resources available on the Web. For example, a web site named Patients Like Me (`www.patientslikeme.com/`) provides a social network forum where patients can specify a search query that describes a condition, symptom, or treatment to find other people who are suffering from the same or similar health problem. This site works very hard to maintain good information, and as of mid-2015 had over 325,000 members discussing more than 2,500 medical conditions. The web page also provides links to research studies that have benefited from the use of the data gathered on this site. Another web tool, the Alzheimer's Association web site (`www.alz.org/`), is also well maintained and is designed to help patients, caregivers, and people who are interested in better understanding the disease. This site also has specialized pages for different geographic areas.

Even with the availability of well-designed sites like these, it can be hard to find the most relevant information. For example, some treatments only work for one biological gender or the other. Other treatments have many different names, making it hard to track whether people are talking about the same disease or not. There are also many treatments that have a lot of variables that cause them to be more or less effective. These are all cases where cognitive computing, brought to the individual level, could potentially have a high impact. However, unlike the medical diagnosis described above, here the AI techniques are mostly focused on helping people find information most relevant to their own case, perhaps as a way of better understanding their problem or of forming some questions to ask their health provider.

Unfortunately, many sites on the Web that a person might find when searching for medical information are not reputable. Medical fraud and "snake oil" certainly predate the Web, but the easy access combined with peoples' difficulty in judging credible information make web-based healthcare sites a potential danger to the uninformed patient. The medical community is well aware of this problem and is providing tools to help nurses, doctors, and patients evaluate the accuracy and reliability of web sites.[9] For example, medical web evaluation tools such as HON (Health On the Net Foundation)[10] are available to help patients and medical professionals evaluate the reliability of a web site and the data it provides. Additionally, some healthcare providers are starting to vet web sites or offer their own sites to their patients.

Although AI systems are being explored to help patients navigate available web information, it would be unrealistic to expect a computer to restrict its searches to only reputable sites since even people will generally not have complete agreement as to which sites are most reputable. For example, in the health area there is a considerable amount of what is sometimes called "gray literature." These are sites such as the aforementioned Patients Like Me site which allows patients suffering from various ailments to share information about what does and doesn't work for them and to make recommendations to each other. Many people report finding very useful tips on these pages that have helped them get through chemotherapy or other difficult medical treatments, although many medical professionals worry that some of the advice may be contraindicated for some patients. However, AI technologies could be developed to access medical web evaluation tools and use them to influence what data is provided back to healthcare providers and patients. Asked whether a potential treatment might be useful, these technologies would present a user with a list of web sites with differing opinions. The computer would not try to judge the correctness, but it would provide a credibility rating or use certain weighting factors to help the human evaluate each option. In general, the goal is for the computer to summarize options and allow humans to pick the best. Here again we see the value of combining human judgment with the power of the computer.

Personalized (Healthcare) Applications

Another emerging area of healthcare includes a wide range of mobile applications that increasingly are devices that belong to an individual. A variety of activity trackers have been developed and marketed to keep track of steps taken, calories consumed, heartbeats, amount of sleep, etc. Specialized tools have been developed to monitor people with

---

[9]NIH, "Evaluating Internet Health Information: A Tutorial from the National Library of Medicine", www.nlm.nih.gov/medlineplus/evaluatinghealthinformation.html, 2016.
[10]Health on the Net Foundation, Health Website Evaluation Tool, www.hon.ch/HONcode/Patients/HealthEvaluationTool.html, 2016.

certain diseases, such as autism[11]. In more significant healthcare situations, implanted medical devices like pacemakers or diabetes pumps can be used to monitor and maintain stability in patients. The cost of these technologies is falling rapidly, and more and more of them are starting to show up as smartphone applications or even on the new "smartwatch" technologies. The availability of these tools is forcing many healthcare organizations to establish standardization and interoperability methods so that the data collected by the individual can be used more effectively by a healthcare specialist.

Another problem with these technologies is that they are currently geared to an "average" user. For example, a step-counting application will generally tell users that they should take 10,000 steps a day. But will that number of steps be as appropriate for an 80-pound teenage girl as a 200-pound middle-age man? Would someone who is generally athletic need more steps or fewer than someone who rarely exercises? Could an AI capability be used to better individualize these applications?

Considering the differences among people, it is clear we need something other than averages. Rather, we need to decide for various properties (age, weight, fitness level, etc.) what is most appropriate for an individual user and communicate that information. Machine learning techniques, a topic we will return to in later chapters, can be used to determine which factors are the best predictors for which outcomes. Consider how you might change your behavior if an application was able to say, "Walking 30 minutes a day would significantly improve your breathing problems," or "Swimming instead of running two days a week would help your knee pain"–advice clearly applicable to very different users. It is the individual, not necessarily the doctor, who will determine how to follow the advice. With the help of an AI system, the overall effect could be better because you would be getting personalized advice, rather than general guidelines that may be too hard to follow or seem unrelated to your own situation.

In addition, the medical community recognizes that a person's health has many dimensions: physical, emotional, psychological, and social. While much of the discussion in this chapter has focused on how AI tools can support the physical health of an individual, there are some tools being created to focus on the social health of individuals. One that has met with some recent success is the Selfhelp Virtual Senior Center (www.selfhelp.net/), which offers online support to home-bound seniors. On the other end of the spectrum is the introduction of smart technology into nursing homes and private homes to enable people to continue to live independently and yet be cared for. In addition, robot technology to support patients in nursing homes, as they receive physical therapy, etc., is being widely explored and may be required to support an expected large population of senior citizens. These robots are becoming more attractive as AI-based technologies are enhancing how the human can communicate with the robot using natural language, gesturing, etc.

So Who Will Be Your Next Doctor?

The examples of AI-based healthcare computing capabilities presented in this chapter were intended to showcase how AI technologies can support and enhance current medical care. In general, AI-based healthcare technology is being developed and offered

---

[11]Fletcher, R., Dobson, K., Goodwin, M., Eydgahi, H., Wilder-Smith, O., Fernholz, D., Kuboyama, Y., Hedman, E., and Pho, M., "iCalm: Wearable Sensor and Network Architecture for Wirelessly communicating and Logging Autonomic Activity", *IEEE Transactions on Information Technology in Biomedicine*, Vol 14, No. 2, March 2010.

as "cognitive assistants," not as a replacement for the doctor, the nurse, the patient, or the medical team in their roles as decision makers. Current results from limited studies of the use of this type of technology indicate that in the case where humans are using the AI-based systems, they are likely to perform better than the people who are using non-AI based technology to perform the same task.

In the next chapters, we will look more carefully at what it is that differentiates how humans and computers "think" and the key strengths of each. We will look at the technologies described in this chapter in more detail to see how they work and what they do best. We will then explore how humans and computers can work together to create powerful social machines that can help us to cope with some of the hardest problems we face as human beings.

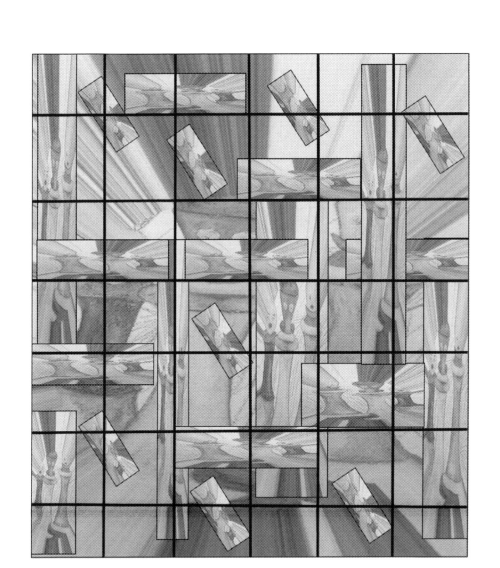

CHAPTER 3

■ ■ ■

The Games We Play

In the medical scenario presented in the last chapter, you saw that there are differences between what humans can do well and what computers can do well. In this chapter, we will explore this in more detail. In particular, we want to highlight the capabilities where human cognition shines, describe the areas that computers are best at, and introduce emerging areas where computers are starting to blur some of these differences. We will explore these issues by looking at the area of game playing, an area where it is easy to see the progress that AI has been making over the years, but also to see areas where machines still have a long way to go.

Obvious Differences?

The fact that there are differences between humans and machines seems pretty obvious. We think of humans as artistic, emotional, intuitive, and creative. In contrast, we tend to think of computers as mechanical, emotionless, mathematical, and repetitive. We pride ourselves as humans for having consciousness and awareness, while thinking of computers as soulless and solipsistic. We are, essentially, aesthetes; they are lifeless and programmed. A modern Jewish prayer thanks the Lord that we are neither "angels nor robots," a blessing of thanksgiving by humans for having the free will denied those other entities.

Yet despite the seeming obviousness of these differences, when push comes to shove, it's actually very difficult to define what these things that make us human, and which we feel distinguish us from computers, really are. When we talk, for example, about feeling emotions, we're discussing something that is so inherent to the way we interact with the world that we don't really have other words to explain it. If your cell phone were to say "I'm feeling happy for you today," what would you make of it? Most people would say it isn't feeling an emotion, but rather is parroting the words. But what if it said "You sound very happy today" at an appropriate time? That's within the realm of current technology. Most of us wouldn't think of that as the computer experiencing happiness in any sense, but if a human said that to you, you would just take it for granted that she knew what happiness was.

This notion that we somehow "know" what is human and what is machine seems compelling, but in fact it is very difficult. When machines take over physical tasks, generally programmed to imitate humans, it can seem obvious. When machines were initially being programmed to run weaving looms using instructions stored on cards, run sewing machines, and to perform other processes that had been done by people, they were

© James Hendler and Alice M. Mulvehill 2016
J. Hendler and A. M. Mulvehill, *Social Machines*, DOI 10.1007/978-1-4842-1156-4_3

still viewed as machines. However, those early automated systems did raise many of the concerns people have about modern AI (and which we'll return to later in this book): being too smart or "humanlike," putting people out of jobs, and causing workplace disruption.

When the digital computer was introduced, and the computation of the machine was encapsulated inside the box, the distinction between human vs. machine capability became less clear. As computers started being programmed to do tasks that had previously required large numbers of people, the question arose as to whether they could someday be intelligent. The term *artificial intelligence* was introduced in roughly the mid-1950s (it is usually attributed to a workshop held at Dartmouth College in 1956), but discussions as to machine intelligence were already ongoing.

In fact, since that time, there have been many debates about what intelligence is and the "philosophy" of AI. There is a rich body of literature on consciousness, mindfulness, emotional reasoning, etc. This literature describes many capabilities native to humans and contrasts machine capabilities with human capabilities. But there are a number of philosophers who are explicitly exploring what machine intelligence would mean, and whether it is even possible in some deep sense.

At the heart of many of these arguments is an allusion to a critical influential idea introduced by the British polymath Alan Turing in a paper he wrote in 1950. Entitled "Computing Machinery and Intelligence," it started with the question "Can machines think?" Arguing that thinking would be too difficult to define, Turing proposed something called the *imitation game*, which he claimed was almost equivalent: if a computer could pass the imitation game, we would have to consider it to be intelligent in some sense. The idea of passing the imitation game became so crucial to both those debating the philosophy of AI and to those performing research in the emerging field of AI that it became known as the Turing Test.

The basic imitation game, as usually defined, is simple: a human communicates with a conversation partner who is hidden behind a screen. The partner might be a human or it might be a machine. If, at the end of the session, the human guessing whether he is talking to another person or to a computer is unable to tell, then we say that the computer has fooled the person and has won the game, thus passing the Turing Test. This seems pretty straightforward; Turing is essentially privileging the ability to communicate in human language, about pretty much any topic, as a clear indicator of intelligence.

It is worth noting that the actual imitation game, first defined in this paper and later explicated in talks by Turing, including a presentation of debates on the topic presented on BBC radio, involved some subtleties. One of these was that Turing knew the computer would be pretending to be something it wasn't, so it wouldn't be fair if the human wasn't also doing that. So Turing essentially proposed that the person in the test would pretend to be a person of the other gender and the computer would imitate a person pretending to be of the other gender. That is, just as the computer might not know what it was like to be a human, a man might not know what it is like to be a woman. So where the computer would need to imagine its answers based on what it thought a human was like (when pretending to be another person), the person would need to imagine what the person of the other gender was like.

Another subtlety Turing addressed was the issue of what could be said. One question he was asked during the interviews was whether the computer could lie. He answered in the affirmative (noting that the human could as well) and that this might be a crucial part of the test. In fact, the test assumed the computer knew it was trying to imitate a human and thus might want to purposely get some things wrong. Asked to perform a complex mathematical calculation, for example, the computer might want to either give a wrong answer or say something like "that's too hard" even though in practice it could know the answer.

Over the years, there have been many variations of the Turing Test proposed. For example, Turing didn't specify how long the conversation should last (although according to reports at one point he opined that 20 minutes might be sufficient). He also didn't want to put limits on the topics that could be discussed. Limited forms of the Turing Test, that set a specific time or topic, have been performed, however. It would seem that getting a computer to discuss some particular topic (like playing cricket or baseball) for some short amount of time would cause us to be impressed, but perhaps not to want to claim the computer really showed intelligence, let alone consciousness or self-awareness.

At the other end of the spectrum, Turing was assuming that the participants would be typing their conversation to each other. As computers have gained voices, the issue has arisen as to whether speech understanding should be part of the test. Others have argued, especially as computer vision and robotics have emerged, that the abilities to recognize objects or to manipulate things in the world are also necessary to the test. The term *Total Turing Test* was proposed around 2011[1] and is based on an earlier proposal by researcher Stevan Harnad in the early 1990s who pointed out that it was unclear whether language (as printed text) alone would be a sufficient test for the computer.

Despite these many proposed variations, most research still focuses on the original imitation game, and as of this writing a computer has not yet passed the test. A claim in 2014 that a computer had passed the test was based on a misunderstanding; the computer had passed a form of limited Turing Test and, in fact, had only fooled about 30% of the judges. An impressive feat, but not yet a real pass.

In fact, the question as to whether a computer can win the imitation game is one where there seems to be little consensus. Some researchers argue that success is imminent, others that it is impossible. Whichever one believes, it is clear that this 1950s idea has had a huge impact on the field of artificial intelligence through to the present time.

As interesting as these philosophical ideas are, in a certain sense they are easy to ignore. In lectures he gave in the 1970s, Professor Herbert Simon, considered one of the founders of the AI field, argued that discussing these things without providing *operational* definitions was not a worthwhile pursuit. If we are just arguing about whether a machine can ever do something we cannot define, for example "feel sad," then how would we ever know whether we were right or wrong? Simon argued it made more sense to come up with examples like the imitation game that would answer these questions. Some behaviors could be easily measured; for example, how well a computer could play chess or some other "winnable" game is easily calibrated by how well it does playing against a human. Other ideas, like emotions, he argued, needed similar kinds of definitions. For example, if we could differentiate what a sad person said and did from what one did who was happy, then we could tell whether a computer could be appropriately programmed to feel that emotion.

It's worth noting that Simon went on to say that it made more sense to talk about "practical" things, like playing a game, planning a trip, or solving a complex problem, than to argue about internal states like emotions. He argued that first we needed to get computers to do things that are useful and often difficult for humans, and to save some of the more philosophical arguments for later.

---

[1]Oppy, Graham and Dowe, David, "The Turing Test", *The Stanford Encyclopedia of Philosophy* (Spring 2011 Edition), Edward N. Zalta (ed.), http://plato.stanford.edu/archives/spr2011/entries/turing-test/.

In the remainder of this chapter, we will follow Simon's advice. In understanding what computers do best *at the current time* and where humans outshine them *today*, we can better understand what each is best at without getting into these deeper philosophical issues.

One area where it is possible to compare human and computer performance operationally, as discussed above, is in the area of playing games. This is a good area to explore because at the current time there are some games at which people are way better than computers but others where machines are now the champions (and some where it's hard to even be sure).

Computers Play Chess

The board game that is probably best known with respect to artificial intelligence is that of chess. Technically chess has the following properties:

- **It is a *perfect information* game**: There are two players and both can see all the pieces at any time, so there's no information that is "hidden." We compare this to an imperfect information game, such as a card game where one cannot see what is in the other player's hand.

- **It is a *zero-sum* game**: This is the technical term to describe the simple notion of a game where what is good for one player is bad for the other. Most common games, especially board games where people play against each other taking turns, are zero sum games, but there are others where some moves may benefit both players, where teams may be involved, or where the game doesn't have a specific "win or lose" character where the players oppose each other.

- **It is a *deterministic* game**: There is no "luck" involved. These games are ones where there is no throw of the dice, deal of cards, or other aspect that introduces randomness into the game.

All of these make explaining the computer play of the game easier, but there is one aspect of chess that makes it much more compelling for us to examine: it's a game that's had a long history of play among humans (variants of chess are known back to the fourth century, and the modern version of the game has been around for at least 500 years). In fact, in the early days of AI, when programmers started to explore chess as a challenge, many people thought the computer would never be able to win.

Ignoring some earlier claimed machines, which were later proven to be hoaxes (having humans inside that actually played the game), the first modern exploration of chess-playing machines started virtually at the same time as the development of the digital computer. A number of well-known early computer scientists, like Norbert Weiner and Claude Shannon, wrote papers about how a computer might be made to play chess. Alan Turing, discussed above, is thought to have developed the first program (described in a paper he wrote in 1951) that could actually play a full game of chess; however, his program only worked on paper because there weren't any computers available at the time that could actually run the algorithm.

There were a number of early machines, and with the development of some new algorithms, which we will discuss later, that started to play credible games in the late 1950s and early 1960s. In 1957, a group at the Carnegie Institute of Technology (now Carnegie-Mellon University) predicted that a computer would defeat the world chess champion within ten years. They were quite wrong!

However, just before those ten years were up, an MIT student, Richard Greenblatt, wrote a program named Mac Hack VI that is generally acknowledged to be the first significant computer chess program in terms of how well it played. By the end of 1967, Mac Hack VI had played in the Boston Amateur championship and became the first computer to ever win a game in tournament play against humans. By the end of the decade, the program was playing at about the level of an average player in human tournaments.

A couple of other interesting events in human vs. computer chess also took place around that time. In 1965, philosopher Hubert Dreyfus wrote a paper called "AI and Alchemy" where he argued that intelligence couldn't be achieved by a digital computer, and he argued against the prediction that a computer would ever be the world champion. In fact, he stated that a computer would never be able to beat a ten-year-old at chess. Taking up that challenge, the MIT team challenged Dreyfus himself to a chess game, which occurred in 1967. It is said that it was a close game, but in the end Dreyfus lost. In a 1972 book, based on that earlier paper, Dreyfus changed the argument to say a computer would never beat a human champion. He was also wrong about that, as we shall see.

For the next 20 years, computers continued to improve, and while they were routinely beating human players, the best players in the world remained humans. In 1968, a master chess player made a bet that he would not be beaten by a computer in the next decade and offered a cash prize. In 1978, he played against one of the best computer chess players in the world, and he won the tournament, validating his claim. However, it is said that after that game he said it would not be very long before computers were playing as well as he could. In that, he was right again. In 1981, a computer called Cray Blitz, so named because it ran on a Cray supercomputer, became the first computer to beat a human master in tournament play.

Computers continued to improve throughout the 80s and 90s, and in the mid-1990s, IBM decided to take up the challenge. Modifying some of their computers to be specialized for chess playing, they developed a program called DeepBlue that started playing well enough that in 1996 they challenged the world's best player, chess grand master Garry Kasparov, in tournament play. In a six-game match Kasparov lost the first game, but then went on to win three and draw two, thus winning the match.

In 1997, using a more powerful computer that had been trained based on many games by Kasparov, the IBM team was ready to try again. In a match that received publicity around the world, Kasparov won the first game, lost the second, and then drew three in a row, leaving the match as a tie going into the final game. In that game, Deep Blue won a decisive victory, and became the first computer ever to beat a grandmaster in tournament play. For the first time, the best chess player in the world was a computer.

IBM retired DeepBlue after that game, but people continued to develop new and better computer chess games. Kasparov continued to play in challenges with some of these machines, including a televised 2003 match against a computer that offered a million dollar prize. Watched by millions of people around the world, the match ended up a draw. Since that time, computers have continued to improve, and so have chess playing algorithms.

Today, computers rarely lose to the best humans. And nowadays, it doesn't even require the fastest machines. For example, in 2009, a program known as Pocket Fritz running on a cell phone won a major tournament, allowing it to receive a higher chess rating than had been achieved by DeepBlue. Today, most human chess tournaments don't allow computers in because they play too well, and today computers, not humans, are the undisputed world chess champions in tournament play.[2]

In the next sections, we will explore some of the basics of computer game playing, and how computers can be made to play chess. First, however, we will start with a much simpler game.

Starting Simple: Tic-tac-toe

To understand how computers play chess, it is important to understand some things about games as seen from a programmer's point of view. Before we can explore computer play at chess, let's start with a much simpler game: the game of tic-tac-toe (also called noughts and crosses, Xs and Os, or exy-ozys). This game is one of the first games that many kids learn. It is a turn-taking game that is played against another person, and the rules are simple. The board is three squares by three squares, as showed in Figure 3-1.

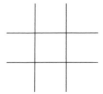

Figure 3-1. *The empty (starting) board for the game of tic-tac-toe*

One player, who moves first, puts an X in one of the boxes; the other player then puts an O in a box. They each take turns adding Xs or Os, and the game is won when one player gets three in a row horizontally, vertically, or diagonally. If no player gets three in a row when the board is filled in, then the game is a draw and no one wins. When properly played, all games lead to a draw, which makes tic-tac-toe a game that is more generally used to explain games, or teach young children about turn-taking, than it is as a challenging game.

Although tic-tac-toe is also not much of a challenging problem for a computer, we can learn a lot about computer game playing by carefully looking at how the game is played. If we don't worry about wins or losses, and just look at the sequence of moves, then we see the following: in the first move, X has 9 places to move. The response by O can be in any of the empty places, but not where X moved, so there are 8 responses. X then has 7 places to move, O then 6, and so on. If we ignore the issue of winning and losing, there are 9x8x7x6x5x4x3x2x1 possible moves, so the complete tree (of every possible legal board) would have about 362,880 possible sequences of moves.

---

[2]Later in this chapter we will look at one kind of non-tournament play where teams of humans and/ or computers play against each other. Things in that space are somewhat more complicated to analyze, as we shall see.

If we look a little more carefully, however, we see that the game is actually much simpler than that. There are many symmetries in this game, so X really only has three moves that can be made: move in a corner, move on a side that isn't a corner, or move in the middle. The second player has more possibilities depending on what the first did. If the X went in the middle, then O can move in a corner or in a non-corner, so there are only two possibilities. If X took a corner, O has 5 other places to move, as opposed to 8; when we remove the symmetries, and when X takes a side, O also has only 5 non-symmetric options. So instead of 9x8=72 possible boards, we have 3 possible first moves, and then 2+5+5=12 possible second moves, a significant improvement! (Figure 3-2 shows the set of possible moves to this point). Further, after a few moves, some of the games are won by one player or another, so those games end before the whole board is filled in. In fact, when symmetries and wins/losses are included, there are actually only 138 possible moves, instead of the 362,880 we computed before.

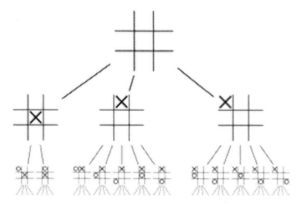

Figure 3-2. *The first two moves of the tic-tac-toe game with symmetries considered (from https://en.wikipedia.org/wiki/Tic-tac-toe)*

Analyzing a game like tic-tac-toe, which is so easy for people to play, may seem somewhat pedantic and far more than we want to know about a simple game, but understanding even a simple game like this can help us to see some of the key ideas traditionally used to program computers to play a game.

To start with, let's look at the "structure" that we can use to represent the state of the game to a computer. If we look at Figure 3-2 again, we see that we can view the game as a tree where the first level is the starting position, the second level is the set of boards after the first move (by X), the next level is the set of board after the second move (by O), and so on. (In showing these trees, we'll use the convention from this figure and use pictures to represent the tree structures. In a computer, we would represent these pictures using matrices or other mathematically equivalent forms.) This structure is called a *game tree*.

To program a computer to play tic-tac-toe, or other such games, we use the game tree with one more convention added. We label those boards that complete a game. In particular, we use the convention of playing from X (the first to move), and thus we can label any board with 3 Xs in as a *win*, with three Os in a row as a *loss*, and any complete board with no winner is labelled a *draw*.

Using this convention, it is fairly straightforward to see how we could get a computer to play tic-tac-toe. Once we have completely labeled the tree with the 138 possibilities, we can see that on some levels X will make a move that is a win, or O will make a move that causes X to lose. If it is X's turn, and one of the moves can lead to a win, then X should clearly make that move. Similarly, if it is O's turn, and O can make a move that causes X to lose, then O should make that move. However, if X sees that some move would lead to O winning, then X should try to avoid that move. So when we reach some point in the game tree, X can see, for every move whether it allows X to win (so it takes that move), puts X in a position where O can win so it avoids that move), or is in a state where it doesn't know.

The key to understanding how computers can play games is to explore what happens when the next step is not obvious; that is, where X has to make a move, but there is no branch below that is labelled a win. Thus, we need to find a way to choose what to do next. In this case, what we see is that the computer can look further down the tree. It looks at its possible next moves, sees all the moves its adversary could make, and then looks at what it would do after that.

In some fortuitous cases, X can discover it has a forced win. That is, as shown in Figure 3-3, if the computer places its X in the lower left-hand corner, then for EVERY move that O can make (the next level of the tree), there will be some move that X can make that would allow it to win. Thus, we can label this board, even though it is not a complete game, a win for X, because no matter what O does, X still can win.

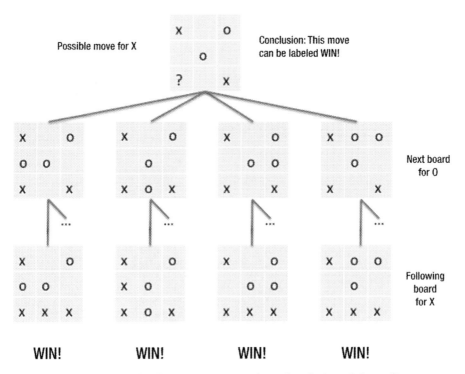

Figure 3-3. *The situation for the next two moves when X has the board shown (lines to ellipses represent boards not being shown)*

A very different case happens if at the next level ANY board for O would be labelled a loss. Consider the situation in the piece of the game tree shown in Figure 3-4. If X were to move in the lower middle, then at the next step O would complete a three in a row and X would lose. So clearly X would not want to make this move.

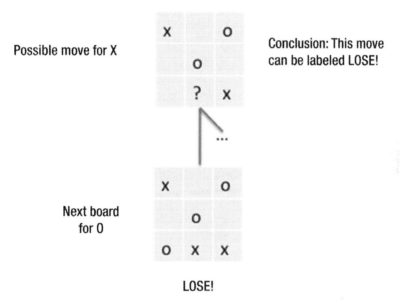

Possible move for X

Conclusion: This move can be labeled LOSE!

Next board for O

LOSE!

Figure 3-4. A losing position for X down the tree

So, when we look at the game tree, we see that in certain cases we can propagate a label up. That is, when X is considering its next move, it can look further down the tree. For any move it can take and *every* board under it leads to a win, then it can label that move as a win. For any move it can take where *any* board under it leads to a loss, it has to worry that O will be smart enough to make that move, and therefore it has to label its potential move as a loss. In a game like tic-tac-toe where draws can occur, we can conclude that given no wins, a draw is preferable, so any move that has everything under it either a win or a draw (but no loses) is a safe move and can be taken (and thus the move can itself be labelled a draw).

It should be noted that to do this for the whole tree, we need to keep going down. That is, at the first move, X doesn't know what to do, so it looks at the tree for the second and third move, and labels anything it can. For any move it cannot label at that level, it looks at the fourth and fifth level, labels everything it can, and then reexamines the third level to see if anything has changed. This continues all the way to the bottom of the tree and, in a game like tic-tac-toe where every board at the bottom is a win, loss, or draw, then it can propagate the boards all the way to the top. (In the case of tic-tac-toe, the computer would discover that every first move can lead to a draw or win, and none leads to a loss, so it can pick one at random and proceed.)

As we consider this algorithmic approach to labeling the game tree (which is technically known as *alpha-beta* search), we can see why it was so important that we performed the analysis of the game. As discussed, when we realized that there were different ways to reach the same positions (the symmetries) and to label the boards, we were able to cut down the number of possible move sequences by a huge amount. In computing through the game tree, if we used the original tree, we would have to consider upwards of 300,000 moves; in the tree after analysis we cut this down to a little more than 100. When doing the propagation of moves, each one we have to compute takes computer time, and so we want to cut down the number of steps anywhere we can.

In fact, this kind of analysis is often very important in getting computers to play these sorts of turn-taking games. Programmers who want to get computers to play games have often attempted to develop these same sorts of analyses to reduce the game tree size. This is very important because game trees can grow very large very quickly, and this kind of analysis can remove a huge amount of potential computation.

SOLVING A GAME

When we can label a tree, like that for regular tic-tac-toe, and determine the value of every move, then we say that a game has been solved; that is, at every move there is a way that one player or the other can win (or draw).

Because of the speed with which game trees grow, solving games can be very difficult. For example, the game of checkers (also known as draughts) is one of the first interesting games in which an AI program was developed. Arthur Samuels wrote a checkers playing program in the late 1950s that used a combination of game playing approaches like those we will discuss below. By the mid-1970s, the program was rated as a "respectable amateur." Jonathan Schaeffer, at the University of Alberta, led a team that developed a computer program to play checkers called Chinook. By the mid-90s it was considered one of the best players in the world. However, it wasn't until 2007, almost 50 years after Samuel's player was announced, that Schaeffer and his team published a paper in *Science*[3] that proved the player moving first in checkers can either win or draw. However, the Chinook checkers player using this strategy isn't guaranteed to play the best game. If the opposing player doesn't make their best move, it is possible to take the program into a part of the tree that is not completely analyzed. This is known as a *weak solve solution*. Once the full tree is identified, the program would play a perfect game (always achieving the best it could, and at least a draw, no matter what the other player does). In that case, it would be, as is the case for tic-tac-toe, a strong solution.

Many games, such as chess, where computers are able to beat the best humans, or Go, where computers are just starting to challenge human experts, are still a very long way from being solved.

[3]Schaeffer, J., Burch, N., Björnsson, Y., Kishimoto, A., Müller, M., Lake, R., Lu, P., Sutphen, S. "Checkers is Solved". *Science* 317 (5844): 1518–22, 2007.

From Tic-Tac-Toe to Chess

In tic-tac-toe, the game tree is small enough that the computer can look down the tree and analyze all the way to the end of the game. In some games, however, the size of the game tree grows too large for that to work. So in these cases, the machine must have some way of labeling the board positions even if it cannot tell if they are wins or losses. One game with an interesting history in AI, the game of chess, easily helps us understand this point.

The first player to move in chess is able to make 20 moves (each of eight pawns can move one or two squares forward, each of the two knights can make two opening moves). The opponent can then respond with the same 20 moves on their side. So the game tree for the first two moves has 20x20 = 400 possible ways that pieces on the chess board could be configured (compare that to the 15 for tic-tac-toe discussed previously). After that, the number of moves is a bit tricky to calculate because the next possible moves are dependent on the first move made (some moves let a bishop or a queen move out, some don't). Roughly speaking, there are about 30 possibilities for each of the next moves in the game. So by the time each player has moved twice, there are 20x20x30x30=360,000 moves. This is already the size of the tic-tac-toe tree where we didn't use any symmetries, and the chess match has barely begun. As the game continues, the number of moves changes, but by the time the game is over, the estimated size of the tree of legal boards using various symmetries and eliminating duplicates (that is, when there are multiple ways to the same position, we don't duplicate that position in the tree) is estimated to be somewhere in the neighborhood of 100,000,000,000,000,000,000,000,000,000,000,000,000,000,000,000 ($10^{47)}$) boards[4]. Even if we were to take all of the fastest computers in the world today and have them do nothing but compute chess board positions, it would still take thousands of years before we could have the whole tree labeled. Yet computers not only play chess, they do it quite well. Clearly, some other techniques must be being brought into play.

The trick in playing games with large search trees is that we cannot search all the way to the bottom of the tree each time we need to make a move, but rather we search ahead as far as we can in the time available and generate a subset of the game tree. The term for each level of a game tree is a *ply*, and we thus can characterize this by saying how many plies a computer can look ahead in choosing its move.

However, for this to work, we need to understand what the computer does when the moves, even down to that level, contain many games that don't have a win, lose, or draw.

The approach to this is to use a variant of alpha-beta search called *minimax*. In this algorithm, what we do is come up with a way to assign every board a value. There is no best way to do this, and the real art of building computer game playing systems is to come up with good scoring algorithms. These can be based on a number of different things. Here are a few common ones:

- Giving individual scores to particular pieces that are left on the board. For example, we might decide a king is worth 1,000 points because losing the king loses the game, a queen could be worth 500 because it is such a powerful piece, etc.

---

[4]These numbers are notoriously hard to compute. The estimate here is from Wikipedia, which claims this number as a provable upper bound. Other numbers that have been proposed range from about 10^{24}, which can be achieved by ruling out a lot of very unlikely situations, to about 10^{43}, which is based on adding in some tournament rules that limit the total number of games possible.

- Rating certain pieces in certain places as having special value (for example, if a pawn reaches the far side of the board, it can become a better piece, so we might give pawns more value as they get further into the game).

- Evaluating game-specific tactics and positions such as having the king be "protected" by other pieces.

And there are many others. A program is written to calculate all these sorts of things and use some function to combine them. We then take the value of the board for the first player and subtract the value of its opponent. So if the first player had a score of 237, and the second player had a score of 125, the value would be 112 for the first player. If, on the other hand, the pieces were reversed (that is, the opponent had the better position), then the number would be -112, with the negative number representing a potentially bad position.

Given a set of numbers for each board in a ply, we use an approach similar to the one we used to compute the WIN and LOSE in tic-tac-toe. That is, when we are evaluating a particular potential move, we look down the tree as far as we can. When it is our turn, we take the move with the highest value. When it is our opponent's turn to move, we assume that the move with the lowest value (i.e. the one best for that player) would be the value. So at our level, we choose the *maximum* value, and at the next ply, we choose the *minimum* (and thus the name *minimax*).

So let's look at an example of a small tree and a few plies. But please keep in mind that in chess each number is the value of a board, the number of possible next boards for each move can range from as low as zero (we've lost) to as high as 278 (the maximum possible at any point in a chess game, although quite rare). So the plies would be much larger, and as we went down the tree, it would expand very quickly. In fact, we'd need a whole book just to encode a few plies of a real chess game.

Figure 3-5 shows the simple game tree at some point in time. The player must determine which move to make to get the best value possible. In this case, the board has been expanded out so that each player gets two moves (or a total of four plies). The values at the bottom ply are those that would be computed by the board evaluator based on rules like the ones above.

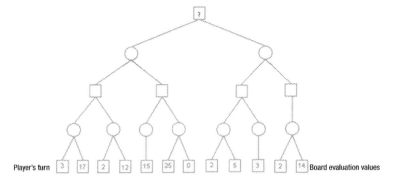

Figure 3-5. *What is the best move that the player can make in this situation, and what is the value of the move?*

The move at the next level up would be the opponent's choice, and thus the minimum value (the one worst for the player) would be chosen. The resulting numbers are shown in Figure 3-6.

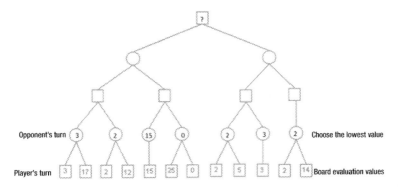

Figure 3-6. *The game tree values brought up one ply. A good opponent chooses the smallest number possible.*

Now it is the player's turn to choose. Of the values available, the player wants to pick the highest values because those are the ones the board evaluator thinks are the better moves. Figure 3-7 expands the tree to show the values at this ply.

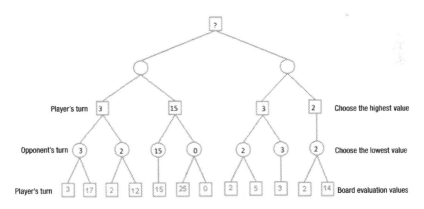

Figure 3-7. *It is now the player's turn at this ply, so the highest value is chosen*

This process is now repeated for as many plies as necessary. In our example, there is only one ply left, and this is the move of the opponent, so again the low value is chosen. At that point, the player has all the information needed to fill in the number at the top: choosing the highest value (in this case, a board worth 3, as shown in Figure 3-8).

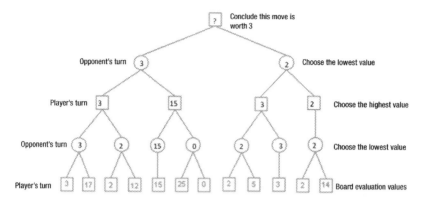

Figure 3-8. *The opponent makes a last choice, again picking the minimum, allowing the player to value the "?" node by choosing the best value that can be reached.*

Notice that in this simple example we computed all the values in the tree and then figured out the best move. Chess grows so fast that to go down a reasonable number of plies, and then compute all the values in this way, is still prohibitively expensive. There are a number of tricks that can be used to improve the performance by not computing the whole tree in advance. Some of these are difficult to explain without a fair amount of math, and really aren't germane to this discussion, but there's one that is important.

In actual computer game play, we can generate the tree in pieces, as it were. That is, for example, we could compute the best moves for a small number of plies. We could then pick only a few of the best values and compute those moves down deeper. For example, if there were 50 possible moves in the first ply, we might evaluate them all for a couple of steps and pick the best ten. For those ten, we could go down a couple of extra plies and recomputed the values. We could do this a number of times, meaning that in the most promising parts of the tree we evaluate down a larger number of plies, thus looking much further ahead then we could if we tried to generate and evaluate the whole tree.

However, there is a problem with this approach: we could end up in a "trap." That is, the most likely looking first moves might actually be taking us into what would be worse positions lower down than some of the other moves. In fact, a good adversary would try to set such traps for us, creating situations where, for example, they might sacrifice a piece now for a position that is better later in the game. Early chess playing programs were often easy to trick because of this feature.

To avoid falling into traps, there are various kinds of tricks and strategies that can be used. For example, the computer could pick some number of the best moves, but then also a couple of other moves at random. Or it could purposely try using what seems to be a worst move to see if there's something that would indicate that it is a trap. Programmers trying to figure out how to avoid traps came up with many clever tricks. So in addition to working out the mathematical approaches to game tree search, designing a good chess playing program requires several things that aren't needed for a simple game like tic-tac-toe. First, the program needs a good way to decide between different strategies for how deep to search and under which values. Second, there's no single board evaluator that is known to be best, so the programmer must design different evaluators and choose between them. Finally, as the computer explores possible best moves, it should look for places where its opponent might be fooled by the numbers; that is, it should be able to lay traps of its own.

But all of those different things make for a lot of parameters that can be varied, and thus it is hard to know what makes the computer play better or worse. One addition to the canon of game-playing techniques that arose out of chess research was the realization that the machine could actually learn some of this in a relatively straightforward way. Basically, the machine would be set to play against itself, using different variants. One approach might look at more moves vs. another that might look deeper. One might use a board evaluator that was primarily based on piece values, another on relative position strengths. By using multiple computers and variants of the different approaches, computer chess designers were able to hone their programs by varying the parameters in systematic ways, seeing which approaches did better than others, and adjusting the parameters towards those that increased success.

Why Computers Are Good at Chess

As discussed earlier in this chapter, in about 50 years computers went from barely able to play against humans to being superhuman chess players. The criticism in the early decades was that computers would never be good at chess; the criticism now is that the sophistication of computer chess programs is one more piece of evidence in the argument discussed in the introduction: that AI could be a threat to mankind. How can we contemplate competing with or even controlling these machines when we cannot even beat them at a game humans created and have played for centuries?

As we've explored how computers play chess, we can see that the power is coming from several different aspects of the ways machines work. Reflecting on the long discussion of game-playing, the following key points summarize why computers do so well at chess:

- **Design of key algorithms**: The chess playing prowess of the computer is based on the key approach of game-tree search as was first described for the much simpler game of tic-tac-toe. The previous section described how that algorithm was extended from the win/loss/draw tree to the numeric tree that allows the computer to pick good moves when it cannot see all the way to the end of the game. There are a number of improvements that can be made to make the search more efficient, regardless of what game is being played. As research has identified new kinds of game-independent approaches, the ability of computers to play chess, and many other games too, has improved.

- **Increased computer power**: Clearly, the ability to beat a world champion required the computer to look far ahead in the game tree; it could evaluate more plies (either fully or partially) and this allowed it to avoid traps and recognize opportunities before its opponent saw them. In 50 years of game play, computers have increased in power by a huge amount. If you have a smartphone, the processor is more powerful than the most powerful computer available to the early chess researchers, and the amount of memory on your phone exceeds the total amount of memory storage that existed in the world in the late 60s and early 70s.[5] Chess tournaments are generally played against some kind of time clock or time limit, and computers can take advantage of their increasing power to do more in the same amount of time. In game play, the faster the computer can run its board evaluators, the more boards it can evaluate in the same amount of time, and thus the further ahead it can look and the better game it can play.

- **Better heuristics**: As well as the game-independent algorithms, we can see that chess playing requires a lot of specialized knowledge about chess. Just as in tic-tac-toe, where we saw the tremendous savings in tree size by noting symmetries, recognizing multiple ways to get to the same board, etc. so too do these things come up in chess. Even more importantly, the chess playing system requires a good board evaluator. When the system is looking at a board some number of plies deep, if it cannot tell good situations from bad ones, it cannot play a winning game (as a thought experiment, think about what would happen to the game tree-based search if we simply inverted the values, that is, switching the scores for the two players and then use the tree search).

- **Application of machine learning**: By having computers play against each other, with some variants, the board evaluators can be improved as discussed. The approaches used in doing this can be very varied, and when very large sets of parameters are involved (such as in adjusting the scores of the many components of a chess board evaluator), the learning algorithms get complex. We will be exploring these in a later chapter, but for now it is important to mainly realize that the kind of learning we are talking about, recognizing how to change parameters in an algorithm, is very different than the kind of learning we talk about when we discuss a child learning to play chess or, in fact, many kinds of human learning.

---

[5]Modern chess computers are made more powerful by storing both strong sets of opening sequences and known winning sequences at the end, so more memory allows more of these to be stored. Current computer chess players make great use of these memory tricks, often saving great amounts of computation by, essentially precomputing large portions of the tree.

CHESS CENTAURS

After Garry Kasparov lost to the IBM DeepBlue program in the 1990s, he began to study computer play and compare it to human play. He argued that the game styles of humans and computers were different, and he proposed an "advanced chess" where a human using a computer would compete against another such team. The idea had been explored in the past, but with Kasparov advocating for mixed teams, the idea gained new ground, and in 1998 a match was held between Kasparov and another chess champion each aided by a computer player.

The term *chess centaur* was coined, analogizing the half-human, half-horse creatures of mythology to the half-human, half-computer chess playing-team. Over the next decade, chess centaurs generally outperformed the best humans or the best computers, showing the power of a combination where the human could choose based on their chess knowledge, and then use the computer to look for potential pitfalls (or opportunities) many plies ahead. By around 2012, however, centaurs started losing to the increasingly powerful chess playing computers as the power of computers to compute more boards more quickly continued to grow.

More recently, an extension of advanced chess known as "freeform" chess has arisen. In freeform, games are played online where the two competing players are able to use any resource, including computers or other chess players. Increasingly large groups of players, many using different computers, have been playing against each other in games with variations on timing or other constraints to limit the total time in play. As this is written in 2016, the best players in the world appear to be the freeform teams, which can now beat the best chess playing machines. It is unclear what the future holds in this space but, as we will argue later in the book, it appears that teams of computers and humans working together create extremely powerful "social machines" that can be hard for either alone to beat.

The approaches we have described, when combined together, have allowed chess playing programs to outperform humans, and as computers get more powerful, their advantage grows. In fact, one question we might ask is "how can humans play chess so well?" While much is unknown about human play, it is evident from both psychological and neuroscientific evidence that it is not done by humans actively evaluating lots and lots of game trees. To understand better how humans do play these kinds of games, we will take a look at another game, the game of Go, a game where, as of early 2016, computers are just beginning to challenge humans for undisputed mastery.

Go, the Current Challenge

Game tree search can do so well at chess because it is a zero-sum, perfect information, deterministic game. Later in this chapter, we'll explore some other kinds of games, and compare human and computer play, but first let's look at another game that is also of the same kind. We will explore the game of Go, which is also played by taking alternating turns, where both players can see the whole board and what is good for one player is bad for the other.

Go is game with very ancient roots; in fact, it was around long before chess. The actual origin of chess is lost in antiquity, but the game Go is referred to in Chinese documents from as early as 400 BCE. The game moved from China to Japan and Korea by the early centuries of the common era, and by somewhere around the 6th or 7th century was being played in essentially the same way as it is played today.

The modern game of Go is played on a board that is a 19x19 grid. Players take turns placing pieces, called stones, of specific colors (one player plays black stones, the other white stones) on a point of intersections of grid lines (that is, where chess pieces are inside the boxes, Go pieces are placed on the lines between them). Figure 3-9 shows a Go game in progress.

In Go, the play involves capturing an opponent's stones by surrounding them with stones of your own. This means that when one player has created a shape that encloses all the space within it (no breaks in the line), then they capture the other player's stones within that area. There are some other complexities with respect to captures (there are certain ways to protect stones even if they are within the surrounding line), but by and large this is the point. The simplest surround is when one player has placed their stones on the four points surrounding one of the other player's stones. The largest surround, which could virtually never happen in a real game, is for one player to place their stones on the entire outer border of the game (all around the 19x19 boxes) and capture everything within.

The end of a game of Go is technically when every place on the board is either covered or captured, but actually such a game would require a very large number of moves. The actual end of the game in Go is when both players agree that there is no point going on (roughly the equivalent of one player conceding defeat).

Figure 3-9. *A game of go in progress (From Wikipedia:* `https://commons.wikimedia.org/wiki/File:FloorGoban.JPG`*)*

The size of a possible Go game is incredibly large. There are 361 positions for the first player, 360 for the second, and so on. Thus, the total possible set of all moves is 361! This is a staggeringly large number (roughly a 10^{768}, a one followed by 768 zeros!) However, like tic-tac-toe, Go has a number of symmetries, a number of boards that are not possible, a number of orders that lead to the same position, etc. Even with all of these reductions, and taking into account that games between humans are usually settled in less than half as many moves as possible (about 150 is a much-quoted estimate), the number remains really large. A common estimate is about 10^{170}, which is much greater than the total number of possible chess games as described earlier. Moreover, where the game tree in chess is bounded at most places by the number of next moves, which is a number generally less than 40, the game tree of Go is bounded by the number of possible Go moves, which is typically in the hundreds in early play (possible places to place the next tile). To put these kind of numbers in perspective, the age of the universe in seconds is way smaller than the number of positions a Go player (whether human or computer) would have to consider to evaluate the whole game tree. In fact, it is smaller by many orders of magnitude. A computer that could evaluate a billion billion billion Go boards a second and that started computing at the time of the Big Bang would still be working on labeling the complete tree. Even using the tricks we discussed for chess, to look forward more than a few plies of Go would strain some of the fastest computers today.

It's worth noting that when humans play Go they usually start on a smaller board (9x9 and later 13x13). On the 9x9 board, the numbers are such that game tree search can work on today's computers, and so the computer can play as well as some of the best humans on the small board. On the 19x19 board (official Go board size) the best computers today are just starting to beat serious human players. In late 2014, a computer did beat a human champion on a 19x19 board. However, the computer was given a significant advantage (allowed to play a number of extra stones at the beginning), the rules were slightly simplified, and the length of the game was limited. In early 2015, two computer programs (one developed by Google and the other by Facebook) started to show significant improvement. As of early 2016, a computer had beaten a human Go champion for the first time in regulation play. The computer program called AlphaGO[6] beat the European champion in a 5-game challenge by a 5-0 score.

According to the current Go ratings, the human beaten was in the top 700 players in the world. However, as in chess, the climb up the top ranks is steep. By the time this book is published, AlphaGo will have played one of the top players in the world, and if it wins, then another AI breakthrough will have been made in game playing[7]. Meanwhile, a separate program, being written by a team from Facebook, is also making great progress in playing Go. In short, this is another game where the increasing power of computers, along with more sophisticated AI algorithms, is challenging to be the top player.

Other Games

Before looking at the differences in how humans and computers play games like Chess and Go, there are still many other games to consider; in particular, there are many other games where people play with, or against, computers. Many of these games don't have the properties of Go or chess, such as deterministic, complete information, and/or zero-sum. There are a tremendous number of games played by people around the world, and even if we ignore games of physical skill like sporting games, there is no way we can explore them all. However, we can examine some key features of these other types of games.

First, even within the category of zero-sum games, where what is good for one player is bad for another, there are certainly games that have some complexities that we do not see in chess or Go. For example, there are games like backgammon, in which the board is

---

[6]Silver, David, Huang, Aja, Maddison, Chris J., Guez, Arthur, Sifre,Laurent, van den Driessche, George, Schrittwieser, Julian, Antonoglou, Ioannis, Panneershelvam, Veda, Lanctot, Marc, Dieleman, Sander, Grewe, Dominik, Nham, John, Kalchbrenner, Nal, Sutskever, Ilya, Lillicrap, Timothy, Leach, Madeleine, Kavukcuoglu, Koray, Graepel, Thore and Hassabis, Demis, "Mastering the game of Go with deep neural networks and tree search", *Nature*, 529, (28 January 2016) p.484–489.
[7]In March of 2016, AlphaGo beat Lee Sedol, the fourth ranked human player, 4-1 in an official championship tournament. While more games will probably be forthcoming, as of now, computers are moving up the curve in Go that they did in Chess. Expect to see "Go centaurs" and other such innovations over the next few years.

fully exposed and the players take turns, but luck becomes involved; players throw dice to determine their moves. These games are referred to as *non-deterministic* games or, more colloquially, *games of chance.*

To humans, the element of luck sometimes seems somewhat mysterious, and many of us have witnessed some game where a very lucky amateur beats a much better player. To a computer, luck actually becomes a matter of probabilities and the game tree can be changed in several simple ways to support this.

For example, when we generate the next set of possible boards for each player, we need to take into account the different ways that the dice can come out. To do this takes two steps. First, when we generate the next set of moves for a player, we can take each of the possible roles into account and generate each of the board positions that is reachable with that particular role of the dice. Since there are 36 ways that two six-sided dice can land, and for each role there is some set of moves the next player could make, we end up with a bigger game tree; in fact, in backgammon the size of the game tree, taking into account the possible roles, is somewhere between chess and Go.

The second step is a little more complicated. In Chess, when we took into account what each player would do, we assumed they would make the best move they could find. But in the game tree for a non-deterministic game like backgammon, we have to take into account the probability that they can make that move. For example, supposing in a game of backgammon the game tree showed a bad (or good) outcome that would happen if the next player could move three spaces ahead[8]. Figure 3-10 shows the various rolls of the two dice, and all of those in which the player could either move one piece three spaces (i.e. at least one die is a three) or where the combined count equals a three. There are 13 different rolls of the dice where this could occur (the numbers shown in bold in the figure). Since there are 36 possible rolls in all, there is a 13/36, or about 36%, chance that the opponent will get to make that move. So we need to take these probabilities into account for each board. The simplest way to do this is to multiply the board value by the probability and use that as the estimate, and then make the best choices, as in a regular game tree search. There are also more complicated things that can be done with these probabilities, but essentially they all involve doing some sort of math between the rolls a user might get and the board evaluations for the positions they could reach.

For any single game of backgammon (or other games of chance) luck may determine a winner, but in a set of games, usually played in some kind of tournament style, the better player almost always wins. Today, backgammon programs use some variant of game-tree search and some game-specific heuristic tricks, and the best backgammon players are, like in chess, computers.

---

[8]The details of backgammon play are not relevant to this discussion, but for those who do play, a bad outcome might be where the other player could hit one of my exposed pieces and a good outcome might be where I've blocked a point and thus it will be harder for the opponent to move.

Die 1/ Die 2	1	2	3	4	5	6
1	2	3	4	5	6	7
2	3	4	5	6	7	8
3	4	5	6	7	8	9
4	5	6	7	8	9	10
5	6	7	8	9	10	11
6	7	8	9	10	11	12

Figure 3-10. *Probability table for two dice; bold numbers are all those where the opponent rolls can reach a spot three spaces away*

Another kind of non-deterministic game is one where a deck of cards is involved. In this case, there are two complicating factors. One, of course, is the luck in what cards one gets dealt. The other is that in most card games there are some cards which neither player knows the value of. This can be in a game like poker, where only some of the cards can be seen, or a game like bridge, where each player sees their own hand and some other cards but doesn't know which of the opponents holds the cards not yet seen. Thus, card games are generally not only non-deterministic, but also games of imperfect information; there are some things each player may not know.

For some games, the cards are all dealt out, the players know the cards they've seen so far, and thus the probability space may not be too big. For example, in the game of bridge, once the card play starts, each player can see half of the deck. As the game proceeds, the card that is played becomes known. Therefore, in just the card play part of the game, a probabilistic game tree search works well. However, bridge has a different part of the game where bidding occurs, and this happens when each player can only see their own hand. The details of bridge bidding are complex, but essentially it is a communicative act between the players, and each one is trying to use information from that stage to make guesses about what cards the other players may have. The number of possible deals in bridge is extremely large (all the permutations of 52 cards dealt to four different players), and the principles of bidding allow a lot of uncertainty.

Because of these two aspects of bridge, it is very interesting to compare computer and human play. In what is called *par contest bridge*, special hands are used and the quality of the play, more than the quality of the bidding, tends to dominate. In 1998, a computer program called GIB, developed by an American computer scientist and bridge player Matthew Ginsberg, beat a set of the world's best humans. However, regular tournament play is much more of a combination of bidding and playing skills, and to date the best humans still beat the best computerized bridge players.[9]

---

[9]Interestingly, one of the ways human players get better at bridge is by looking at particular deals and seeing what is the best that could be done. In this case, since all the cards are known, the game becomes a deterministic, perfect information game, and computers can easily evaluate the game tree much better and faster than humans can. So even though the best humans play better than computers, many of them train using computers to analyze the hands.

Other card games, especially poker, are much more interesting to explore. For certain kinds of poker, all that a player knows is their own hand and the probabilities of various types of hands. In these games, computers do well, although comparison between the human and computer is very hard because it involves determining not only probabilities, but the betting scheme. Assuming a fairly long period of time, the computer, using the probabilistic information, will eventually win; it simply does or does not use the probabilities to make a bet.

Another interesting poker game, where some cards are known and shared, is called Texas Hold-em (among other names). There is currently a lot of interest among humans in this game, and there are many high stake tournaments around. In this game, computers have steadily been making progress, and in January of 2015, the computer poker research group at the University of Alberta published a paper in *Science* magazine claiming they have essentially weakly solved this game. This implies that, except in rare cases, the computer should win. However, there is a huge amount of randomness in the game, and in a tournament played with a limited number of chips (thus being essentially of finite length) it is unclear that the theoretical result will translate to a practical one. As of 2016, a set of human vs. computer tournaments are being set up to test whether the computer will be as good in practice as it is in theory.

Similar to card games are various kinds of strategy games. Some are played as board games with various amounts of luck vs. skill, and in many of these computers can do quite well. Some, however, like a game called Infinite City, have very complex sets of rules, very high levels of combinatorics, and depending on situations there are times when one player can make multiple moves in a row, adding another kind of complexity. To date getting computers to play these games are at best in the early research stages.

There's one more type of game that we haven't looked at, which are known as *non–zero-sum games*. These are games where there isn't a competition between the players where what is good for one is not good for another. Very few games that are commonly played are non-zero-sum (although with the growth in new kinds of table games, some are beginning to show up in specialized game stores). However, there are many games that are technically zero-sum because they are competitive, but they're not so much played for the win as for the enjoyment of the game. For example, party games like charades (a game played by trying to essentially act out common phrases) often have two teams that are essentially competing, but in many cases the score isn't really the important thing.

Similarly, there are many online games that are often played by humans playing together in a game mediated by a computer. Some of these are games like Grand Theft Auto in which humans essentially play against a computer, but also against each other to amass a score, so the computer isn't trying to play the game the same way. Other games, like League of Legends or World of Warcraft (each of which has million of players around the world), are also mediated by a computer, but people play in teams and have social relationships. These games are hard to even categorize by the traditional terms of non-determism, zero-sum, etc; especially where computers may be the adversaries (for example, they power the monsters in the World of Warcraft) the point of the game is to do well against the game's AI.

Finally, there are also games that are more about using imagination and creativity as opposed to being competitive per se. These games are increasingly popular, and they too are often played for fun rather than for competition. As an exemplar of this kind of game, consider Dungeons and Dragons, a game that has been played by people in countries around the world for over 40 years (and is now available in dozens of languages). In this game, one player, known as the Dungeon Master (DM), creates a fantasy landscape and a quest that a set of other players take part in. These players take on roles of various types ranging from thieves and rogues to wizards and healers. The rules of the game dictate many properties of players and the monsters they face on their quests, but one of the fun aspects of the play is that the humans can make up creative things to try, and the DMs use their judgment to decide what may and may not work. Knowing about the physical properties of the real world (weights and measures, for example) coupled with properties of the fictitious world of the dungeon makes the game a fun challenge for the players. The game is played primarily through a combination of language (communication between players and DMs) and luck (many different dice of many kinds are used in different situations), and experience becomes an important feature of game play. To date, computers are occasionally used as resources by some players during play (although many people use the game as a reason to turn off the machines and interact with other humans), but to date no computer D&D player of note has been devised.(A recent doctoral thesis explores how a Watson-like architecture can play these more complex games[10]. In it, the author states his aim as the eventual design of a computer that can play an interesting game of Dungeons and Dragons.)

How Do Humans Play Games?

In thinking about AI and games, it is useful to look at how humans have managed to play games so well. Why did it take so many generations of computer technology, looking ahead more and more plies down a game tree, until it could beat a human chess player? Why is it difficult for a computer to beat a human player at Go? In fact, we might want to ask "how is it humans can play Go at all, given the complexity of the game?"

Ironically, these are hard questions to answer largely because we know more about how computers play than how humans do. That's not to say that human game playing hasn't been studied; it's been an active area of research for a long time, and new studies are going on all the time. The real problem is that we can analyze a computer's algorithm in detail, since we can examine the specific code it runs, but we don't yet have tools to look inside humans' cognitive processing at that level. While some of the newer tools in neuroscience and psychology are being used to explore game play, modern tools still aren't close to letting us analyze what is happening in the human brain at the level of detail we would need in order to accurately understand the human's cognitive process. Several experiments have been conducted in order to determine what humans are doing while they play games.

Some of the earliest experiments on human game-playing were done more than a century ago. Alfred Binet, the scientist who developed the IQ test approach we still use today, was interested in human memory. One of the things he explored was *blindfold chess*, where a human chess player plays against an adversary without being able to see the board; he's just told the moves. Binet surveyed many chess players, especially masters, asking them various questions about how they performed the task. He was especially interested in whether the players used "visual imagery" (keeping a sort of mental picture of the game) or some other memory trick. His results were not conclusive but indicated that most of the better players didn't mentally visualize the board, but rather used some abstract method to represent the board.

---

[10]S. Ellis, "When Watson Gets Board: Cognitive Computing as a Basis for AI in Tabletop Games", Doctoral Thesis, Computer Science, Rensselaer Polytechnic Institute, 2016.

The approach used by Binet, and many later psychologists following his work, is referred to as *protocol analysis*. People are asked to describe out loud to an observer what they are doing while they perform a task or to describe in detail what they have done. The researcher uses the results to draw conclusions about what was observed. In the middle of the twentieth century, the field which we now call *cognitive psychology*, started to come into its own, with an increasing emphasis on experimental methods with rigorous comparisons between groups.

One of the first people to apply the protocol analysis method to chess playing was the Dutch psychologist Aadrien de Groot, who was himself a strong chess player. In 1965, De Groot ran an experiment by taking a position from a game of chess (i.e. the board at some point in the middle of the game), exposing it to people for a short amount of time, and asking them to recall the pieces. According to de Groot's results, the best players could remember over 90% of the pieces, while average players did much worse, barely remembering more than half the pieces. In a further experiment, de Groot showed that when he took the same number of pieces and placed them on the board at random, instead of in game play positions, the difference largely vanished, with stronger and weaker players remembering about the same number of pieces. Later experiments by de Groot's colleagues showed that people with little or no chess experience remembered about the same number, regardless of whether they were from real or random positions, as the chess players did on the random boards. De Groot concluded that this confirmed the idea, going back to Binet, that abstract representations, based on the structure of the game of chess, were being used by players, as opposed to just visual memory.

In 1973, a paper published by William Chase and Herbert Simon[11] explored this idea in great detail. Chase and Simon exposed chess boards with pieces on them to their subjects, in the same way de Groot did, but controlled many factors including the part of the game the boards were from (early-, middle- or end-game play). They also controlled for the number of pieces for particular kinds of chess positions that could arise in play (for example, when one player's piece could threaten two of another player's, a situation known in chess as a *fork*), and other chess-specific factors. They were able to show that better chess players were able to remember more of the "meaningful" positions and to explore which kinds were better remembered.

They concluded that chess players, especially the better players, were able to remember "chunks" of positions with multiple pieces, as if they were single units. Thus, where a non-chess player might remember that a particular piece was at a particular place on the board, an experienced player was able to remember sets of pieces that represented:

> 1. *A variety of chunks consisting of Pawns (and possible Rook and minor pieces) in common castled-King positions;*
>
> 2. *A variety of chunks consisting of common first-rank configurations;*
>
> 3. *A variety of chunks consisting of common Pawn chain, Rook pair, and Rook and Queen configurations;*

---

[11]This is the same scientist mentioned earlier in the chapter as arguing for the operationalization of AI. In his early work, he explored computer and human chess play, with this paper being his most famous from his chess research.

4. A variety of common configurations of attacking pieces, especially along a file, diagonal, or around an opponent's castled-King position.

—Chase and Simon, Cognitive Psychology 4 (1973), p. 80.

Simon, his colleague Allen Newell, and several of their students generalized this idea of reasoning via "chunks" into a computer model called Soar, which has been widely used to model different aspects of human cognitive behavior. While some other researchers have rejected the idea that chunking is as fundamental to human thinking as the Soar model proposes, there is clear evidence, and general agreement, that for chess and similar games, it is an important aspect of human play. However, exactly how humans learn the patterns in these chunks, how they use them at the right time in chess play, and how experts apply them to learn to play against different opponents with different styles all remain open questions.

In studying Go, there has been less formal experimentation reported, with much of the work still being at a similar level to that of early chess studies (analyzing the descriptions of games by the masters). Many very famous early works on Go, from hundreds of years ago, taught the game through "proverbs" that would help players learn to recognize certain kinds of patterns or strategies that could improve play. These proverbs include general advice about moves, such as "play on the point of symmetry;" ways to recognize very specific situations, such as "learn the eye-stealing tesuji" (a particular pattern of about ten stones); and general statements of game strategies such as "big dragons never die" (which essentially recommends linking up smaller patterns into larger, harder to surround, groups).[12] It has been argued that these proverbs essentially correspond to the same idea as chunking in chess, although it is hard to prove this given both the greater complexity of the game and the fact that a number of these proverbs use metaphors rather than specific patterns (compare the tesuji and dragon proverbs above).

Beyond chunking, one of the things most discussions of human Go playing seem to agree on is that Go is very dependent on the ability to see patterns emerging on the board. In fact, part of what makes Go so interesting and so challenging is that, according to many players, when playing a good game of Go, if a player can recognize "non-local" effects, that is, a stone that is relatively far from the center of action, that recognition can be crucial to the outcome. (In fact, even talking about the "center of action" is wrong, as strong players competing at Go appear to be playing in a number of centers of action at the same time.)

Somewhat generalizing, it is this latter hallmark of Go that is pointed at when people talk about how humans outperfom computers not just at this game, but also at a number of other tasks. While computers can do deep searches and use complex rules in narrow domains, humans still tend to do better when it comes to "synthesis" of results over multiple domains, or where recognizing a key aspect of a pattern that is spread over a wide set of entities is involved.

In addition, the sort of proverbs used to help train Go players relate to another area where humans seem different than computers. The ability to find correspondences between stones on the Go board and general patterns, and to relate these patterns to concepts way beyond Go, like dragons, seems to be an important part of how humans play Go. Similarly, in chess, concepts like *forks*, *traps*, and *lines of*

---

[12]A collection of Go slogans can be found online at http://senseis.xmp.net/?GoProverbs.

defense let us use our memories of things we know from outside the game domain to help us to process (and particularly to chunk) what moves to make next. This ability to reason by analogy between one situation (like a chess position) and another (such as a real-world concept like a trap) is an important strength of humans that computers still cannot approach (as we will discuss in a later chapter).

Finally, Go points out one more ability that seems to still be significantly easier for humans than computers. Not only does Go require seeing patterns, the best players are the ones who can see the patterns *before* they form (predict emerging patterns). Top Go players report that they place tiles based on where various potential surrounds may occur; they see the dragons before they emerge, not after they form. This ability is still something AI systems have been unable to duplicate outside of very specific areas with a lot of specialized knowledge. The vague kinds of patterns that seem crucial to Go are still challenging the current state of the art. Programs such as AlphaGo, for example, are not able to generalize their pattern recognition the way humans can. For example, if a game was played on a 21 x 21 board, AlphaGo, which was trained on 19x19 would do poorly, while a human expert would be able to continue to play at a high level.

Beyond Games

We started this chapter by exploring the idea that while it seems clear to us that humans and computers are different, nailing down the differences and what they mean with respect to how humans and machines differ at a cognitive level is difficult. However, as we've explored human vs. computer game play, a number of differences have emerged as important. AI systems exploit the computer's large memory, mathematical algorithms, and various kinds of search techniques to play games against humans. Humans take advantage of being able to recognize emerging patterns, to recognize somewhat abstract positions such as the chunks in chess, and to relate what is happening in games to aspects of life in the real world to better organize their thinking about what is happening (as we see in the Go slogans).

If you think back to the previous chapter, you saw examples from medicine that had similar features. The computers were able to process large amounts of texts using the large memories available, to process mathematically the probabilities among symptoms and diseases, and to use specialized algorithms to identify items that were hard for humans to identify in images. Doctors, on the other hand, were able to take into account features of what they perceived in patients learned from experience, to "chunk" various kinds of medical situations in reasoning about how to diagnose diseases, and to look at a wider context than medicine in determining how to prescribe their treatments.

As we continue to explore the AI technologies that are making computers more powerful than ever, it is useful to keep these kinds of differences in mind. In the next two chapters, we will explore some of the other differences in capabilities between humans and computers, looking at the weaknesses of each as they try to deal with the complex interactions in the world in which we live.

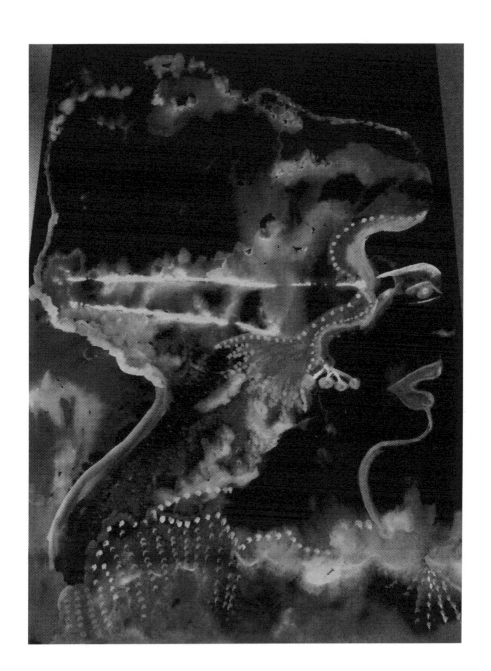

CHAPTER 4

■ ■ ■

The Limits of Humans

People are amazing, especially when it comes to creativity and adaptability. Many of the cognitive skills that humans regularly use to solve problems, imagine, play, and create still stump computer scientists to even define, let alone program. Humans are, by evolution, amazing pattern recognizers, including our ability to see patterns not yet formed. However, the cognitive machinery that gives us this breadth also limits our ability to concentrate on a single thought deeply through many, many alternatives. While some people (like skilled planners or chess players) are better at generating and keeping track of numerous alternatives, the number of alternatives that most people can efficiently handle is well below the thousands of alternatives that computers can routinely generate and manage. Additionally, cognitive skills vary across people, are dependent on our genetics and experiences, and tend to degrade as we age.

In the previous chapter, we discussed some limits of computers, and we will return to that theme in later chapters. In this chapter, we will discuss some of the limitations that humans have, how automation can augment some of these limits, and how some emerging technologies, such as deep learning, are giving the computer more human-like capabilities in perception. Later, in Chapter 6, we will further explore this idea of augmenting humans with the help of artificial intelligence.

Problem Solving

Human problem solving is a skill that has evolved collectively over many generations, and continuously evolves over the lifetime of each individual. We are all born with a set of sensory systems that allow us to detect and interpret many forms of data (such as visual, auditory, and tactile). Based on instinctual survival needs, or learned through training, we each develop our own methods for filtering incoming data (such as prioritizing and biasing) so that we can better interact with our environment and solve the many different types of problems we encounter in our day-to-day lives.

Figuring out how to make sense out of all of the different forms of data that we encounter takes time. During the process involved in learning about our world, we often receive feedback (both negative and positive). For example, when a child first sees fire, the child might find the colors and the movement of the flames so fascinating that they touch the flame. If the child gets burned as a result of touching the flame and feels pain, this feeling of pain (which is a type of negative feedback) will help the child to associate touching a flame with pain and will bias the child to avoid touching a flame in the future. Moreover, the child will also learn to be wary of any source that generates high heat,

© James Hendler and Alice M. Mulvehill 2016
J. Hendler and A. M. Mulvehill, *Social Machines*, DOI 10.1007/978-1-4842-1156-4_4

thus generalizing the experience for the future. This ability to identify patterns, make associations, build up general concepts from experiences with different patterns, and in general accumulate and use knowledge, is enabled by our physiology (brain and body composition), motor skills, sensory, cognitive, and memory capabilities.

The ability to form patterns from input data and use those patterns to build up categories that can then help us interact with the environment appears to be an innate ability. Building links between observed patterns and the associated context (such as time and space) and building pattern or concept categories is a process called *concept formation*. This process is both influenced by and continuously refined through our individual experiences, either through our exploration with the world around us (a form of unsupervised learning) or by being coached (a form of supervised learning). Playing is an example of exploratory unsupervised learning. Being explicitly taught words for objects is an example of supervised learning.

Once we have learned a pattern for something and have experienced the usefulness of the pattern for interacting with the environment, we don't have to keep relearning the pattern. Instead, our minds are able to somehow represent and store the pattern so that we can use it in the future. This ability to solve a new problem or recognize a new pattern by matching it to some previously solved problem or observed pattern is called *pattern recognition*. Pattern recognition relies on the ability of our sensory, perceptual, and cognitive systems to extract features from input data; identify some regularity in that data (build a pattern); determine if a new pattern is similar to other patterns we have encountered (build categories of patterns); and compare new patterns to known patterns as needed to support learning and problem solving.

Having a set of patterns somehow encoded in our memories and being able to use them during pattern recognition is a type of reasoning. Unfortunately, sometimes a pattern that we have encountered in the past doesn't exactly match some pattern that we are currently observing, and when we try to take an action to respond to what we are currently observing, it doesn't have the same result. For example, an apple is a fruit that a parent might give to a child to eat. Initially, the parent might instruct the child to eat the apple by biting into it. The child does so and enjoys the taste of the apple. So, the child learns that the pattern or concept of apple is related to something that has a particular shape and color and can be eaten. Now imagine that the child sees a bowl of fruit on a table and one of the pieces of fruit in the bowl looks like an apple. The child picks up the apple and takes a bite. But, the texture and taste is different because this is not an edible apple; it is a wax apple. The child will probably stop trying to eat the wax apple. How does she learn to differentiate inedible apples from edible apples? In general, this happens with experience. As the child encounters both edible apples and decorative non-edible apples, she learns to differentiate the two different types of very similar patterns (apples) by the features of texture, taste, and any other feature that seems important. Moreover, unlike a cat or dog encountering this kind of situation, as the child accumulates more experiences and becomes more verbal, she learns to understand the concept of real vs. artificial, and to generalize it to many more things than just apples. This type of learning and associated reasoning relies substantially on our ability to recognize patterns and to identify certain distinguishing features of those patterns, and is often referred to by terms such as *learning by experience, analogical reasoning,* and *case-based reasoning.*

Although all humans have an ability to recognize patterns and use their knowledge of patterns to solve problems, our abilities are not equal or interchangeable. Genetics and life experiences play a large role in what each of us comes to know and what skills we each possess. Additionally, each of us has the ability to choose to learn more or less about different problem domain areas, and each of us can develop unique methods for solving problems. This is partly what enables some of us to become expert at a particular skill or craft, or to become expert at solving some particular type of problem.

Researchers in the 70s and 80s who were using Artificial Intelligence (AI) techniques to build expert systems explored why some people are considered an expert. Many of the early expert systems were developed to encapsulate the knowledge of some person who was considered an expert in a particular problem domain and was planning to retire. Early expert systems were generally composed of a knowledge base and an inference engine. Once operational, many of the successful expert systems were used to train novices or to provide recommendations or reminders about how to solve some particular problem set.

One way to build an expert system is to interview an expert and collect stories about how he/she came to become an expert and to solve specific types of problems. This interview process is called *knowledge acquisition*, and when done properly results in the development of a domain-specific knowledge base and a set of rules and procedures (heuristics) to support inferencing. However, while many experts can generally describe how their experience over time helped them to perceive domain patterns and build up their domain knowledge, they often have difficulty articulating the details for how they solve a problem[1]. Many experts will talk about the little tricks they have developed to more efficiently discover patterns in the data or some novel methods they used to classify patterns based on both similarities and differences. However, when it comes to describing how they actually solve a problem, they might describe strategies that sound like formulas or rules, or they might just say that it was their intuition that allowed them to solve the problem.

What does it mean to use intuition to solve a problem? Is the expert's problem solving ability so ingrained that it has become an automatic behavior like a habit and therefore appears to be intuitive? Assume that you are good at driving a car. When you drive your car, do you consciously think of how to perform tasks like applying pressure to the gas or brake pedals, or turning the wheel as you drive? In general, you don't consciously think of each of these actions because your driving has become automatic, or intuitive. However, if you are in a very stressful driving environment, like a very busy interstate intersection where you have to quickly think and drive (multitask), you will likely become more aware of your actions.

The fact that some people can become masters or experts at solving certain problems emphasizes how individual differences enable unique capabilities. While many of us can drive a car, only some of us have the interest in and go on to develop skills that are required to drive at high speeds on a professional raceway. Additionally, although it's generally possible for people to get good at one or two things, few people can be great at many things. This may be one of the reasons why people form groups. In a group, people can use their unique skills to support others in the group, thereby enabling the group to do many of the things that a single individual can't do.

Unfortunately, some of us will never be able to perform certain tasks, let alone become experts at some task, because of certain cognitive and/or physical limitations that we are either born with or that we acquire at some point in our lives. While many sensory, perceptual, and cognitive deficiencies can be remedied with synthetic devices

---

[1]Collopy, F., Adya, M., and Armstrong, J. S., "Expert Systems for Forecasting", In *Principles of Forecasting: A Handbook for Researchers and Practitioners* (Ed. J. Scott Armstrong), Kluwer, 2001.

like prosthetics, hearing aids, and glasses, some disabilities like cerebral palsy and some forms of autism are not so easily corrected. Fortunately, humans are very adaptable and often develop a set of alternative skills to compensate for skills that they lack. For example, people who are deaf often learn to communicate in sign language and may also develop enhanced abilities to interpret gestures and bodily movements. In addition, while being deaf might be considered a limitation in general, in some environments, for example where there is a lot of noise, being deaf might be an advantage because a deaf individual's ability to problem solve might not be affected by the noise[2]. So while certain physical, sensory, perceptual, and cognitive differences can typify a human limitation, some differences can result in extraordinary intelligence and skills.

In the following paragraphs, we describe several other human attributes that may present as limitations either within a particular context or as a person ages.

Memory and Aging

Years of research about memory and the brain indicates that memory is a reconstructive process. A single memory of an experience is not located in one particular part of the brain; parts of that memory are distributed across different areas of the brain. Memories can be imagined as a complex web in which the threads symbolize the various elements of a memory that join at nodes or intersection points to form a whole memory of a person, object, or event. This kind of distributed memory ensures that even if part of the brain is damaged, some parts of an experience may still be retained[3].

Unfortunately, during memory reconstruction, people may "mutate" their memories, and in some cases introduce errors as they reconstruct what they remember from the past. For example, researchers studying autobiographical memory[4] discovered that suggestions, false beliefs about the past, and knowledge from sources other than one's own experiences can provide unreliable building blocks. Additionally, the more incorrect information a person uses when constructing a memory, the more erroneous the memory will be[5].

Memory reconstruction also tends to get worse as we age. As people enter their senior years, they might start to have age-related limitations such as: degraded sensory capabilities (poor vision), motor skill problems (difficulties with balance), and cognitive problems (memory loss). In some cases, there can be a ripple effect with degraded sensory capabilities leading to incorrect perception and cognition, which can result in poor concept/pattern formation and higher tendencies to distort memories. For example, as a person ages, they might have diminished olfactory capabilities, which means that they can no longer rely on their sense of smell to detect food that has gone bad. As a result, they might stop eating some type of food if the food makes them sick, or they might start to use another sense (such as vision) to identify bad food (since food often has a certain color when it is fresh and this color changes as the food decays). Unfortunately, because age can also impact the visual capabilities, this kind of compensation itself starts to become less reliable.

---

[2]Sparrow, Robert, "Defending Deaf Culture: The Case of Cochlear Implants", in *The Journal of Political Philosophy*, Vol. 13, Number 2, 2005, pp. 135-152.

[3]See www.human-memory.net for a good introduction to human memory and its organization.

[4]Loftus, Elizabeth F., "Illusions of Memory", in *Proceedings of the American Philosophical Society*, Vol. 142, No. 1, pp. 60-73, March 1998.

[5]Hyman, Ira E. Jr. and Loftus, Elizabeth F., "Errors in Autobiographical Memory", *Clinical Psychology Review*, Vol. 18, No. 8, pp. 933–947, Elsevier Science Ltd., 1998.

In addition to having problems sensing and perceiving the environment, some people might not be able to remember much or even anything about what they are perceiving. This problem is often faced by people with certain types of dementia such as Alzheimer's, and these memory limitations can affect their behavior and performance well before the age of 65. As we age, and especially if we develop dementias, we also tend to lose our ability to effectively multitask. While we might still be able to do two things at the same time, we might be a lot slower at executing these parallel tasks. For example, many seniors with balance problems have difficulty walking and talking at the same time because they need to focus on balancing so that they don't fall. Some of the research about multitasking indicates that multitasking is a skill that varies across individuals, is acquired over time, and seems to be associated with the individual's ability to plan and manage available attention and cognitive resources (such as memory and language understanding) and to execute task-coordination strategies. Because multitasking is a skill, babies often have trouble walking and vocalizing at the same time. Research about multitasking indicates that high-level cognitive processes appear to interfere with seemingly automatic processes like walking and the mutual costs accrued by such interference are pronounced at opposite ends of the lifespan. Some researchers are currently developing games to improve multitasking. One widely reported example is the video game NeuroRacer[6] which, according to research results published in 2013, shows that this type of game could improve multitasking performance in older adults, and might actually reverse some age-related memory and cognition deficits (Figure 4-1).

Figure 4-1. *Using games to enrich memory (Gazzaley Labs)*

---

[6]Gazzaley Lab, "Video game training enhances cognitive control in older adults", http://gazzaleylab.ucsf.edu/neuroscience-projects/neuroracer/.

Currently, several other companies are also working to create games or web sites based on this and similar ideas.

Emotion and Stress

One of the amazing qualities of human beings is their ability to communicate complex concepts through emotion. When we interact with other people, we interact physically, intellectually, and emotionally. Each of us has a number of basic emotions including anger, fear, surprise, disgust, happiness, and sadness, to name a few. From these, we can learn to identify the emotions of others and discern hostile from friendly intent; happiness from anger; fear from sadness, etc.

People express emotions in a variety of ways, both verbal and non-verbal (through bodily movements and facial expressions). People learn how to interpret displays of emotion. For example, a look of anger might warn us to stay away from someone, while a facial expression of happiness might encourage us to interact with someone.

The meaning of some facial expressions and body movements that seem to convey basic information can vary across cultures. For example, in some parts of India, people often nod their heads in an up/down motion to indicate refusal or an objection to something. Alternatively, in the United States, this same type of nod often connotes agreement. This difference in the interpretation of a physical motion can cause subtle misunderstandings when people are interacting interculturally.

Emotions can be used to convey a variety of information about a certain context. Early Greek theater used comedy and tragedy masks to help the actors convey happiness and sadness about actions being displayed in the play to the audience. Today people use a variety of emoticons to convey their emotion when they are sending text and e-mail messages. There are many different types of emoticons available, an indicator of how complex emotions can be. Somebody might choose one emoticon to convey happiness but a more complex emoticon if they want to convey both happiness and excitement.

Our memories are also highly affected by the emotion that is associated with our experiences. The emotional content of an experience can influence how we store the experience as a memory, our ability to reconstruct a memory, and how the remembrance of that memory affects future action. For example, bad emotional memories might encourage us to avoid certain places or people and minimize our willingness to take certain risks or perform certain tasks[7].

There are many books and journal articles dedicated to explaining how our emotions bias our interpretations of the environment and affect our behavior. Emotions influence how we solve problems, whom we bond with, and the choices we make in our lives. While emotional bias can enhance our chances for survival, it can also limit our curiosity[8], our willingness to explore, and our ability to accept changes in our environment.

---

[7]Neisser, Ulric, *Memory Observed, Remembering in Natural Contexts*, W. H. Freeman and Company, 1982.
[8]Kahneman, Daniel, *Thinking Fast and Slow*, Farrar, Straus, and Giroux, NY, 2011.

A recent movie (released in 2015) called *Inside Out* by Disney illustrates how different emotions can influence our interpretation of the world and our actions. In this movie, individual animated creatures are used to represent several basic emotions of the main character, such as joy, sadness, fear, disgust, and anger. During the movie, certain situations arise and we get to watch how differently those situations are interpreted and responded to by different emotional creatures. The movie represents memories as colored orbs that are stored in long-term memory. Reacting to a situation is affected by a control console that can be directed by any of the emotional creatures. The movie shows how one emotional creature, *Joy*, might try to prevent another emotional creature like *Sadness* from storing a memory or using a stored memory as the basis for a response to some situation. While simplified for the purpose of the movie, this film shows how a number of key aspects of emotional content can affect memory and behavior.

Many environmental situations can invoke certain negative emotional responses such as fear and anger, which can impair how we function. Sometimes these negative emotions can even lead to physical distress and illness. We often refer to this influence on a person as *stress*. Certain types and amounts of stress are highly correlated with a human's ability to make certain types of decisions. For example, most of us would agree that preparing for, being in, or talking about some natural or man-made disaster evokes emotion and possibly some level of stress, especially if the problem situation can personally impact us or someone we know or care about. Weather reports are often filled with information about impeding or currently occurring natural disasters, such as hurricanes, snow storms, tornadoes, earthquakes, etc. If we are planning to take a trip and one of these types of disasters is forecast to occur, our travel plans, such as airplane flights, might be delayed or cancelled. The delays or cancellation can cause stress because we do not have control of the situation or of the potential side effects.

The two most notable and common reactions to stress are flight and fight. For example, if we live in some geographical location and a natural threat is predicted, our instinct for survival may cause us to leave the area (flight). However, if we have lived in this area for a long time, and have survived similar threats in the past, we might decide to stay and take some local actions (board up windows) to prevent harm (fight). Fight and flight are basic reactions across the animal kingdom, but in humans they are intrinsically tied to complex planning and the ability to make decisions about alternatives to pursue.

As an example, in August of 2005, Hurricane Katrina hit the United States (Figure 4-2). Katrina caused severe destruction along the Gulf coast from central Florida to Texas, much of it due to storm surge and infrastructure failure. Roads for evacuation were overwhelmed by people trying to escape.

Figure 4-2. Hurricane Katrina moved ashore over southeast Louisiana and southern Mississippi early on August 29, 2005, as an extremely dangerous Category 4 storm. (Credit: GOES Project Science Office[9])

Although advanced warning allowed some people to prepare for the storm and many to leave the areas that were likely to be hit, many people did not leave and were forced to stay in cramped shelters while the hurricane played out. The Superdome, which was sheltering many people in New Orleans who had not evacuated, sustained significant damage. Many people lost their lives and their homes as a result of this storm.

One might think that disaster relief support would arrive quickly in a country like the United States. Unfortunately, providing support to any area hit by a disaster takes time, requires a lot of logistics coordination, and tends to be impeded by local government regulations and by physical infrastructure damages that have affected the area. This delay in disaster relief for Katrina resulted in anger in many of the people affected. Not only did people not get evacuated quickly, but many had to deal with other problems that are common after a natural disaster, including increases in crime (such as looting) due to insufficient food and water availability, and health problems due to overcrowding and a lack of good drinking water and proper sanitation.

Even months or years after a disaster occurs, many people continue to deal with emotional and economic issues associated with the loss of their loved ones and/or of their property. Many people who lived and worked in the area affected by Katrina were left without housing and many became unemployed. Statistics published at https://en.wikipedia.org/wiki/Hurricane_Katrina show that before the hurricane, the region supported approximately one million non-farm jobs, with 600,000 of them in

---

[9]More about Hurricane Katrina at www.livescience.com/22522-hurricane-katrina-facts.html#sthash.3WK2g1ht.dpuf.

New Orleans. The site authors estimate that the total economic impact in Louisiana and Mississippi could eventually exceed $150 billion.

In addition to reacting differently to stressful situations, each of us react at different speeds to problems that cause stress. Some of us are able to make decisions quickly while others go into a type of shock and become incapable of making any decisions. Under severe stress, some people develop post traumatic stress disorder (PTSD). For example, researchers who study the economic, sociological, physiological, and psychological effects of hurricaines, such as Hurricane Katrina, discovered that many of the people who were personally involved in the storm and its aftermath experienced PTSD symptoms, and that some people had symptoms that lasted for a long time after the disaster ended. Stress is such a common and limiting problem for humans involved in disasters that a variety of web sites (for example, http://www.mentalhealthamerica.net/conditions/coping-stress-natural-diasters) have been developed to provide the general public with tips on how to recognize and cope with stress.

Coping with disasters is just one example of a problem context where people can become challenged in their ability to take physical and/or cognitive actions because of limits introduced by the complex interplay of emotion and stress. Coping with the different challenges that a natural disaster can pose currently exceeds the capability of any current single type of technology. Networks of different types of technologies appear to be able to provide some help. For example, cell phone systems and computer bulletin boards are being used more commonly to help families find their loved ones. Specialized robots have been developed and effectively utilized to search for people lost in the rubble after a disaster. Several sophisticated planning software decision support systems have been developed and utilized by the military and local governments to more effectively react to and manage disaster relief activities. In other words, some computerized tools to support humans during emotional and stressful situations are being provided through a society that is made up of both humans and technology.

Socialization and Mobility

We are born with the ability to crawl and reach so that we can more easily explore and interact with our environment. Some of us learn to walk, drive a car, and fly in an airplane to other places, and even into outer space. Some of us learn several languages so that we can communicate and socialize with others across cultural barriers. We form social and emotional bonds with other people and often join a variety of groups (soccer team, book club, professional organization). However, compared with a computer, we have limitations on our physical mobility (a computer can connect to a computer in China in milliseconds, while a person in the US still takes a day to get there on our fastest planes).

Machines and automation in general have been augmenting our ability to move and socialize for a long time. While the automobile and airplane have made it easier for us to travel geographically, information technology has provided an alternative form of mobility that allows us to explore, communicate, and maintain social relationships through phone calls, e-mail, texting, Facebook, Skype, and a variety of social tools. Virtual reality technology, once considered science fiction or confined for use in research laboratories, is currently being marketed as a method for mobility[10], especially for people who have limited abilities to physically move or travel. For example, virtual environments such as the Virtual Senior Center (http://selfhelp.net/virtual-senior-center) are being used to enable home-bound seniors to interact with friends and participate in social groups. Early findings indicate that many elderly individuals report that they are happier being able to socialize virtually through this technology than they are without this capability. In general, interaction with others, whether in person or virtually, tends to improve a person's quality of life.

Humans are social creatures. Some of the research about how people react during natural disasters indicates that people tend to band together in a disaster to reduce stress and feelings of vulnerability. Many of these issues have been explored in a 2012 *Scientific American article*[11]. Much speculation now centers on evaluating and determining whether the use of these technologies for socialization can help ameliorate some of the limitations of humans caused by physical distance.

Humans and Tools

Humans have been creating tools to augment their capabilities and support their needs for a very long time, as evidenced in findings from archeological investigations of early civilizations. Humans experienced major shifts in automation during the Industrial Revolution and the more recent Information Revolution. The loom was created to help enhance the production of cloth; the telephone changed the way humans communicate with people at a distance. Computer technology has helped people perform many different types of computational tasks including monitoring and managing factories; analyzing medical data; supporting command and control; managing financial records, photos; and so on. Computer technology will also continue to evolve.

The World Wide Web, along with its browsers and search engines, has brought education, the library, and shopping into our homes. Although some people are considered to be *early technology adopters*, others are reluctant to accept and use new technology because they don't understand how it works, they don't trust it to be correct, or it costs too much to acquire and/or maintain. For example, the number of households with computers has increased dramatically since the 1970s. Part of this increase is due to the reduction in the cost of having a computer and the improvements made in computer interfaces. However, other common reasons include the need for children in a household to use a computer to do their homework, and more commonly, the use of a computer to make purchases and manage income and expenses.

Accepting AI technology is no exception. Although many people are not aware of it, AI is currently being used reliably in many of the systems and devices that we commonly use, such as the cars we drive, the airplanes that we fly in, and many of the devices that we use in our homes, like our heating systems. Additionally, AI technology has been used to develop many of the algorithms that are used to manage air traffic, traffic lights, to make hotel and flight reservations, and to support advanced logistics systems.

---

[10]Kamieth, F. et all, "Exploring the Potential of Virtual Reality for the Elderly and People with Disabilities", cdn.intechopen.com/pdfs/13659.pdf.
[11]www.scientificamerican.com/article/how-the-stress-of-disaster-brings-people-together/.

Today's educators and some parents are trying to use technology to provide early training to their children about engineering, science, and technology. This has resulted in a number of specialized educational programs that are currently introducing science, technology, engineering, and math (STEM) topics into many school systems across the United States. Some parents are introducing their pre-school children to toys like *Robot Turtles* (Figure 4-3; www.robotturtles.com) so that they can learn about skills associated with science and engineering while they are engaged in play.

Figure 4-3. *Robot Turtle Game from www.robotturtles.com*

Toys and specialized technology (www.therapyshoppe.com) are also being developed for children with many different types of learning needs such as autism.

Artificial cognitive computing technologies, such as smart home sensing systems, memory reminding devices, and robots are also being developed to support elderly humans. For example, specialized robots are being developed and programmed to assist seniors with physical exercises, to help them take medicine, or perform a variety of housekeeping tasks. Home care robots are being developed in many countries like Japan, where there is a large aging population, to provide a variety of support services for elderly individuals who are living in their own homes.

Can Machines Augment Human Limits?

In this chapter, we have described how humans, as amazing as we are, can still be limited by physiological, psychological, emotional, or social conditions. Several examples have been provided that describe how technology can be used to augment or eliminate some of these limitations. Cognitive computing technologies, introduced in Chapter 2, are an important aspect of this work. These technologies appear to have the capability to provide expertise to people when they need it (replacing older forms of knowledge-based systems), and there is good evidence to indicate that these types of systems could provide support to people who suffer from a variety of human limitations, like memory decline, which, according to the Alzheimer's Association could become epidemic in the future. According to information provided on the Alzheimer's Association web site (http://www.alz.org/facts/), the number of Americans with Alzheimer's disease and other dementias will grow each year as the size and proportion of the U.S. population age 65 and older continues to increase. By 2050, the number of people age 65 and older with Alzheimer's disease may nearly triple, from 5.1 million to a projected 13.8 million, barring the development of medical breakthroughs to prevent or cure the disease.

Humans are creative problem solvers and they will continue to extend and enhance intelligent computing systems. One technology that shows promise for developing future cognitive computing systems is a type of machine learning called *deep learning*[12]. Deep learning software uses several novel representation schemes and neural network-based machine learning techniques to learn and improve by experience. Many large companies, ranging from web giants like Google and Facebook to traditional business leaders such as GE and IBM, are experimenting with the usage of this technology. Until recently, no machine learning technique was able to beat a human at the game Go, which requires the ability to see patterns not yet formed and to learn from experience. However, in 2016, Google announced that a version of its DeepMind system called AlphaGo was able to successfully defeat Europe's reigning Go champion. Google's algorithm was able to use information provided to it by humans, and to learn on its own by playing against itself (http://www.wired.com/2016/01/in-a-huge-breakthrough-googles-ai-beats-a-top-player-at-the-game-of-go/). (See Chapter 3 for more discussion about AI and games, and we will discuss deep learning further in later chapters.)

Our social system currently tries to solve many human limitations through medical approaches (using medications or providing prosthetics), through social supports like various types of senior housing, and through a variety of technological devices (like wearable alert tools). Advanced decision support technology shows potential to help people overcome many kinds of limitations, especially cognitive limitations, as discussed in this chapter.

Over the next few chapters, we will explore some of these technologies in more detail. We will see how computers are being taught to perform some of the cognitive tasks, including better handling of human language and handing recognition and vision problems that require perceptual capabilities long thought to be beyond the capacity of machines. We will also explore some of the future directions in which these systems are moving.

Before that, however, we note that these cognitive computing systems are still in an early stage. We don't yet have any firm evidence to determine how well they will perform over time or across a wide domain space. There are open concerns and issues that need to be investigated. If cognitive computing technology uses experience and a multitude of data sources to solve problems, could this technology eventually become sensitive to some of the same types of memory problems that humans exhibit? For example, as a cognitive

---

[12]Jones, Nicola, "The Learning Machines", *Nature*, Vol. 505, pp. 146-148, January 9, 2014, provides an informal introduction to this technology. We will reference other more technical articles in later chapters.

computing engine fuses together information from multiple sources, might it not also become prone to generating erroneous solutions if some of the sources that it is using to generate a solution are incorrect? How will emotion be incorporated and/or represented by these types of systems? Will a cognitive computing system grow to understand a wide range of information or will a set of cognitive computing systems network with each other to support distributed computing? How will humans interact with sophisticated cognitive computing systems? Will interfaces between the humans and computing systems change so that some of the computing technology is worn (like GoogleGlass) or embedded as a chip or prosthetic device? These are just a few questions that researchers, systems developers, and government organizations will need to address as they determine how advanced cognitive computing technology, sensor technology, robots, autonomous systems, and virtual social webs and tools become commonly available for use. Following the discussion of these technologies, we will return to some of these issues, and explore some of the potential dangers that are triggering the warning about emerging systems that was discussed in Chapter 1.

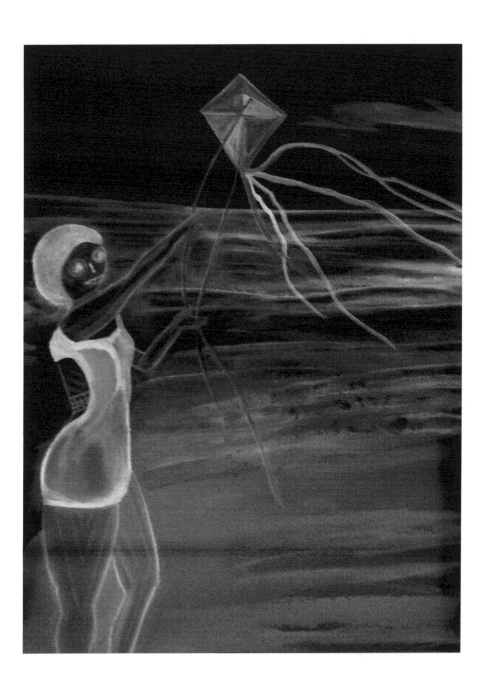

CHAPTER 5

■ ■ ■

What Computers Can't Do–Yet

Artificial Intelligence is what computers cannot do–yet.

> Attributed to various early AI researchers,
> particularly Larry Tesler,
> ca 1970

As mentioned in Chapter 1, over the years there has been considerable change in the attitude towards what artificially intelligent machines can and cannot do. Pretty much every attempt to express some sort of inherent limit by defining a task "computers will never do" has either failed over time (such as happened to the claim that computers would never beat humans at chess or, more recently, Go) or runs the risk of being falsified as AI research proceeds. Other claims on the limits of AI systems, based for example on philosophical or religious principles, are interesting fodder for discussion and potentially important in the long run, but really don't speak to the issues of performance. That is, an argument over whether machines can ever be said to be conscious beings, for example, doesn't have a lot of practical consequence in the near term when debating whether they should be allowed further control over the cars we drive, control of air traffic, military use, etc. (Later in this book we will explore some of these issues from a more practical approach, looking at the dystopian views of artificially intelligent systems and what we might do to prevent them.)

It is also the case that it is very hard to set boundaries on many of the things that we might say a computer is bad at. For example, one of the real issues we have with modern artificial intelligence programs, as we will discuss below, is the desire to improve their ability to interact with humans in natural language. While it is still clear that there are significant issues that remain in this field, continued progress is being made. In the past few years, systems like Siri, the Apple iPhone agent that can handle many queries in a limited domain, has become widely used. We saw a major breakthrough in 2011 when the IBM Watson program beat the world's best players in the question-answering game show Jeopardy!. Systems that organize information extracted from newspaper articles, social media posts, and spoken conversations are improving at a rapid rate. Even if one believes that a computer will never pass the Turing Test (see Chapter 3), might we not reach a point that it is close enough for all intents and purposes?

© James Hendler and Alice M. Mulvehill 2016
J. Hendler and A. M. Mulvehill, *Social Machines*, DOI 10.1007/978-1-4842-1156-4_5

In this chapter, therefore, we will take a somewhat different spin on this issue. In the previous chapter, we looked at human limitations in the aggregate (not all people suffer from all the issues) and with an emphasis on those where computers may be able to help people overcome them. In this chapter, we will consider some of the things that AI programs still struggle with, what some of the potential improvements may be, and explore in particular where combinations of humans and computers working together may have the most benefit.

Getting Machines to Understand the Way People Use Language

One of the biggest complaints people have today when using computers is that the machine can never seem to understand what they are really asking. As an example of this, consider the quote at the start of this chapter. As we were looking for what to name this part of the book, we remembered a quote that we'd heard long ago: "*Artificial intelligence is what computers cannot do-yet!*" Since we didn't make up that expression but wanted to quote it, we of course wanted to find out who said it first so we could give appropriate attribution. It seemed like it would be a relatively simple search.

We started by typing the question "who said artificial intelligence is what computers cannot do yet?" into various search engines. We tried various ways of asking this question to several of the different online systems. Most of the search engines took us to the same places: sets of pages with quotations about the AI field. Yet none of those pages had this actual quote on it. We also repeatedly found a 2014 blog whose title was the same as the quote (but didn't say where it came from) and a number of news articles, blogs, or stories that used the expression. Many of these documents did include the quote, but none said where it came from.

Frustrated, we posted the query on Facebook and Twitter. Within a few minutes, opinions started coming in. Several people pointed us to the Wikipedia page entitled "AI effect" (https://en.wikipedia.org/wiki/AI_effect) that included the following text:

> *Douglas Hofstadter expresses the AI effect concisely by quoting Tesler's Theorem: "AI is whatever hasn't been done yet."*

This had a footnote stating

> *As quoted by Hofstadter (1980, p. 601). Larry Tesler actually feels he was misquoted: see his note in the "Adages" section of Larry Tesler's CV.*

That section of his *curriculum vitae*[1] reported his adage with the following statement:

> *Tesler's Theorem (ca. 1970). My formulation of what others have since called the "AI Effect". As commonly quoted: "Artificial Intelligence is whatever hasn't been done yet." What I actually said was: "Intelligence is whatever*

---

[1] http://www.nomodes.com/Larry_Tesler_Consulting/Adages_and_Coinages.html

> *machines haven't done yet". Many people define humanity partly by our allegedly unique intelligence. Whatever a machine—or an animal—can do must (those people say) be something other than intelligence.*

which seems to be the closest to what we were looking for, and thus is what we used in the start of this chapter.

However, it is worth noting that in both Twitter and Facebook we received many other suggestions and comments. People remembered hearing it in the early days of AI from a number of famous people, various of our friends thought they could recall it from books or papers (most of which are now out of print), and of course many side comments discussed the quote and pointed at other facts about it, for example that it was obviously some kind of response to the Dreyfus book discussed in earlier chapters, which was entitled *What Computers Can't Do*.

It is not just search engines that have trouble with this. Using a version of a program based on the Watson Jeopardy system (not the IBM Watson, but a system designed using similar principles[2]), we asked the same question. The system suggested several AI researchers, including some our colleagues mentioned, and could identify some sources, but it was not able to embark on the sort of problem-solving reasoning that our friends could. That is, like the search engine, it could identify sources, but it was not able to enter into any sort of discourse that might lead to enlightenment.

This simple anecdote is a good one for exploring some of the complexities that computers face when trying to interpret human use of language. First, today's AI technologies largely work by trying to find documents (written by humans) that can help answer a question or help a person solve a problem. As anyone who has used a search engine knows, even this is very hard; often we are very frustrated by what the system returns. The documents don't seem to line up with our expectations. Second, human language use goes beyond just looking for documents or questions: humans use language in many different contexts. Additionally, while we see tremendous strides being made in the areas of question answering, computers that can truly "converse" in the way that meets the standards of the Turing Test face even further challenges. We address these issues below; exploring the search, question answering, and discourse systems research and development that is being undertaken in current AI research.

SPEECH RECOGNITION IS NOT THE SAME AS LANGUAGE UNDERSTANDING

It is important at this point to recognize an important distinction that is often blurred when talking about computers interacting with people using human languages. The general field is sometimes called *human language technologies*, but AI researchers make a differentiation between recognizing words said by a human in a spoken context, a field called *speech recognition*, and understanding what the words mean, a field usually called *natural language understanding*.

---

[2]This system was described in http://www.slideshare.net/jahendler/watson-summer-review82013final and developed prior to the IBM release of Watson APIs to developers.

To see the difference, consider a famous example, which, like the quote that opened this chapter, is disputed as to who said it first. Consider a human saying out loud to a cell phone or other speech recognition system "Can a computer recognize speech?" This phrase is notoriously close in standard pronunciation to the phrase "Can a computer wreck a nice beach?"[3] In fact, depending on one's accent, context of use, and the noise in the environment when speaking, computers still have trouble distinguishing the two.

While this is a somewhat special case, speech recognition is the ability to recognize the words that are spoken out loud. Systems that recognize speech have made huge strides in the past few years, and now speech interfaces are getting much more robust. A number of companies now offer speech recognition as a service, and speech-to-text systems are getting robust enough that many people now use them as an alternative to typing. Speech recognition systems are being developed in a number of languages, and the legendary frustrations people have had with automated phone answerers, for example, are rapidly becoming a thing of the past.

That said, there is still significant room for improvement in these systems. The problems can arise from a number of issues. Some of these are issues in signal processing; for example, current state-of-the-art speech recognition systems have serious problems when trying to recognize children's speech, speech in noisy environments, speech when multiple people are talking, or accented speech, especially by non-native speakers of the language being recognized.

Another problem for speech recognition systems has to do with pronunciation issues *per se*. For example, in English one can change a statement to a question by changing the intonation (generally a rising tone at the end of a sentence will imply a question). Similarly, in English if you say a sentence like "do you like ice cream?" with the emphasis on different syllables, the words will be the same but the meaning may be subtly different. An emphasis on the "you" would imply that the question is asking particularly about the person being spoken to, while an emphasis on the "ice cream" would imply the question is more about the food than the person. Some speech systems are being devised to recognize these subtleties, but most will simply transcribe the words the same way. In many languages, such as Chinese, intonation can be crucial to understanding, and actually changes the meaning of the words being said. For example, the syllable "da" in Chinese can mean, depending on how intoned, "to hit," "to answer," "big," and "to hang over something," and each of these can be transcribed into different written words.

---

[3]This example has become well-enough known that "How to wreck a nice beach" has become the title of books, films, and blogs about the speech recognition problem.

However, once the words have been recognized, there is still the issue of understanding what they mean, and how the computer should respond. In the remainder of this chapter, we will focus on that aspect of language processing, and not focus on the issues of speech recognition. It is worth noting, however, that some of these apply to both. For example, we will discuss ambiguity in language understanding in the next section; some of these issues also come up in speech when dealing with words that are pronounced the same but spelled differently (and have different meaning), like "sight," "cite," and "site". Many current speech systems, for example, will properly transcribe "how do I cite a website" by using aspects of language that go beyond just the speech signal being received, but also include some of the techniques we will discuss.

Ambiguity in Language

One of the main challenges in getting computers to understand human language is the tremendous ambiguity in the way the same words can be used to mean different things. This ambiguity comes from a number of sources: the same word can have multiple meanings, the sequence of words can have different meanings depending on how they are combined grammatically, and the same set of words can have different meanings in different contexts. (While we will use examples from English in this section, it is worth noting that these problems come up in almost every human language commonly spoken today. Some may have one problem more than another, but they all serve as similar challenges to computer understanding.)

Consider the English word "run," which is commonly used as an example of an ambiguous term with many meanings. The word can mean to move rapidly ("run, don't walk"), to operate something ("run the machine"), to stand for election ("run for office"), to perform an activity ("run an errand"), and many others. Some of these are subtle variants of each other (consider "run a race" vs. "run upstairs," which both refer to moving rapidly but have different implications to the activities), others only occur in some syntactic forms of the word (for example, run can imply a liquid state as in "the butter ran" or "the soufflé was runny"), and still others only have meaning when occurring in phrases (for example being "run down" can imply tiredness or having been hit by a car, but usually wouldn't include a meaning related to running for an elected office). And those are only some of the ways the term can be used; in fact, dictionary definitions of the word "run" can run into hundreds of meanings.

English has many words with multiple meanings; some with only one or two meanings, but a large number of them have multiple meanings in different contexts (the technical term is "polysemy"). The word "tank," as a noun, can be something that can hold fish, a place to store gas or liquid, or a military weapon. Asked "where can I buy a tank?" a computer is faced with determining which thing you are looking for. The different search engines we tried made different suggestions, some favoring military vehicles, some favoring propane or water storage tanks, and none offering fish tanks among the first choice. (This is likely because although the most common of these in purchases are the tanks that fish are put in, a typical query would say "where can I buy a fish tank" rather than just tank.)

The problem gets worse when multiple words, each of which have multiple meanings, are put together. There is a famous example of this which is, again, of unclear origin (but often attributed to a 1966 *Scientific American* paper by researcher Anthony Oettinger[4]), which looks at the adage "*Time flies like an arrow.*" As the author points out, "time" can be a noun or a verb; "flies" can similarly be a plural noun or a verb; and "like" can be a verb. Given this, four distinct meanings can be given to this sentence:

1. *Time flies in the same manner, metaphorically, that an arrow flies,* which is the generally accepted meaning that is attributed to the adage (i.e. time moves quickly).

2. *Time flies in the same way that you time an arrow.* This would be taken to mean that the listener is being asked to perform the task of measuring how fast some flies (of type insect) are moving in the same way that they would measure how fast an arrow moves.

3. *Time the flies the same way an arrow would time the flies.* While seemingly nonsensical, these words can combine to mean that a user is being asked to perform an action in the same way that something else would perform that action.

4. *"Time flies" are an entity that enjoys an arrow.* This seemingly silly version, which is syntactically legal, is what gives this example its staying power through the years; it yields the humorous line (sometimes claimed to have been spoken by Groucho Marks) that "Time flies like an arrow; fruit flies like a banana."

This example may seem frivolous, as only one of these is likely to be meant by a human using these words, but in reality this type of ambiguity can arise numerous ways. Consider the first sign shown in Figure 5-1. This picture, taken at a marina in the South of England, needs the phrase "waste oil" to be interpreted the way "time flies" is in the fourth meaning above (like "fruit flies"). Without combining the two nouns, which is what caused the problem previously, readers would be entitled to think that they were being encouraged to waste their oil at this spot.

A somewhat more subtle example of the problem can be seen in the second sign in Figure 5-1, which was taken near a prison in the Midwestern United States. If the reader interprets the sign to mean that the hitchhikers might be "escaping inmates" (as intended), they will not stop and pick them up. However, wrongly interpreting the combined phrase would imply that the hitchhikers may be trying to escape from inmates, in which case it would be bad not to pick them up. Here the word *escaping* is being used as a gerund, which is a case in which a verb (escape) functions as a nominal modifier by the addition of the "ing" ending. However, this would not necessarily be the preferred meaning in other situations.

---

[4]Oettinger, Anthony, "The Uses of Computers in Science", *Scientific American*, Volume 215, September 1966, p. 168.

Figure 5-1. *These signs show how the same word used as a verb vs. a noun can significantly change the implied meaning*

For example, if we read that "refugees may be escaping retaliations," we don't hesitate to realize that this is the reverse of the previous case.

For a computer to correctly interpret these examples, we would need to develop a rule for the computer that would recognize that in the case of the "time flies" it is wrong to combine the terms, but for "fruit flies" it is correct; that "waste oil" is generally a noun phrase whereas "waste" is more typically used as a verb ("waste time"); and that "escaping inmates" is a phrase that makes sense when used as a gerund-noun combinator, but this is not always the case.

There are other kinds of ambiguity that also cause computers a lot of problems. For example, one that causes many problems for search engines is the ambiguity of names. This can be caused by the fact that names are not unique (there can be many people with the name Joseph Smith that a user can be looking for), or the fact that many people are named after each other. In a talk presented by Peter Mika of Yahoo! Labs in 2014, the difficulty search engines have using machine learning to recognize individual entities was presented.[5] In his talk, he gave two humorous examples of mistakes that needed to be fixed as Yahoo! extended its search engine. In one, he showed how the rapper Ice Cube is used as a photo on a page describing small pieces of frozen water. In another example, shown in Figure 5-2, he showed how a famous painter and his comic book namesake are confused.

Michelangelo

Artist

Michelangelo di Lodovico Buonarroti Simoni , commonly known as Michelangelo, was an Italian sculptor, painter, architect, poet, and engineer of the High Renaissance who exerted an unparalleled influence on the... wikipedia.org

Born: March 6, 1475, Caprese Michelangelo

Died: February 18, 1564, Rome

Parents: Ludovico di Leonardo di Buonarotto Simoni, Francesca di Neri del Miniato di Siena

Feedback

Figure 5-2. *Names can cause many ambiguity problems, as in this amusing mistake made by a system attempting to use learning to label entities. (From a talk by Peter Mika, reprinted with permission.)*

[5]http://www.slideshare.net/pmika/semantic-search-at-yahoo, April, 2014.

Another famous example of ambiguity causing a problem for a computer came about in the televised Jeopardy! competition between IBM's Watson computer and its human opponents in 2011. In the final question on one of the days, the category was U.S. Cities and the clue was

> *Its largest airport is named for a World War II hero; its second largest, for a World War II battle.*

Watson guessed incorrectly "Toronto" (a city in Canada). This is a mistake that no human would be likely to make and, in fact, both of the human players got "Chicago," the correct answer. The lead of the Watson team, in explaining this mistake, said that the likely cause of this error for Watson was an issue of naming ambiguity.[6] He explained that Watson's confusion resulted in part from the fact that there are cities named Toronto in the US (although none has an airport), that "America" is often used as a synonym for United States, but America can also be used for the continent that contains other countries including Canada, and that the Toronto in Canada has a baseball team that plays in the "American league" where all the other teams are US cities.

In short, ambiguity remains a very hard problem for computers, even though it is easily understood by humans, to the point where many of the examples shown in this section seem humorous until explained. The solution appears to somehow be found in the fact that humans have more knowledge about the words and their meanings than just the sort of lexical, syntactic, and associative knowledge described so far.

Understanding the World We Live In

In understanding language, and being able to handle examples like those described above, it is clear that an understanding of the world we live in helps. How do we know that "time flies" aren't a species that we've simply not encountered? How do we know that wasting oil is a bad thing? Why wouldn't we want to pick up hitchhikers if we think they are inmates who are escaping? Why wouldn't we make the mistakes Watson made in categorizing Toronto inappropriately? It seems somewhat obvious that it is our knowledge of the world in which we live that causes these examples to make sense to us.

A critical aspect of human cognition is our ability to appropriately use our knowledge of the world when needed. This can be something as mundane as remembering how to start one's car each morning or as complex as working out what to do on that particular morning when the car doesn't start. In this latter situation, we naturally start to ponder alternatives: is it better to leave the car fixing for later and find another way to get to work, or should plans be changed to get the car to the shop first? We also reason about the effects on other people: does this car problem make it so I cannot get my kids to school or to make it to a meeting at work? If so, whom do I have to inform? Are there other people who can help me out, and if so, how might they be impacted? What about longer term: if the car's going to be in the shop for a few days, what's in my plan for the week that may have to be changed?

---

[6]`http://asmarterplanet.com/blog/2011/02/watson-on-jeopardy-day-two-the-confusion-over-an-airport-clue.html` presents the explanation by David Ferucci, who at that time was the lead researcher of the Watson project.

As exasperating as a situation like this is, the mental effort involved in planning what to do is generally straightforward. It seems natural that you would remember an important meeting you have that day; that you would recall that you have a neighbor with an extra car they sometimes lend to friends; that you would know that you have a mechanic you always use, or that you don't, in which case you'd also know where to go to look for recommendations. Your cognitive abilities as a human are naturally honed for you to be able to make decisions like this in a relatively straightforward way, and problems like this don't tend to cause us major difficulties in terms of planning what to do.

In fact, humans are so good at this sort of thing that you are not only able to figure out what to do in a situation like this, but you can read the proceeding two paragraphs and understand them. In doing so, you may have recalled a specific situation like this that happened to you in the past. You will have thought through the implications to the person dealing with the problem, understanding how the issue of transportation can impact the many things someone might have to do in a day. You have essentially put yourself in the position of the person dealing with the situation, and are able to recognize not just the specifics of the problem (that the person has to deal with the car), but also how frustrated a person in this situation is likely to be feeling. In short, you've somehow imagined yourself in the situation, known what problems it could entail, and started to figure out some of the solutions, such as considering public transportation or a partner who might help, etc.

These abilities, both for dealing with problems that arise with respect to a planned activity (in this case, driving to some destination) and being able to put yourself in the place of someone else and figure out what they might do when faced with such a situation, are hallmarks of what is known as *common sense reasoning*, the ability to understand the way we interact with the world in our day-to-day events.

Encoding World Knowledge

In the early days of AI, many predictions made about what AI could do didn't hold up. For example, given the successes of AI systems at games like checkers, there was an assumption that AI systems would soon outplay the world's experts. However, as we saw in Chapter 3, it was many years before that prediction came true; people simply hadn't realized that one game was so much harder than the other.

A similar thing happened in the area of language and understanding. One early and incredibly important use of computers was in breaking codes. During World War II, a number of systems were devised that combined analog and digital technologies to decrypt what were thought to be unbreakable codes. The breaking of German and Japanese codes were clearly critical to the success of the US and UK war efforts. After the war, cryptographic research continued, and some of the first fully digital computers were developed specifically for this task.

A key part of code breaking was to look at the features of the target language and use them as hints to breaking the code. Thus, if one were trying to break a code in English, it would be useful to know that the letters *E* and *T* occur very frequently as compared to say *J* and *Z*. (Note that in other languages the frequencies might be very different, but still significant). Using a computer to simply count various kinds of occurrences was a starting step. (The real code breaking systems were much more complex, as the codes were designed to try to obscure these features). Based on these early successes, some researchers reasoned that if we could turn codes into language, then translating from one language to another wouldn't be too hard.

However, it wasn't long before the sorts of problems discussed previously started to arise. The ambiguities of language turned out to be much more complex than anticipated and language translation was deemed to be much harder than expected. As more research went into the area, it became clear that there was another set of problems beyond the ambiguity. Language translation research was found to hinge on other difficulties, including different cultural aspects of language use, the different use of clichés and idioms in different languages, and very deep issues in the philosophy of language (for example, does someone who lives in a culture that sees the rainbow as having seven colors, as it is said to be in most English-speaking countries, actually perceive colors the same as someone whose language refers to an eight-colored rainbow, as is the case in Russian and various other Cyrillic languages). It became clear that translating language required a deeper level of "understanding", and that in turn required a deeper knowledge of the way things worked in the world.

To deal with this problem, researchers in artificial intelligence looking at language started to explore how computers could be made to understand language by using question answering as a paradigm. That is, could a computer read a story and then answer questions about what it had read? If those questions included information that had to be "inferred" from the story, and the computer could answer correctly, it seemed like one could claim progress was being made in understanding the world.

As people working in language translation and question answering continued to explore language, it became clear that even very simple sentences required a lot of underlying information in order to be correctly understood, and that stories were even harder. For example, if you consider a story from a mid-1970s AI research project (called SAM, for Script Applier Memory, led by Roger Schank and Richard Cullingford), it might go something like this:

> John was hungry. He went to a restaurant. He ordered lobster.
> He ate and left.

The system would then be asked a question like "What did John eat?"

While it would be clear to most people that the correct answer should be "John ate lobster," it is important to note that the story doesn't say that explicitly. Rather, you need to bring in "world knowledge," which is information about people, culture, the world we live in, etc. Answering the question requires that you know what restaurants are (that one eats meals there), and how things go in restaurants (that typically you are served what you order and eat what you are served). A more complex question, like "Why might John have ended up eating something else?" helps make the problem clearer; we not only have to know what typically happens, but also some of the ways things can go wrong in these situations (perhaps the restaurant service was so bad that John got angry and left, maybe they were out of lobster and John had to order something else, maybe when it came the lobster was poorly prepared so John sent it back, etc.).

Trying to figure out how to get a computer to be able to bring world knowledge to bear requires figuring out a way to get that information into the computer. There are two obvious choices: we somehow get the computer to learn it, which we will address later in this chapter, or we find a way to encode that knowledge and program it in. This latter approach is known as *Knowledge representation* and it has remained a key part of AI research throughout the field's history.

Early attempts to think about how to get computers to understand the world focused on encoding the information in some sort of logic. Essentially, the computer could be given a set of rules of some kind, and it could apply these rules to reason about situations. However, it became clear pretty quickly that these rules could not be very simple because the real world has so many exceptions. That is, a simple rule like "you get served what you order in a restaurant" is clearly true much of the time, but not always.

Over the years, many different kinds of logics were explored, and to discuss them all would be way beyond the scope of this book, but the key point to take away is that in order for computers to interact with humans, they must have knowledge about the world in which the humans live, and encoding that knowledge remains a significant challenge for AI researchers, meaning that machines are still seriously limited in the kinds of inferencing they can do.

THE EXPERT SYSTEMS PARADOX

The main theme of this chapter and the previous one is to outline some of the key differences between human and machine cognition. A lesson learned again and again in the AI field has been that often what we think will be easy for a computer, because it is easy for a human, is really hard. Conversely, however, it also turns out that in the AI area, some things that are really hard for humans are not that difficult for AI systems. In the late 1970s and early 1980s, this was often referred to as the *expert systems paradox*.

This name came about because while many AI researchers were wrestling with the sort of "easy" stories like the one about Jack and the lobster, some AI researchers started to look at problems where encoding knowledge seemed harder for a human. For example, as early as the mid-1960s, a project at Stanford University called Dendral[7] was developed to help organic chemists identify the molecules from their mass spectrometer readings, a task that was difficult for humans but turned out to be amenable to an AI solution. Throughout the 70s, there was a growth of so-called "expert systems" that successfully handled medical diagnosis, the configuration of complex mechanical systems, the repair of electronic devices, etc.

AI scientists learned that by eliciting knowledge from the experts in certain ways, it was possible to turn that knowledge into the kind of rules that computers could follow. In fact, these expert systems were often referred to as "rule based" because of how the information was encoded. By the early to mid-1980s, people were understanding that the AI systems could do a great deal with these rules, as long as the domain of the system, that is, what the system reasoned about, was relatively narrow, such as configuring particular types of computer systems or diagnosing particular illnesses, but not reasoning about large-scale systems, all of medicine, *etc.*

---

[7]Wikipedia has a good article on Dendral, and a number of systems that derived from it, at https://en.wikipedia.org/wiki/Dendral.

Configuring a telephone system is a very hard task for a human; AI systems can do it better. But reasoning about "simple" everyday things like the restaurant knowledge needed to understand about John and the lobster remains difficult. In short, AI systems could be built to do really complicated sounding tasks, but reasoning about the common-sense world in which we live was still beyond them.

That, in a nutshell, is the expert systems paradox.

Knowledge and Memory

One of the things that humans do effortlessly, and without conscious thought, is pull up relevant memories from their own lives and experiences that can be useful in dealing with a new problem. In the example of the car not starting, one of the kinds of knowledge that people bring to bear is the memory of similar times this has happened in the past. This memory can also be of something that hasn't happened to them, but of something they observed, read about, or were told that happened to someone else.

This ability to reason not just about the specific things that have happened in our past, but to generalize to other situations or to "remember" what has happened to others is something that AI researchers have been trying to build into computers for a long time. As opposed to the rule-based reasoning used in expert systems, another tradition grew in AI called *memory-based reasoning*: trying to solve problems by finding a solution to a previous, similar problem and then using rules or other techniques to figure out how to identify the differences between the old and new situation and then map the solutions. Sometimes this could be done by merging multiple old solutions; other times it required problem solving to simply fix the small differences, rather than solving the problem from scratch.

Let's consider again the problem with going out in the morning and finding out that the car won't start. In a rule-based system, one might do some kind of reasoning like "My goal is to get to work. I cannot use my car to get to work, so let me find another way to get to work" and then work to solve that problem by applying other rules about transportation and such. In a memory-based system, it might be more like "The last time my car didn't start, I called AAA, and they came and started it, so I'll call AAA."

Of course, it may not be as simple as this. For example, perhaps we decided to allow our membership in the American Automobile Association to lapse. So now "Call AAA" won't work. However, if one also remembers that the reason that the AAA was called was to get someone to come to start your car, then a rule in memory-based reasoning might say that "If something in a past situation worked because it caused something else to happen, then we can substitute in another way to make that same thing happen." Thus, for example, we might reason that the local service station could start the car, so we'd call them instead.

The difference between these two paradigms can be subtle. In the best case, the advantage of the memory-based system is that patching the differences is often simpler than solving the new problem. For example, having determined that a different way is needed to get to work requires, essentially, solving that problem from scratch: what other transport means are there, how do we use them, and so on? For a rule-based system, this can be hard because the broader the situation that is being attacked, the more common sense knowledge is needed. For the memory-based system, the "patch" (i.e., just find a different place to call) may be easier and not require such general purpose knowledge.

When using simple examples like this car one, it may not be so clear where the advantage is, so let's take a real life example. The two authors of this book actually started working together in the 1990s to develop a memory-based reasoning system for military logistics planning[8]. What we discovered was that a lot of detail and thought is associated with providing logistics support for disaster relief situations where quick responses are often required. For example, if an earthquake occurs in some region of the world, people are likely hurt and some of the infrastructure has probably collapsed as a result of the earthquake. A rule-based system might know that if people are hurt, then they will need medical supplies, and if buildings and roads have collapsed, then trucks and heavy equipment are going to be needed to help rebuild the roads and clear rubble. A harder problem is determining how much medical supplies are needed and what type of equipment is needed. Again, rules and formulas can be used to estimate these needs.

But this is just the tip of the logistics iceburg. Medical personnel will also be required, and they will need some place to treat patients, and some place to live, and they will need food and water for themselves, as well as for any support staff that they have. So, as you are planning to send in the medical supplies and personnel, you need to also plan to send in some engineers who can construct or fix some existing structure that can be used to provide medical care, and you need to start to think about what supplies the medical staff and their support teams will need if they are to live and work in the disaster area.

While each of the associated items can also be computed using certain rules or some existing planning template, we learned from the human planners that we interviewed that it took a very long time to build a plan from scratch. So, they used their collective memories to determine if the current situation was somehow similar to some disaster that they, or someone that they knew, had supported in the recent past.

Our research provided a mechanism for storing historical plans or specially-developed, logistic-plan templates. We provided search tools that allowed the planners to find one or more similar plans, and we provided a set of comparison tools that allowed them to determine how plans were similar and different. Once they found a similar plan, we provided tools to remind them where and how to modify the historical plan so that it could better support the current situation. For example, assume that the planners found an old logistics plan in the repository that was used to support disaster relief for an earthquake that occurred in a large city in Alaska during the winter months. Now assume that the current situation is also an earthquake in a large city, but the city is located in South America and it is the summer. The plan developed to support the earthquake in Alaska likely provided supplies to support the disaster relief staff in a cold environment, while the new plan needs to provide clothes and supplies to support a hot, tropical environment. We were told stories of troops being deployed to hot, tropical areas being provided with clothes intended for sub-zero temperatures because the clothing logistics requirement is not easy to find in a logistics plan. Most of the logistics requirements are specified with codes that have either no or very brief textual descriptions that explain the requirement.

The human planners learned by experience that the temperature of the place where the disaster is located is a very important factor to consider when building a logistics plan to support disaster relief. Humans use social knowledge and experience to reason and remember. If the human shares this experience with the memory-based system, then that system can use it to bias how it solves problems. For example, once we learned about the

---

[8]Mulvehill, A., Rager, D., and Hendler, J., "ForMAT and Parka: A technology integration experiment and beyond"', Proc. Intl Conference on Case-Based Reasoning, Providence, RI, 1997.

importance of location and time of year from the human experts, we were able to update our algorithms to provide prompts to the human operator to check on certain items like medical supplies and clothing as a function of the time of the crisis and the place where the disaster is occurring. Note that humans must update the algorithm; it was the human planners who recognized the patterns, not the computer.

Understanding What They Perceive

Another major challenge to computers is to perceive the world. Where humans are born with a built in sensor suite, as it were, AI systems must use sensors such as microphones, cameras, and accelerometers that are integrated into the system. There's been tremendous progress in the past years in improving these sensors, especially those based on video inputs, but weaknesses still remain. The problem is similar to the ones with language: even if the computer can learn to recognize objects, it needs to be able to reason about those objects and the contexts in which they occur.

Consider the picture shown in Figure 5-3. The video coming into the computer is turned into an encoding of 1s and 0s and then the computer is trained on the video images through a training process known as "deep learning," which we will explain in more detail in Chapter 7. Using this technique, the computer can learn to recognize areas of the photo, and to associate them with objects in the real world. Doing this with full generality, the way a human does (recognizing the subtle differences, objects that might be obscured, etc.) is still beyond the ability of machines, but at least they can now recognize many common objects in images and videos.

Figure 5-3. *An image in which a computer has been trained via "deep learning" to label various components. (Nvidia blog, 2016, with permission)*

However, having recognized the different objects, the question becomes whether the computer can reason about these in any meaningful way. As people work on self-driving car technologies, knowing which objects are most important and how they are moving is critical, and that problem is getting a lot of attention. Similarly, if we look at some of the medical image recognition tasks discussed in Chapter 2, computers may get better than humans at recognizing particular kinds of cancer, finding the borders of tumors, etc. Looking further out, however, this doesn't seem sufficient. It's not enough to be able to simply recognize objects; it's understanding the implications of how they interact that would let a computer make the sort of inferences necessary to function in the world without human interaction.

The following anecdote, from co-author Hendler, may help to explain this better:

> When my daughter was little, the first word she learned was "cat," not surprisingly as most children with pets in a house learn to associate a word with their animal friend. Not long after, I brought her a present of a little pull-toy. She learned its name, "duck," pretty quickly. Amusingly to her parents, having those two words meant she would categorize things in her world into cats and ducks. Some people she would identify as "cat," others as "duck," and common objects sometimes would get those names. Some of the categorization she made seemed straightforward; for example, seeing an airplane flying above us she said, with a huge smile, "duck." Clearly she'd figured out that flying things should be ducks. (Note that as obvious as this seems to us, it's still somewhat mystifying; after all, she'd learned to recognize ducks from a pull toy that waddled on the floor, not from things that flew).

> Of course, as time went by, she rapidly learned new words, and the world went from cats and ducks into thousands of different objects and concepts. At the time of this writing, she is a graduate student, and like those of you reading this book, clearly literate enough to understand many of the complexities of the world.

> However, just for fun, I recently asked her to tell me the difference between a cat and a duck. Once she realized I wasn't joking, she said "cats are mammals, ducks are birds." The ability to learn categorizations is something humans do quite well, but is still a challenge to machines. However, learning these kinds of categories is an active area of research, and machines are getting better at it all the time.

> My next question to her, however, was more significant. I asked her, "If you had to explain to a child how to tell a cat from a duck, what would you say?" She replied, "If I was telling it to a kid, I'd probably say something like 'the cat has fur and four legs and goes *meow*; the duck is a bird and it swims and goes *quack*.'"

While there is much active research in both AI and psychology about language acquisition, it is this ability to not just differentiate cats and ducks (a dog can differentiate those even better than a human), but to learn how to categorize the world and form functional descriptions of things that is still way beyond the capabilities of computers.

Learning about what we see is obviously not the only thing humans do. Clearly, all of our senses come into play as we learn our way around the world. In every sensory mode, we also interpret things similar to the cat vs. duck phenomenon. Consider the following: if a child at some point in their young life puts their right hand against a radiator and gets burned, even lightly, they will typically not do it again. But more importantly, they will also not put their left hand against a radiator, and in fact will avoid touching any part of their body to something they perceive to be hot. Again, animals also have this capability built in, and learn similarly, but computers don't. Further, as in the case with vision, the human can learn to explain these differences, and even teach them to others through language (telling their own child, "don't touch that, it's hot!")

It's worth noting that although we describe the way humans learn by giving verbal examples, it goes deeper than that. The human is able to use this information to plan their way through the world (for example, deciding to take bread with you to go feed some ducks, while knowing that might not be a good thing to try to feed bread to most cats); to understand and recognize not just what other people are doing (dodging to avoid touching the radiator) but why (to avoid being burned); and to apply that knowledge "metaphorically" to other problems, such as understanding how to interpret the phrase "big dragons never die" as a proverb that can help you learn to play the game of Go (as discussed in Chapter 3).

In short, learning to sense and perceive the world is something computers are rapidly getting better at doing, but the ability to link a perception with an ability to interact with the world being perceived, in the ways humans do, is still one of those capabilities that is a long way off for artificial intelligences.

The Problem of Context

Since the early days of artificial intelligence research, many approaches have been designed to try to develop better ways for computers to understand the sorts of problems with language and perception discussed so far. These attempts can roughly be separated into three categories:

I. Writing "procedures" that the AI should use to handle situations encoded as programs that the system runs when various conditions hold

II. Defining "declarative" knowledge that expresses the information about the world and what the computer should do in certain situations

III. Creating learning routines that in some way train the computer to develop the knowledge of appropriate actions to take

In all three cases, a computer program (algorithm) is used to get the machine to make choices as to what actions to take (or words to say, etc.), but the nature of the program differs.

Procedural Systems

Consider the chess playing programs discussed in Chapter 3. The program we described for playing chess was an algorithm that used a game tree to search for moves. The system evaluated the board positions available via a program that was tailored to chess board evaluation, used a tree search algorithm to decide the best move, and played that move.

If we want to know why the computer made that move, there really is no better explanation than that some number of plies down the game tree that move maximized the expected board value. To change the behavior of the program, one can change the values in the board evaluator, change some of the parameters of the search, or come up with a better algorithm. The system will play better or worse depending on those changes, but we'd be hard-pressed to explain its play in terms of understanding the game of chess. A human asked to explain a move might describe "avoiding a trap;" the computer is unable to do more than compute the right move mechanistically.

Declarative Systems

For many AI tasks, however, the question has been raised as to whether this sort of "procedural" approach can work. An alternative that was proposed was to write some sort of algorithm that could apply some form of rules, and then to use those rules to generate actions. The program in this case becomes "simple," just a rule-application device, and the system's knowledge is encoded in some explicit "declarative" way, making it so that the human programmer can explicate knowledge about the problems the system is expected to solve, without having to worry about rewriting the program to solve problems in a different domain.

One kind of declarative system proposed early in AI was that of using some kind of logic engine as the underlying program, and then expressing rules to the computer as statements in some logic-based language. For example, in traditional logics there is a common form of rule, known technically by its Latin name *modus ponens,* which states that if A implies B and A is true, then B is also true. For example, if I were to say "If Mary is John's mother, then John is Mary's son," and then I was to say "Mary is John's mother," you should clearly believe that John is Mary's son. In this case, we could say *modus ponens* is one kind of inference rule because using it we can express one fact and use it to produce another.

A logical system is a set of these inference rules (known as the axioms) and a set of beliefs to which they can be applied. Using a theorem prover, a computer can solve problems by determining whether there is a valid set of inferences that connect some statements to some other statements; this is the traditional notion of a logical proof. Thus, by writing some sort of theorem prover that knows how to combine the axioms, and given some set of beliefs, the system could come up with a proof of a new fact. (An early form of such systems were based on a set of simple "syllogisms" in which one could express facts like "If all men are mortal" and "Socrates is a man," then "Socrates is mortal.")

Rather than going into a logical tutorial, it's enough to say that early in AI, the assumption was made that one way to get computers to understand the world could be by creating rule systems in straightforward logics and then encoding information about the world in beliefs that the system could manipulate. However, it was rapidly realized that the logics that would be needed were not so straightforward.

For example, we know that ducks are birds. We also know that birds fly, so clearly if we know something is a duck, we can infer that it flies. However, we also know that penguins are birds, but penguins don't fly. So a simple rule like "All birds fly," which would seem straightforward, isn't. The rule starts to change to something like "All birds that aren't penguins, or ostriches, or kiwis, or ... fly." That is, we start to encode a number of exceptions. But there are also lots of other things that could cause a bird not to fly: a broken wing, being covered in oil from a tanker spill, and many others.

There are many ways to create more powerful logics (technically called *non-monotonic logics*) that can handle these situations: logics with exception rules (All birds fly unless you know a reason they cannot), logics that take probabilities into account (Most birds fly), and logics that have special operators that handle particular kinds of special cases. These latter include what are called *modal* logics which can include terms for things like "Something is necessarily true," "Something is possibly true," etc. To date, the development of logics powerful enough to encode complex situations in a way that computers can use is still an active area of artificial intelligence research.

One kind of rule system that became popular in the 1980s, and is still very much in use today, is called a *production rule system*. In these systems, instead of trying to use formal rules of logic, the system reasons by applying rules in some kind of order, and allowing the results of the rule application to cause other rules to be used. Production rule systems are often called *blackboard systems* because they work via a computational mechanism that is like being able to write and erase information on a blackboard.

One of the common uses of such systems is in medical diagnosis, building the kinds of information systems used by doctors today (as discussed in Chapter 2). Let's take a very simple example.

Suppose we had the following rules in a diagnostic system:

If patient has the symptom of *cough*, then write *possible diagnosis flu* or *possible diagnosis cold*.

> If a *possible diagnosis flu* but patient does not have the symptom *fever*, then remove *possible diagnosis flu*.
>
> If *possible diagnosis flu*, then write *prescribe antiviral* drug.
>
> If *possible diagnosis cold*, then write *prescribed decongestant*.

We would start the system by writing on the blackboard the symptoms. For example, let's assume John comes in with a cough. That symptom would go on the blackboard, so it would contain just

`[cough]`

The system would now look for a rule to use, and it would find the first rule is applicable. This would cause the blackboard to now contain

`[cough, possible diagnosis flu, possible diagnosis cold]`

The system would now look for a rule given this new state. The first rule would still be applicable, but since we already used it, we'd prefer to find another one, and we would find the second rule is applicable since fever is not one of the symptoms listed. Thus, the blackboard would now look like

[cough, possible diagnosis cold]

Again, the system would look for a rule, and again would find the first rule, which was already used, but now also the fourth rule, and the blackboard would contain

[cough, possible diagnosis cold, prescribe decongestant]

The system would find no other rule that hasn't already been used, and thus it would end its reasoning. The blackboard now contains the symptom, the possible diagnosis, and a prescription that is recommended. The patient with a cough was determined to have a cold and would be prescribed a decongestant–easy enough.

Another patient comes in, and this one has a cough and a fever. This starts the same way, with the first rule chosen to create the blackboard status, showing

[cough, fever, Possible diagnosis flu, possible diagnosis cold]

In this case, however, when the system looks for the next rule, the second rule is not applicable, so it must use either the third (because flu is still possible) or the fourth (because a cold is still possible). One of these would be chosen, and then the other, so the final blackboard would be the product of all the rules, showing

[cough, fever, Possible diagnosis flu, possible diagnosis cold,
 prescribe antiviral, prescribe decongestant]

If these were all the rules in the system, it would now prescribe this patient both an antiviral and a decongestant, treating the two possible diagnoses: a cold or the flu.

Of course, this is a super-simplified example. In a more complex situation, the system could have many hundreds of rules, there might be probabilities associated with them (for example, given a cough we might say it was 80% likely to be a cold and 20% likely to be the flu), we might have some method of determining what to do when multiple diagnoses were possible (for example, we might say that if the third rule is applicable, the fourth could not be used, thereby only prescribing the antiviral), and there are many other ways such a system could be used. The great flexibility of production rule systems give them their power, but also make them difficult, in practice, to develop and maintain.

Learning Systems

In the section on perception, we discussed learning systems as an important aspect of how a computer can be made to perceive the world. Similarly, reasoning systems can also take advantage of learning. Consider the expert system example in the previous section. Clearly, knowing the probabilities of whether you were more likely to have a cold or the flu could help the system make a better decision.

A number of powerful systems have been designed that use probabilities for reasoning. One particular technique is *Bayesian reasoning networks*, which is used heavily in science and engineering applications, as well as in medical reasoning systems and many others. Although they are quite powerful, there is always a problem similar to one in the expert systems domain: just as one needs to create the rules there, in a Bayesian system one needs to create the probabilities.

One way to approach this problem is to have the machine learn the probabilities. For example, given a population of patients, we could count how many have colds and how many have the flu, and assume that the counts represent the correct probability. Similarly, given a larger collection we could compute the many different diseases and have a distribution of all of them. In principal, we could then calculate how many of them had which symptoms, and we would end up with a model of what symptoms and diseases go together. In principle, this is the idea behind many kinds of machine-learning systems.

This may sound straightforward, but in practice it is not this easy. To start with, if it was just cold and flu (and fever or not), we wouldn't need that many patients to figure out what was going on. But when we consider that there can be many other diseases and many other symptoms, we realize we have to start to consider lots of combinations. If we want to decide between five diseases and ten symptoms, we would need to take all 50 combinations into account. For hundreds of possible diseases and hundreds of possible symptoms, as would arise in the real world, we'd be looking at tens of thousands of combinations. Each of these combinations needs a meaningful number of cases to check; if there are only one or two patients in some categories, it is hard to tell what is real and what is random. In short, to do this right, we would need information about millions of people.

To make matters worse, many people don't have just one single disease. For example, when we were discussing medical systems in Chapter 2, we mentioned a patient who had anemia and a skin infection. This *comorbidity*, as it is called, must also be taken into account, which means we would need to consider all the people with two diseases, three diseases, etc. The combinatorics grows very quickly, and the bottom line is that to do this right one would need the data on millions and millions of patients, as well as a program that could compute all these probabilities and use them to make a diagnosis.

Although there are a number of kinds of machine-learning programs that have been devised for many purposes over the years, the most common type was designed to handle essentially this kind of problem. There are many variants, but basically what the algorithms try to do is find which things in the data correlate with which others, and then to assign probability numbers that try to predict the correlations being observed.

As an example, machine-learning algorithms are often tested with something called the *shopping cart problem*, named after some of the early uses of the algorithms. In many stores, both online and brick and mortar, as people buy things, the items that they buy are recorded and then correlated to find things that are often bought at the same time. The stores can then use this information for placing items on the shelves (putting things often brought together near each other can increase sales) or in online systems to generate recommendations (the famous "people who bought that also bought..." kind of recommendation). These recommendations can also be personalized to know that certain customers who buy certain things may be more apt to buy others, leading to the generation of personalized advertisements and the like–a major online business.

To see how this works, consider the following example: let's assume that people coming through the line are buying only a few items in our little store that only sells a few things. Here is a list of who bought what:

Person	Item 1	Item 2	Item 3
P1	Chips	Fruit	Soda
P2	Fruit	Steak	Vegetables
P3	Chips	Steak	Vegetables
P4	Soda	Steak	Vegetables
P5	Chips	Soda	Steak
P6	Chips	Fruit	Steak

Let's now look at this data a different way. Let's generate a matrix of which things were bought with which other things. In this case, we would see

Also Bought	Chips	Fruit	Soda	Steak	Vegetables
Chips	6	2	3	2	1
Fruit		6	1	2	1
Soda			6	2	1
Steak				6	2
Vegetables					6

(As the matrix is symmetric, we're only showing the upper half, clearly anyone who bought steak and soda also bought soda and steak). Looking at the matrix, we see that the most common pairing, occurring three times, was chips and soda; after that were several other pairings that occurred twice (chips and fruit, chips and steak, fruit and steak, steak and vegetables) and the others appeared only once. We can now turn these into probabilities by dividing the total (six people) by the co-occurrence numbers. So 50% of the people who bought chips also bought soda, 33% of the people who bought chips also bought vegetables, etc.

This information could now be used in making decisions. We might want to put chips near soda, while perhaps we wouldn't need to put chips and soda near vegetables. Similarly, we might want to make sure that if we had a sale on chips, and we saw someone was buying soda, we could advertise the chips sale since the person might be more likely to also buy chips. This kind of learning is often called *data mining* because it tries to find the "gold nuggets" hidden in data.

Once the probabilities are computed, using this or similar methods, the question becomes how to combine the probabilities into a system that can reason about them together. There are various ways to do this, and the math can get fearsome, but the basic idea is simple. If we can compare the individual probabilities of things occurring (flu but not cold) and compare to the probabilities of them happening together (cold and flu), then the system can combine the various probabilities to determine the most meaningful correlations in the data. (There are also methods for combining these combinations of probabilities into networks where one can reason about multiple events and how they might affect each other. There are a number of ways to do this, and the interested reader is directed to read about Bayesian probability[9], the most popular of these.)

This example seems pretty simple, but in the real world it is much harder because of a number of variables. We may have many, many more brands, not everyone buys the same number of items, we may have some inaccuracy in our scanning of items, etc. When properly identified, all of these variables can be taken into account in this sort of math, and as a result, these systems are used in many applications. For example, if instead of the various kinds of foods, if the data was about different types of diseases, symptoms, how the diseases were co-occuring, etc., then we could use that type of data in a medical application. We can also tie things in the shopping carts to things occurring in the larger environment. For example, in one famous case, in the mid-2000s WalMart announced that their data-mining algorithms showed that sales of strawberry Pop Tarts rose by about seven times before hurricanes (correlating buying an item with weather).

There are many other variants of data mining and machine learning that build on the sort of approach described above. For example, consider if the shopping carts had people buying potato chips and Pepsi and potato chips and Coke fairly often. If the computer had a way to learn that Pepsi and Coke are both kinds of cola, then the association between potato chips and cola would be higher than vs. the individual brands.

To learn these sorts of relationships, different kinds of machine-learning algorithms are used. In this case, the computer basically creates "clusters" around things that are related based on some criteria. One of the most common uses of this approach is in *text analytics*, one of the key technologies that underlies web searches, recommendation systems, and ad matching on the web.

The idea is somewhat similar to what we described for shopping carts. Take each document and treat it like it was a shopping cart full of words. Instead of comparing the items to each other to see the probabilities of them co-occurring, we could instead look to see which items have the most correspondence to similar other words. For example, we might find that "cat," "dog," and "hamster" often occur with similar words like "pet," "food," etc. Clustering is a mathematical technique that finds these correspondences and puts the words into groups that have similar words they occur with.

This sounds relatively straightforward, and the idea is, but in language many words are ambiguous (remember "waste water") and thus may occur in multiple contexts. Telling the difference between the word *tank* occurring with words about fish vs. the same word occurring with military words causes many problems for these systems, and much of the reason why search engines still have retrieval problems is because they can still not adequately deal with these kinds of ambiguities.

The same kind of math can be used to cluster other things. For example, medical epidemiology systems try to cluster patients with some disease against other factors like where they have been or what they have eaten; advertisers try to cluster users into groups who may have similar preferences; politicians try to cluster people to determine what they may or may not want to vote for (or what might sway them to vote for a particular candidate), and many other applications.

---

[9]Wikipedia's article is a good place to start:
https://en.wikipedia.org/wiki/Bayesian_probability

In short, modern learning systems generally try to reason by taking data (or words) and looking for those that correlate closely together. Detecting such patterns can be very useful for machines, and this is an extremely active area of AI research.

It is worth noting that in the context we've been discussing learning, that of providing information for inferencing systems, the work tends towards the mathematical systems described above. However, there is another kind of learning, based on very different principles, that is becoming quite important in AI. This is the technique called *deep learning*, which we alluded to earlier in this chapter, and which we will discuss in a later chapter.

What About Creativity?

In the discussion so far, the astute reader may have noted that we have avoided discussing "creativity" as one of the things that differentiates humans from machines. Clearly this feels like something we as humans are good at, and that machines aren't. However, it is also notoriously hard to define creativity.

Generally, definitions of the term come in a couple of forms: one is the way the term is used to talk about people developing something new and valuable. For example, this can be in the arts, where we talk about someone creating a painting or a piece of music, etc. Similarly, we can talk about it as a scientist creating a theory, an inventor coming up with a new method to do something, etc.

A second use of the term, however, may be more germane to this discussion. In this use, creativity is defined as an ability to come up with possibilities that may be useful in solving problems, generally implying coming up with ways that are either novel (a creative solution to a puzzle) or out of context. This latter would include, for example, using a coin to turn a screw when one doesn't have a screwdriver or a rock to drive in a nail when one doesn't have a hammer. While this kind of creativity isn't all about tools, it is the use of tools that many anthropologists believe led to our creation of language and culture. In fact, the use of tools in complex new ways is often used to distinguish humans from other animals.

In short, one of the things that defines human behaviors from those of non-humans is the ability to use a solution from one context in another or to invent a solution (originally an appropriate tool) when in a new context. This is why this chapter has dwelt on context. While AI is bringing machines along in many ways, the ability to reason across a large number of contexts remains limited.

In the next chapters, we will explore how humans and computers may be brought together in ways that could overcome some of the limitations of each and we will also explore technologies in which humans and computers together are powering new breakthroughs in artificial intelligence. However, despite these increasing capabilities, it is worth keeping in mind that humans have an amazing ability to reason across contexts–a capability that still distinguishes us from AI systems, and one which many researchers believe will remain that way for a long time to come.

CHAPTER 6

▓ ▓ ▓

Augmenting Human Capabilities with AI

We are already starting to see some of the ways that AI technologies can augment our human decision making, enhance our physical performance, influence how we conduct transactions, and affect how we interact with others. AI technologies are already demonstrating how they might play a larger role in our personal lives and offset some of the human limitations that were described in Chapter 4, such as helping people make decisions when they have physical or cognitive disabilities, or are fatigued or stressed. In Chapter 5, we described some current limitations that machines have, including problems acquiring world knowledge and accurately using context to influence problem solving. While these issues are the subjects of active AI research and development, in this chapter we will describe how some machine limitations can be offset through human interaction.

In order for machines and humans to more closely interact, and develop a more productive, efficient, and trusting symbiotic relationship, the interfaces used to support interaction will need to change. In this chapter, we will describe how interface technology has evolved and describe some of the challenges that interface developers are facing as they design interfaces for the future.

As humans interact with machines, each has the potential to overcome the weaknesses of the other. In a utopian world, this would be a true benefit, but there are also dystopian futures where the weaknesses of each compound the other. We will look at the possibilities inherent in the combination. In a later chapter, we will explore some of the challenges and even dangers that need to be avoided as these technologies continue to develop.

Human Enhancements: Now and the Near Future

Advanced computer technologies, including those that use AI, are currently being used to enhance human problem solving, especially in situations where a human has to process a huge amount of complex data or where a human must make a critical decision quickly or under extreme stress. AI technology is also being used to help individuals manage daily tasks, make purchasing decisions, and manage finances. For example, AI-based tools are being used in educational settings to provide training and they are being used in nursing homes to monitor a person's routine, determine what is normal, and to contact someone if a difference is detected in the routine.

© James Hendler and Alice M. Mulvehill 2016
J. Hendler and A. M. Mulvehill, *Social Machines*, DOI 10.1007/978-1-4842-1156-4_6

Enhanced Problem Solving

AI-based systems that help humans analyze data, diagnose problems, and make decisions have been being developed since the 1980s. Decision support systems, like expert systems, medical diagnostic systems, or planning and scheduling systems, have historically been developed to aid, not to replace, the human in making decisions. Many AI-based decision support systems are custom developed to support a particular problem domain. General decision support tools are becoming more available as a result of advances in knowledge representation, machine learning, related AI technologies, and changes to computing devices and storage.

In order to effectively operate, many decision support systems or applications need to be primed with certain types of information, such as information about the entities and events that constitute the problem domain space (typically stored in a knowledge base), information about how computation or inference should be done in order to solve problems, and information about user preferences. Many knowledge bases and inference techniques (such as rules to support inference) are built for the machine by humans. Although machine learning techniques are fast becoming very efficient in performing this activity, building knowledge bases to support automation is still primarily performed today by humans.

It can take years to build up a knowledge base that can effectively and correctly support problem solving in some particular domain. It can take many years of usage before the users develop trust and confidence in the decisions or recommendations generated by the tools.

As an example, the clinical decision support system DXplain[1] currently has a knowledge base of about 2,400 diseases and 5,000 symptoms as a result of continued use and development since 1984.

Advances in machine learning techniques are reducing the time needed for AI tools to acquire knowledge. A clinical decision support tool called Isabel[2] (which can be accessed over the Internet or used via a downloaded app) can automatically increase its knowledge base by using statistical natural language processing software to mine data from databases and text. Cognitive computing technology, is being used in the Watson project[3] to autonomously perform searches over the Internet to acquire the data that is needed to answer questions in a variety of problem domains.

Another type of system that is now widely available to support decision making is called a *recommender system*[4]. Recommender systems obtain their domain knowledge by mining usage behavior, including user ratings and personal usage history. A number of downloaded recommender apps are currently available to help an individual make decisions about purchasing wine, cooking, managing investments, managing health, arranging travel, and so on. Recommender technology is also used to match advertisements to web users, and thus is the focus of much current development in the field.

---

[1]Massachusetts General Hospital, "DXplain, Using Decision Support to Help Explain Clinical Manifestations of Disease", www.mghlcs.org/projects/dxplain/, 2016.
[2]Isabel, "Isabel Symptom Checker for Patient Engagement", www.isabelhealthcare.com/home/default, 2016.
[3]IBM, "Meet Watson, The Platform for Cognitive Business", www.ibm.com/smarterplanet/us/en/ibmwatson/, 2016.
[4]Bobadilla, J., Ortega, F., Hernando, A., and Gutierrez, A., "Recommender systems survey", *Knowledge-Based Systems*, Volume 46, pp. 109–132, July 2013.

Fatigue and Stress

As people become tired or get stressed because of too many choices or because they don't have enough time to make a decision, the quality of their decision making can be affected. Many studies have been conducted to measure how cognitive functioning and skill performance are affected under stress and fatigue[5]. The studies indicate that in addition to having trouble making a decision, people also have trouble recalling facts that are required to make the decision. Some studies refer to this state as *cognitive* or *ego depletion*[6].

The military conducts many performance studies to determine how a highly stressful environment, like the military battlefield environment, can impact the physical and cognitive performance of a soldier. An active battlefield environment is a highly stressful environment where soldiers must make decisions even when they are tired and overwhelmed by frequent changes in the environment and/or constant aggression from an enemy. Battlefield stress can also trigger both physiological and emotional changes, which can inhibit effective decision making.

Computers, unlike humans, do not tire easily and are not overcome by emotion, so in stressful situations like those encountered in an active battlefield, computers can help the soldier assess their environment and consider options, risks, and tradeoffs.

KEEPING HUMANS IN THE LOOP

Although computers can undeniably outperform humans in many types of stressful, complex, and/or highly uncertain situations, humans need to remain in the loop because they often introduce solutions that most currently technology can't compute. Consider this true story where a missile launch was deferred because of human intervention. In 1983, Stanislav Petrov was working as a duty officer at a command center for a nuclear early warning system, when the system reported that one or more missiles were being launched from the United States. Petrov's job was to react appropriately: any weapon launch by another country required launching a weapon in response. However, because this action could have high risk if it was made in error, before responding, he reviewed some other data, including data from ground indicators. When Petrov was later interviewed about his decision, he indicated that the influences on his decision to not launch a missile included the following: that he was informed a U.S. strike would be a full strike, so five missiles seemed an illogical start; that the launch detection system was new and, in his view, not yet wholly trustworthy; and that ground radar failed to pick up corroborative evidence, even after minutes of delay[7].

---

[5]Staal, M., "Stress, Cognition and Human Performance: A Literature Review and Conceptual Framework", NASA/TM-2004-212824, http://ntrs.nasa.gov/archive/nasa/casi.ntrs.nasa.gov/20060017835.pdf.

[6]Baumeister, R. F., "Ego depletion and self-control failure: an energy model of the self's executive function", *Psychology Press*, 2002.

[7]https://en.wikipedia.org/wiki/Stanislav_Petrov.

If a computer had been autonomously performing the job, and if the computer had a rule that said "if you see a sensor that indicates a weapon launch, respond with a countermeasure," the action of the computer might not have been the same response as the human. Why? It could be that Petrov felt that it was his personal responsibility to make the correct response, and if he made a mistake, he would be responsible for the mistake, so he decided to act in a way that had less general negative consequences for himself and for people in general. In a 2013 interview, Petrov said that at the time of the incident he was not sure that the alarm was erroneous; instead, he felt that his civilian training helped him make the right decision. So one of the benefits of having computers and humans work together is that they can provide options to each other and counterbalance elements of decision making.

Humans are accustomed to making decisions even when they don't have all of the facts (incomplete knowledge) or they are unsure about some of the facts (uncertainty). Through their experiences and guidance from formal training or other humans, they learn how to weigh the factors that are relevant for a particular decision and how to calculate risks and benefits that might occur as a result of a decision in the near term or future.

While a computer program can be programmed to consider uncertainty and evaluate risks before executing an action, can a computer be programmed to handle all situations, including ones that have never happened before? Let's imagine a slightly more complicated scenario. Imagine that someone hacked into the nuclear early warning system that Petrov and other operators were using, and, whether by purpose or accident, they changed a few bits so that more sensors were displaying launch confirmations. We tend to build very good fail-safe systems into our automated systems as a function of what we know or what we anticipate could happen, but there are often other factors that we may not have considered. Thus, to deal with these sorts of complex issues, we argue that we need to keep humans in the loop, so that they have the opportunity to act outside of preprogrammed logic, taking common sense information into account. Just like the doctor case discussed in Chapter 2, for the foreseeable future, humans appear to be better able to take into account the wider contexts and to make decisions about what is most appropriate in complex ethical situations.

Many decision support systems have been developed to aid the warfighter in intelligence analysis, planning, and mission-execution monitoring. These problem solving areas are challenging because there is often limited or conflicting intelligence, coordination is often required across multiple organizations or individuals, plans must be developed quickly, and plans need to adapt to a variety of potentially changing constraints such as limited resources. As an example, the deployment planning tool discussed in Chapter 5 was developed to help military decision makers quickly develop logistics plans to support an emergent crisis, such as a natural disaster. In many crisis situations, the planners might not be able to get the best resource in place quickly, so the tool helps them to determine what is needed, when it is needed, and if a preferred resource is not available, what other solution might be used initially.

In order to measure stress and other physical conditions that might affect how a soldier makes decisions, researchers have been investigating the usage of wearable computing technology[8] since the early 90s. Military wearable technology[9] provides the soldier who is traversing the battlefield with lightweight wearable decision support technology. It can also collect physiological data to determine when the stress or fatigue level of the soldier indicates depression, other psychological disorders, or more severe trauma, such as post traumatic stress disorder (PTSD) or traumatic brain injury (TBI) that requires intervention.

Wearable technology is also becoming readily available to the general public to help individuals determine when they are becoming fatigued or are experiencing some type of cognitive depletion. Some devices can help individuals determine when they should delay engaging in certain types of problem solving or decision making, or when they should take some action to regain their equilibrium. Some devices can be used to tell a person when another person needs assistance. For example, baby clothes that contain sensors embedded in the cloth are becoming available to collect physiological data about the baby, such as temperature. The sensors send information to other monitoring devices that can signal the parent that the baby needs attention. Similar clothing is also being used to monitor the stress level and general health of seniors.

Individualized Support Technology

In Chapter 4, several of the limitations that a human can face during a typical lifetime were described. Many different types of technologies have been and continue to be developed to help humans with a variety of physical and cognitive limitations. One type of technology, called *assistive technology*[10], is intended to support people who are born with or develop physical handicaps as they age, such as dementia. Some of this technology utilizes AI technology like machine learning, speech analysis, and image analysis in devices that can aid cognition, help with mobility, monitor vital signs, provide physical therapy, monitor living environments, etc.

Several assistive technologies, like activity monitors and sleep monitors, are also being developed to support healthy humans.

---

[8]Bass, L., Kasabach, C., Martin, R., Siewiorek, D., Smailagic, A., and Stivoric, J., "The Design of a Wearable Computer", CHI 97, http://icie.cs.byu.edu/cs656/papers/Wearable-bass-CHI97.pdf, March 22-27, 1997.

[9]Howard, Courtney (Editor), "Widespread Use of Wearable Technology", *Military Aerospace Electronics*, Vol. 26, Issue 9, www.militaryaerospace.com/articles/print/volume-26/issue-9/technology-focus/widespread-use-of-wearable-technology.html, September 21, 2015.

[10]Ashok J. Bharucha, A. J., et al, "Intelligent Assistive Technology Applications to Dementia Care: Current Capabilities, Limitations, and Future Challenges" *American Journal Geriatric Psychiatry*,17(2): 88–104,www.ncbi.nlm.nih.gov/pmc/articles/PMC2768007/, February, 2009.

The drawing in Figure 6-1 is an artistic rendition of how this type of assistive technology might augment humans in the not so distant future. The human displayed in Figure 6-1 is wearing several devices to enhance his sensory input and to monitor his physiology, including different types of bio-bands on each wrist; a bio-belt that is monitoring some of his internal organs; an implantable monitor on one of his arms that can display feedback to him about what the sensors are collecting and computing, such as information about his insulin levels[11]; sensor-embedded clothes that monitor certain joints, like his hips and knees for distress or that monitor his body temperature; and a skull device to enable him to mentally control certain devices or communicate with other people or applications, including those that are interpreting the data received by the sensors that he is wearing.

Figure 6-1. *The future of wearable technology (A. Mulvehill with permission)*

Some of these devices exist today; others are ideas that can be found in the literature and might be generally available soon. Just imagine, that instead of getting a text message or hearing an alarm that says that you need to drink some water because you are becoming dehydrated, perhaps that message might be presented like a whisper in the ear[12], or maybe even like a thought!

---

[11]Bourzak, K., "TR10: Implantable ElectronicsDissolvable devices make better medical implants", *MIT Technology Review*, www2.technologyreview.com/article/418543/tr10-implantable-electronics/, April 20, 2010.
[12]Shinavier, J., "Web Semantics For Multisensory Integration", PhD Thesis, Department of Computer Science, Rensselaer Polytechnic Institute, September, 2015.

Additionally, in the not too distant future, applications will likely be able to analyze your physiological sensor data and determine when there is a potential for a health issue to arise.

Instead of recommending that you book an appointment with your doctor, the application might utilize what is becoming known as *e-health technology* to arrange and facilitate the appointment. E-health is currently being introduced as a new method for providing healthcare to people in a global society. It leverages sophisticated technologies like AI decision support systems, wearable and smart home devices, and telecommunications capabilities to enable medical facilities and services across countries to share data so that patients can have healthcare no matter where they are located. The e-health application might arrange to have you transported to your doctor's office or to a hospital in a robotic car, or it might communicate with home robotic assistants, like the ones being developed in Japan to act like nurses for people in a home environment[13], and have those robotic assistants provide health services.

Although robot development is not a focus of this book, many robots rely on AI-based planning algorithms in order to navigate in the environment and to help them perform tasks. Many hospitals are already using robots in a variety of ways, from delivering meals to augmenting a surgeon in performing an operation. Robots can directly utilize data from sensors in our living spaces and/or sensors that we wear in order to monitor our physiological selves. Hosted in a robot or in some other wearable or mobile device, an AI cognitive computing system could provide the human with personalized clinical decision support anywhere and anytime; diagnosing the human's symptoms and making recommendations about what to eat, what pill to take, what physical activity to perform, etc.

Building User Interfaces

Humans generally communicate with computers through some type of user interface, like a keyboard, a touch screen, mouse, speech, etc. As people become more comfortable using different types of computing devices and applications for a variety of purposes and in a variety of contexts, they want the interfaces to be more natural. User interfaces have frequently changed to keep pace with changes in computer technology. Punch cards were the primary way for humans to enter data into a computer through the early 70s[14]. The mouse became available for use in the late 60s to support data entry, and by the mid 80s computer interfaces were being developed to enable a user to interact with the computer and its contents through a variety of mixed media including maps, charts, text, and so on. User interfaces have been evolving to become more natural and, in some cases, to become almost an extension of the user, or in effect to augment the human user. Think of how the keyboard and mouse have become extensions of your hands when you type a paper or create a presentation.

---

[13]Japan: a national strategy for e-health based on robotics. *Le Mag* Article, http://esante.gouv.fr/en/the-mag-issue-12/japan-a-national-strategy-e-health-based-robotics, September 23, 2014.
[14]IBM 100, "The IBM Punched Card", www-03.ibm.com/ibm/history/ibm100/us/en/icons/punchcard/, 2016.

In the 90s, mixed-initiative interface research was focused on developing an interface to enable a human and one or more software agents (an automated software entity that can perform some particular task) to collaborate with each other to solve problems. In mixed-initiative systems, the interface goes beyond the surface mechanism used to support communication between the user and the machine; it includes software that helps the machine understand the goals and intentions of the human[15].

The requirements for the design and implementation of a specific computer interface are generally driven by the needs of the user population. Although standard interface styles and widgets are available, interfaces often need to be custom-developed to support a complex cognitive problem such as air traffic control, military planning, financial analysis, seismic analysis, etc. For example, custom interfaces are typically developed to support individuals with specific learning and/or physical disabilities. At the other end of the spectrum, designers are challenged to develop interfaces for devices and applications that do not have a specific user audience; these interfaces must be designed for use by almost anyone and on almost any task.

Interfaces are needed to enable communication between all different types of human users and many different types of computing devices and applications. The interfaces need to provide the computing device or application with input, some direction or preference for processing, and some way to output a result to the user. In addition, in our current computing environment, the interface also needs to be able to maintain the privacy of the individual. This is particularly critical in order to realize personal AI assistants. Currently, researchers and advanced system developers are investigating the requirements for such interfaces. The challenge is that a lot of the standard methods used to build a good user interface today (with good user privacy protection) can't be used because creating the technology that is needed to make personal AI assistants a reality is still primarily a research challenge.[16]

As discussed previously, people are also becoming more comfortable with wearable technologies, which is resulting in a demand for the devices to become lighter and smaller, and for new interfaces to be created to facilitate interaction. Insertable and implantable devices, often developed for health monitoring, can require biological compatibility and some way to interface with the device through the human body[17]. More futuristic interfaces are also being investigated. For example, *wetware* is a term used by researchers to describe how a biological system, using a direct brain-computer interface,[18] can allow a human to use thought to communicate with and control an artificial limb or an external machine[19]. Holographic projections and virtual reality are also actively being researched as not-so-distant future interfaces between humans and machines.

---

[15]Horwitz, Eric, "Principles of mixed-initiative user interfaces", in CHI '99 Proceedings of the SIGCHI conference on Human Factors in Computing Systems, pp. 159-166, 1999.

[16]Nardi, B., some problems are described in "Designing for the Future – But Which One?", *Interactions of the ACM*, pp. 27-33, January-February 2016.

[17]Holz, C., Grossman, T., Fitzmaurice, G., and Agur, A., "Implanter User Interfaces", CHI'12, Austin, Texas, USA, May 5–10, 2012.

[18]John Hopkins Medicine, "Mind-controlled prosthetic arm moves individual 'fingers'", www.sciencedaily.com/releases/2016/02/160215154656.htm, 2016.

[19]Schmidt, A., "Biosignals in Human-Computer Interaction", pp. 76-79; ACM Interactions, January-February 2016.

Human Enhancements: Near Future and Beyond

Because of reduced costs to build computer technology and ever improving ways to deliver it, many of the sophisticated decision support, analysis, and computational technologies that were once available only to government and large organizations are now commonly available. Sensor capabilities and data analysis technology is now available to individuals for monitoring and managing resources in their home. Cars often have computer technology that helps the driver navigate, park, avoid accidents, and even be rescued if the technology detects that they are involved in an accident.

Assistive technologies like virtual assistants are starting to be provided at airports to provide airport visitors with information about gate transfers, where to catch a bus, etc. Holographic assistants are becoming widely available to support a variety of tasks. The hologram in Figure 6-2 is an example of virtual promoter that is being used to sell cosmetics.

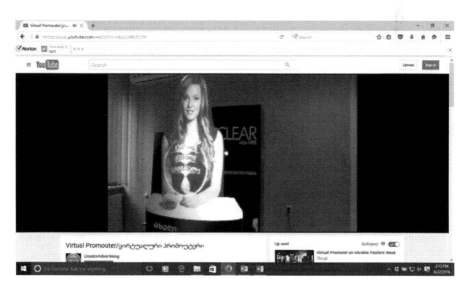

Figure 6-2. Holographic virtual promoter selling cosmetic products (www.youtube.com/ watch?v=mXyuUWUfxLM)

Humans have become accustomed to using technology for administrative, educational, and recreational support. Applications on smartphones are regularly used to find location information, get recommendations about places to eat, and directions on how to get there. These devices and applications, once novel to many, are now considered a common need. As they become more common, our expectations for what they can provide us will likely grow. For example, in the not so distant future, more people will have homes that will have multiple smart devices. These devices will also notify the home owner when they need maintenance. As entertainment systems learn more about the viewer, they will start to recommend entertainment that more closely satisfies the viewer's preferences. Planning and scheduling software will provide reminders about appointments and family events. Home security systems will provide alerts about intruders and notify external agencies as necessary.

While many of these future technological amenities are easy to imagine and are in the process of becoming commonly available, the following technologies might take some time to become reality.

Personal Assistants

There are many possible futures and social changes that AI technology might influence[20]. Determining when a device that uses a particular technology might be commonly available for use is difficult. Take, for example, the voice interaction technology that is commonly available with tools like Siri[21] on smartphones and tablets. In a 1990s television show called *Time Trax*[22] this type of technology was being used to support a futuristic policeman as he pursued criminals.

In this show, a policeman was able to use speech to interact with his computer. His computer was not a cell phone; instead it was the size and shape of a credit card and it embodied a smart, AI-like computer program called Selma, which stands for "Specified Encapsulated Limitless Memory Archive." In addition to being able to talk to Selma and listen to her replies, he could actually interact with a visual form, since Selma could holographically project herself in the form of a human woman if needed to improve their communication.

Basically Selma was acting as a personal assistant. She was augmenting the human user, extending his access to knowledge, and helping him make decisions, and even proposing some suggestions and solutions that were based on her understanding of the current context and her ability to make projections about the future.

So, what was presented as science fiction in 1990 partially became reality in the 2014 time frame, and will become more of a reality in the near future as several of the largest technology companies are actively involved in creating virtual assistants. In addition to Siri, new virtual assistants like the concierge service called M from Facebook through its Messenger app, Google Now, Microsoft's Cortana, and Amazon's Echo (a voice-activated living-room device that can control the ambience of your home) are being developed or enhanced to help augment human decision making[23]. In each case, these virtual assistants use AI technology to learn from the human so that they can become better personal assistants.

---

[20]Hodjat, B., "Artificial Intelligence: What Will the Next 20 Years Bring?", The Huffington Post, www.huffingtonpost.com/babak-hodjat/artificial-intelligence-w_1_b_8894418.html, December, 2015.

[21]www.apple.com/ios/siri/, 2016.

[22]Wikipedia, "Time Trax", https://en.wikipedia.org/wiki/Time_Trax, 2016.

[23]Murgia, M., "The race for virtual AI assistants is on, but the ultimate prize is you", The Telegraph, www.telegraph.co.uk/technology/news/11874511/The-race-for-virtual-AI-assistants-is-on-but-the-ultimate-prize-is-you.html, September 18, 2015.

As some of the problems with context and natural language understanding (described in Chapter 5) get solved through scientific research and development, personal AI-based cognitive assistants will increasingly be marketed. AI-based personal assistants will be able to communicate with us to understand our goals. Instead of having hundreds of apps and multiple devices to juggle, the assistant will use information about our goals to find and fuse together relevant information, along with recommendations for actions, in a form that we can trust and understand.

Robot systems, coupled with AI reasoning abilities, will likely be available and more affordable for home usage. Instead of typing on a keyboard, the human will be able to interact with the robot through an interface that might include speech, gesturing, and emotion recognition. Specialized robots will be able to provide personalized care or companionship as needed. If a person falls, the robot will be able to help the person get up and get to a medical facility for help.

Computers will also likely continue to enhance how people interact with each other across geographic distances. Instead of typing into a laptop or using Skype to teleconference with someone, perhaps a person will be able to walk into a special room in their house where they can be immersed in the entire environment of another person or group of people that they are interested in talking with. Real-time language translation is also starting to make its way out of the lab and into practice, which means this communication will not require everyone to speak the same language. In addition, instead of personally attending some meetings or performing certain tasks, a person might be able to delegate these tasks to smart engines or agents that know the user's preferences and objectives, or the AI personal assistant might be able to provide oversight and administration. A person might be able to send a virtual AI to a meeting as their representative. Looking further out, perhaps some of the meetings of the future will be solely attended by AI representatives who have the ability to negotiate and make decisions for their humans.

IMPLANTABLE COMPUTERS

Tools are currently being developed to transform many of the tasks currently performed by laptops or hand-held computers to machines that we can implant into our bodies. Insertables (small implanted devices that can be removed) are gaining popularity. Just as we can place microchips in our pets or in farm animals to support livestock monitoring, insertable devices are being developed to improve our cognitive and physiological capabilities and to support some very specific tasks, like granting permission to a person to enter some secured physical space. Instead of moving a special card over a sensor, the person can just wave their hand near the door, and if their credentials, as recorded in the implantable, are appropriate, the door will open[24].

---

[24]Heffernan, K. J., Vetere, F., and Chang, S., "Insertables: I've Got IT under My Skin", *Interactions of the ACM*, January-February, 2016.

As these devices are developed, tested, and become widely available, we assume that regulations to evaluate and maintain the technology, as well as services to support their host humans, will also improve. For example, the Federal Drug Administration currently has a program in place to track and evaluate new medical devices that is called the Unique Device Identification (UDI) system[25]. The UDI's information about medical devices is a way to track and manage medical devices. Data that is collected through this system can be used to evaluate how devices are being used, problems they have, how many have been recalled, etc. The goal is to create standards and government regulations that will be used to impose requirements for quality control and the distribution and usage of these devices, thereby increasing patient safety. The relationship of these implantables with AI technologies is one that is both promising and a bit scary–an area we will return to in Chapter 8 where we discuss some of the challenges with emerging AI technologies.

Enhancing Memory

Memory is a very personal part of a human being and is often highly associated with what we think of as our personal identity. We rely on our memories to solve problems and to reminisce about or relive the past. People's memory abilities vary. For some, memories can be replayed like a movie, with every little detail contained in a scene. For others, memories appear as snippets or individual facts. Memories can come to mind on demand (like getting a result when you do a computer search) or automatically surface when in some specific context. Memories tend to be very biased since people experience the world through their own sensory systems and from their own perspectives. Some memories you want to forget and others you never want to forget. Unfortunately, as people age, many develop memory problems. Sometimes a person just gets a little slow in retrieving some fact. Sometimes a person doesn't remember the correct fact. Sometimes a person can't seem to remember at all.

While search engine technology has been a valuable memory aid to many people, it is insufficient for helping a person who has advanced dementia. Although a search engine can help a person with mild memory problems fill in blanks or jiggle their memories so that they can remember and continue a discussion, some people with advanced forms of dementia cannot even use the search engine. Memory assistive technologies are currently being developed to support people with mild forms of dementia. These devices can help a person keep track of the day and date, and help them to plan and manage tasks and events. These tools can remind a person about when to eat, go to an appointment, talk to a loved one, etc.

---

[25]U.S. Department of Health and Human Services, U. S. Food and Drug Administration, "Unique Device Identification UDI", www.fda.gov/MedicalDevices/DeviceRegulationandGuidance/UniqueDeviceIdentification/, 2016.

Other memory assistive devices can analyze wearable monitor data, use data from sensors that might be monitoring a person's living environment, or use directives from doctors to provide the person with personalized reminders about when to take medications, perform physical therapy, and so on. Some memory assistive devices can provide more personalized services like helping an individual keep track of personal items that tend to get misplaced, such as keys or a wallet or helping them to recognize people in old photographs. In fact, some technology that is currently being developed can recognize distorted faces, which is useful since people can look different if they wear makeup, and their appearance tends to change as they age. A description of several of these memory assistive technology devices as well as other information about memory problems and solutions can be found on the Alzheimer's association web site[26].

As we continue to use various technologies to monitor our health, to support problem solving, to communicate and socialize, and as cognitive computing algorithms become more reliable at finding relevant information, tagging the information that is sensed, and in general recognizing patterns within a context, they could become the new media for collecting, storing, and recollecting the memories of an individual, in effect archiving the lifetime of a human.

Perhaps at some point in the future this type of assistive technology will take the form of an implantable device, like a brain pacemaker, and be used to augment human cognitive and capabilities. Brain pacemakers are currently being developed to support Alzheimer's and to treat Parkinson's disease[27], which can be accompanied by some form of dementia. The first brain pacemaker was implanted in a human patient in 2012[28] and research is continuing to determine how well these devices work for people with different levels of cognitive decline. Current research also involves enhancing these devices with more AI to help fill in details of a person's current and past life. Much of this research is in a very early stage, but it will clearly become more important in developed economies with an aging population (such as the US and Japan).

Beyond the Individual

The integration of AI technologies and the individual user is an emerging area, getting significant attention. As we've described, the technologies are becoming more available, and many are being tested today. The first place we are likely to see many of these is in assistive devices for the elderly or those with disabilities, where the great need for assistance can outweigh some of the reservations that are found in bringing these techniques to the more general public.

---

[26]Alzheimer's Association, "Assistive technologies – devices to help with everyday living", http://www.alzheimers.org.uk, April 2016.

[27]Strickland, E., "How Brain Pacemakers Treat Parkinson's Disease", http://spectrum.ieee.org/tech-talk/biomedical/devices/new-clues-how-does-a-brain-pacemaker-control-parkinsons-symptoms, 2015.

[28]Ohio State University Wexner Medical Center, "First brain pacemaker implanted to treat Alzheimer's", *Science Daily*, www.sciencedaily.com/releases/2013/01/130123164906.htm, January 23, 2013.

Another area where the use of AI is also growing is in the development of new technologies that enable multiple people to work together to solve hard problems. Going beyond the crowd sourcing we see today in web sites such as Kickstarter and Wikipedia, these new applications become social machines that enable humans and computers to work together as powerful teams. We will discuss the emerging world of social machines in the next chapter.

CHAPTER 7

■ ■ ■

Social Machines: Embracing the Blur

Real life is and must be full of all kinds of social constraint—the very processes from which society arises. Computers can help if we use them to create abstract social machines on the Web: processes in which the people do the creative work and the machine does the administration...

Tim Berners-Lee and Mark Fischetti[1], 1999

In the previous chapter, we explored how AI systems are increasingly being used to enhance the capabilities of humans. However, in our increasingly networked world, the people using the applications, and the applications themselves, can interact, allowing more and more complex "systems of systems." In this chapter, we will explore this interaction at scale, looking at ways in which people are networking using machines, machines are enhancing the networking of people, and how as this all comes together it offers increasingly powerful mechanisms powered by the integration of people and computers. Where the last chapter looked at human enhancement, this one will look at humans enhancing AI in return.

WEB 2.0

Around the turn of the millennium, a new bit of jargon started to emerge. The term *Web 2.0* started to be used to indicate what seemed to be a second generation of web technologies (using the sort of numbering scheme popular in many computer applications and programs). The argument was that the development of new technologies that were making it easier for users to enter information, without having to create their own specialized web sites, was changing the nature of the interactions on the Internet. New technologies in the early 00s included software that

---

[1]Berners-Lee, T. and Fischetti, M., *Weaving the Web: The original design and ultimate destiny of the World Wide Web*, Harper Collins, New York, 1999.

© James Hendler and Alice M. Mulvehill 2016
J. Hendler and A. M. Mulvehill, *Social Machines*, DOI 10.1007/978-1-4842-1156-4_7

made it easier to make and create blogs; wikis, which were pages where anyone could enter text and have it become part of the site; and tagging sites like Flickr that made it possible for people to add keywords to help others find their materials. Also emerging around the same time were what we now call social network sites, such as Friendster, Orkut, Myspace, and TheFacebook were created in the English-speaking world, while sites like Renren launched in China. Dating sites arose, where people could look to meet others on the Web (by 2013 it was reported that about 1/3 of US marriages started with online dating). Over the rest of that decade, the renamed Facebook rose in popularity, eventually eclipsing the others and becoming the first social network with over a billion users. Sites also arose that provided other means of networking, especially those based on messaging and microblogs, such as Twitter and the Chinese Sino Weibo network and later sites such as Snapchat, Messenger, and WhatsApp.

(Some people have used the term *social machine* to refer to these microblogging and messaging sites, Twitter in particular. However, as we shall see below, the phrase, as derived from the quote at the start of this chapter, is more typically used for a very different kind of web interaction.)

With the growth of the social network, and the social changes being wrought by the literally billions of people who could now communicate with others through the Web, the term Web 2.0 started to ebb; people argued this was the Web itself (not needing a number) or was becoming a new generation (although the term *Web 3.0* never quite caught on). Whatever name is used, the world has changed to one where ubiquitous messaging and social networks are part of the fiber of many people's day-to-day lives.

Social networking software has become increasingly pervasive in people's use of the World Wide Web and mobile applications. Facebook, Twitter, SnapChat, Tumblr, Instagram, and many others have become a standard part of many people's lives. As more and more social interaction happens on the Web, the companies that run these sites and applications have access to large amounts of user data and have the ability to do more and more analytics to try to understand users' intent. This information is used to match people's (inferred) interests to what is happening in their social media streams (the average user only sees a small fraction of the information even in their own social media feeds) and for the money-making purpose of trying to match advertisements to users.

This information can also be used in other ways, and that has become an important pursuit of AI research. For example, in Chapter 2, we mentioned Google Flu trends, which was an early attempt to predict real-world situations based on people's search behaviors. Social media analytics, predicting users' characteristics based on what they say and do online, is becoming increasingly important to the economics of the World Wide Web. What different users may see in their search results, their social media feeds, the ads presented to them, and so on are all determined by these companies' use of user data to infer what it is that people want to see online, or what will best motivate them to take some action (click on an ad, go to a web site, buy something in the real world, etc.) However, as discussed previously, computers still fare poorly at determining user contexts, and AI systems still benefit from human interaction and intervention. In social media and other large scale systems, however, it is hard for individual humans to provide these contexts or determine the details of their interactions. The problems don't go away, and in fact are made worse at scale, often causing user frustration with the very systems that are trying to help them. For example, the use of advertisement blockers on the Web, and on mobile apps, is increasing as people find that ads being matched to them are not often useful in the contexts they are in. When looking to buy something online, a search may be helpful, but ads that seem unrelated to needs just get people annoyed. Getting AI systems to understand the complex behaviors of people at scale is still a challenge, and major investments are being made by the largest online companies to try to overcome this.

THE NETWORK EFFECT: METCALFE'S LAW

As the number of people involved in any communications technology (including social networks and large web sites) increases, there is an exponential growth in the amount of possible communication paths. This is known as the network effect and it comes with both good and bad properties. From the positive side, very large numbers of users can interact, enabling many of the social networking and other kinds of web sites and applications we will discuss in this chapter. On the negative side, with more potential interactions there is a greater tendency for people to try to exploit others, which has led to problems such as spam, attempts to bias search engine results, people trying to promote a particular cause, etc. While these same issues come up in real-world life, the number of people one interacts with in physical space can be dwarfed by the number of people involved in large scale social networks and online sites (for example, Facebook reports well over a billion users on their site).

This network effect is best quantified by what has come to be known as Metcalfe's Law, based on a graph developed by Bob Metcalfe in the early 1980s which, according to Metcalfe, was created to better explain to customers of his company's Ethernet boards why they needed more of them than they were buying. Metcalfe hypothesized that while the cost of the network grew linearly with the number of connections, the value grew as the number of connections squared. Every computer on a network that had an Ethernet card could talk to each of the others. Thus, if you bought 20 cards, you would have 20 computers, each of which could communicate with 19 others, so the number of possible communications was 20 x 19 = 380. However, if you had 40 computers, each could communicate with 39 others, for a total of 1560 connections. Basically, the number of connections grows close to the square of the number of machines (380 vs. 1560); however, the cost of the boards rises at a linear rate, so twice as many boards costs twice as much, but gets you nearly four times the number of connections. Ten times as many boards, at ten times the price, gets you a hundred times as many connections, etc.

Metcalfe's law has been used to explain the growth of many items ranging from phones, cell phones, and faxes to web applications and social networks, especially online social networks. The intuition clearly holds that as the number of people in the network grows, the connectivity increases, and if people can link to each other's content, the value grows at an enormous rate.

Recently, there has been some interesting debate with respect to the validity of Metcalfe's law. On the low end, a 2006 column in *IEEE Spectrum* opined that value in a network grows much more slowly, basically arguing that not all connections are of equal value.[2] At the other extreme, a 2001 article in the *Harvard Business Review* (2001) claimed that the value of the network grew exponentially in the number of connections.[3] This argument was essentially that in a largely connected network, such as a social networking web site like Facebook or Twitter, the value is in the creation of subgroups, and the number of these subgroups (i.e. the subnetworks of size 2, size 3, ... size n) grows exponentially with n (a number that grows much faster than the square). While neither of these effects has been proven in practice, nor is it clear that all networks will have the same value increase, it is clear that the network effect is quite real, and even the most pessimistic view still provides for significant value as the number of connections in the network grows.

At the same time, another trend has been growing on the Web that is more successful at capturing human intent: this is to get people to perform a task based on purposive behavior about something they want to do, in a context they understand. There are two common forms of this kind of system. The first, which has come to be known as *crowdsourcing* has become quite familiar on the Web. In these systems, a number of people each doing a "small" amount of work are able to create something large by dint of the common effort (an example of this is Wikipedia, which we will discuss later). Other examples may include people each contributing a small amount of money so that together they can fund something they find meaningful at a level none could do alone. Web sites such as Kickstarter, Indiegogo, GoFundMe, and many others have been built to make this possible and have together raised literally billions of dollars for causes people believe in. Before we discuss crowdsourcing and the many forms it comes in, however, there is a second approach to exploiting the interactions of many humans aided by machines that we need to explore.

Human Computation

This second approach to taking advantage of people working together is called *human computation*, a term that was originally used to describe people creating benefit to a web site or service provider based on things they were doing for their own benefit or enjoyment. The term is generally credited to researcher Luis von Ahn, whose seminal

[2]Briscoe, Bob, Odlyzko, Andrew, and Tilly, Benjamin, "Metcalfe's Law is Wrong", *IEEE Spectrum*, July, 2006.
[3]Reed, David P., "The Law of the Pack", *Harvard Business Review*, 23-24, February, 2001.

doctoral thesis started a whole new way of thinking about how large numbers of people doing small amounts of online work could, when all of the work was summed up, generate a large amount of total effort for the sake of achieving a purpose.[4] This purpose might be a side-effect of the work people were doing that they weren't aware of, or it could be something they were contributing to knowingly as part of a larger collective effort.

A good example of the use of human computation, and one of the first pioneered by von Ahn, will be familiar in form to most users of online systems. Often, the designers of a system want to know, before sharing information, that the user requesting the data is a human, and not a computer that is just trying to scrape a site to gather information. Von Ahn and colleagues were involved in designing *CAPTCHAs*, which are words or images that were manipulated in such a way that they could be easily recognized by a human, but hard to process by a computer. Figure 7-1 show an early CAPTCHA, one in which a human might be asked "what letters are here" and would reply with the correct answer (6138B), which would be easy for a human to recognize but hard for a computer system to do at that time (as discussed in Chapter 5, computer recognition of such things has improved significantly in the past few years, and thus CAPTCHAs have had to get more sophisticated too).

Figure 7-1. *A CAPTCHA, which is text that is easy for a human to recognize but hard for a computer*

As more and more people use captchas on web sites, von Ahn realized that the time they were spending could, in aggregate, be put to a useful purpose. That is, although it might only take a few seconds for a human to process a CAPTCHA, if you took all the time that all those humans were expending, it could add up to a large total. Was there a way to put all of that time to work doing something useful?

In an effort to try this out, van Ahn developed what was known as a ReCAPTCHA, shown in Figure 7-2. This form, which the reader has probably encountered many times, takes the idea of a capture, but instead of a random set of digits or such, shows the user two words. The user types those words, and if she get them right, is admitted to the web site or allowed to do whatever it is she was requesting. However, in the background, something very important was going on. All of the users using ReCAPTCHAS were helping computers get better at recognizing words in texts.

---

[4]von Ahn, L., *Human Computation*, Doctoral Dissertation, School of Computer Science, Carnegie Mellon University, December, 2005 (Published as CMU report CMU-CS-05-193).

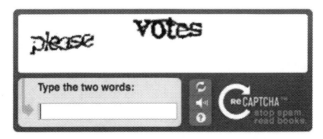

Figure 7-2. Example of a ReCAPTCHA, the extension of the CAPTCHA into a successful form of human computation used to help process texts for optical character recognition (Used with permission)

Consider the image in Figure 7-3. This is an enlargement of an article from the front page of a 1914 issue of *The New York Times*. The articles from this newspaper had been digitized and put online, but the content was not searchable. Using optical character recognition (OCR), a process by which a computer scans the page and tries to turn what it is processing into letters and words, the *Times* could get some of the content, but a great many words were hard to recognize. The words in these old texts could be stained, smeared, crooked, etc., which produced problems for the computer. The *Times* contracted with a company von Ahn had formed, and which had been bought by Google, to use ReCAPTCHAS to help. Using various kinds of processing, words were identified in the output of the OCR that were "suspicious" for various reasons (they couldn't be recognized at all, the word didn't seem to make sense in the sentence, different OCR programs recognized the word differently, etc.).

Russia Announces Its Wish to Remain at Peace Yet Is Determined to Guard Its Interests.

ST. PETERSBURG, July 28.—The Russian Government tonight issued the following official communication:

"Numerous patriotic demonstrations of the last few days in St. Petersburg and other cities prove that the firm pacific policy of Russia finds a sympathetic echo among all classes of the population.

"The Government hopes, nevertheless, that the expression of feeling of the people will not be tinged with enmity against the powers with whom Russia is at peace, and with whom she wishes to remain at peace.

"While the Government gathers strength from this wave of popular feeling and expects its subjects to retain their reticence and tranquillity, it rests confidently on the guardianship of the dignity and the interests of Russia."

Figure 7-3. An article from the front page of The New York Times from 1914

To translate the suspicious words, the system would pair the questionable word with a known word, and then the two words would be shown together to a user who was trying to access a site protected by a ReCAPTCHA. The human would type their best guess at what the two words were. If the human typed the known word correctly, then their guess for the second word would be taken to be more likely correct. If a number of people were shown the same suspicious word (coupled with different test words), then over time the computer could track the guesses, and if most of them ended up the same, it would assume that was the correct word. Given that ReCAPTCHAS were being used by literally millions of people on major sites, the system was able to recognize huge numbers of these words in a high quality way. Thus, the humans using the system, who got value by being admitted to the sites they wanted to get to, were also helping *The New York Times* to transcribe these articles.[5]

Over the course of the years that ReCAPTCHAS have been deployed, literally hundreds of millions of users have in this way helped Google and others to transcribe many millions of words of text and to make many documents searchable online. It should be noted that while many users of ReCAPTCHAS were not aware that their effort was being used in this way, the ReCAPTCHA form did include a link to information that would provide this information.

In a more ambitious effort to move from transcription to translation, von Ahn and his students created a new human computation web site called Duolingo. First made public in 2011, Duolingo offers users a chance to learn a foreign language for free. In exchange, as the users learn the language, they have a side effect of helping to translate documents or to do other services relating to translation. In this project, users are putting in significantly more effort, spending minutes to hours a day on the language learning, and Duolingo makes its profit from finding ways that the collective effort can be used for services that they can sell on the back end (language certification, translation, etc.).[6]

Games with a Purpose and Citizen Science

Von Ahn is also well known for another aspect of human computation that has become widely used, what are now called *games with a purpose* (GWAP) or *human-computation games*. The first of these was called the ESP game and was developed by von Ahn in 2004. The idea of the game was to get images marked with descriptive terms, but to do so in a way that was less idiosyncratic than what was occurring on image sharing sites like Flickr. These sites had a problem: people would upload their own photos, but often put no or very few tags. Even worse, many of the tags weren't very useful. For example, a tag like "Mom" or "my best friend" makes sense if you know the person whose photos they are, but are not very useful if you don't. This is another case where context causes problems for computers, as we discussed in Chapter 5; without knowing the context, it is hard to know what the tag means.

---

[5] `www.nytimes.com/2011/03/29/science/29recaptcha.html`
[6] Von Ahn's TED talk on Duolingo is a good starting place for those interested in more information about the system and how it works: `www.ted.com/talks/luis_von_ahn_massive_scale _online_collaboration`.

Von Ahn attacked this problem by making marking up photos into a competitive game that could be played online. As shown in Figure 7-4, a player would be shown a photo and a set of "taboo words" and then would type guesses. Another player elsewhere would see the same thing. The players would each then input words they thought might describe the picture (but could not use the taboo words). The sooner the two players typed the same word, the higher the score they would receive. The computer used various techniques to make sure people wouldn't "cheat," including giving different users the same photo (sometimes with different taboo words) to check for common tags, using known photos to make sure people included words that had been input by the designers of the game, and so on.[7] The game turned out to be fun to play, and points worked well as rewards (with leader boards and other such features added as time went on). As a side effect, millions of photos were tagged with a high quality of annotations. Google acquired the game in 2006, and used it, and variants thereof, to get people to put annotations on non-textual items like images, tunes, and videos. In addition to this game, von Ahn went on to develop many others, and a number of other people have also developed similar games.[8]

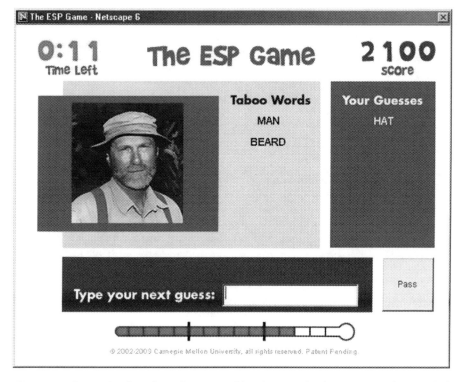

Figure 7-4. *Screen shot from the early version of the ESP game (with permission of L. von Ahn)*

---

[7]Von Ahn, Luis and Dabbish, Laura, "Labeling images with a computer game", *Proceedings of the SIGCHI conference on Human factors in computing systems*, ACM, 2004.
[8]A good selection of such games is described in Wikipedia: https://en.wikipedia.org/wiki/Human-based_computation_game.

With these kinds of games coming to the Web, it was fairly natural that people would develop an interest in merging them with what were known as "serious games." These kind of games, which originally predate computer games, were best known for being used in educational settings. In early computer days, they became programs designed as simple games to help teach people to do things. Early examples included computer games for children that would teach math, geography, or other such topics. Many of these games, such as The Oregon Trail and Where in the World is Carmen San Diego?, became quite popular and were heavily used on early personal computers. As well as for education, serious games have been developed to enhance training for the military and industry, to help injured patients to recover mental or physical skills, etc.

It is unclear what the first example of merging serious games and GWAPs was, but the first to really make a major scientific impact was a site called Galaxy Zoo that was originally developed at Oxford University by Christopher Lintott and Kevin Shawinski, and then supported by a large team of astronomers and programmers from a number of universities around the world.[9] Inspired by some other efforts to get multiple people to jointly identify objects in astronomical photographs, Lintott and Shawinski decided to build a site to get people to help classify images taken as part of the Hubble sky survey. The Hubble telescope took many photos of the universe, and among them were many images containing pictures of galaxies. The astronomers had a collection of over 900,000 galaxy images, and they estimated that using graduate students to classify these images would take years of effort at a high cost (As discussed in Chapter 5, humans remain better at recognizing such patterns than computers, and efforts to develop an automated classifier had largely failed.) They decided to use the combination of ideas from serious games and GWAPs to develop a site where volunteers would look at images and classify what kinds of galaxies they saw.

Figure 7-5 is an example of what the Galaxy Zoo screen looked like. A user could register and take a short course on identifying galaxy types. They would see a photo from the sky telescope and would be asked a couple of questions: to choose which kind of galaxy (spherical or spiral) and other features (symmetric and the like). It was fairly easy to learn to use Galaxy Zoo, and a large number of users discovered it and cooperated. The site was so successful that the team reported that in the first version of Galaxy Zoo, more than 100,000 volunteers marked up the types of the 900,000 galaxies within 175 days. To validate the classifications, Galaxy Zoo used methods similar to those used by Von Ahn to prevent cheating: showing the same galaxy to multiple users to raise the certainty of the classification (and get an "inter-rater reliability" score) and showing the same galaxy to the same user at a later time (to check the rater reliability of the particular user).

---

[9]Lintott, Chris J., Kevin Schawinski, Anže Slosar, Kate Land, Steven Bamford, Daniel Thomas, M. Jordan Raddick et al. "Galaxy Zoo: morphologies derived from visual inspection of galaxies from the Sloan Digital Sky Survey." *Monthly Notices of the Royal Astronomical Society* 389, no. 3 (2008): 1179-1189.

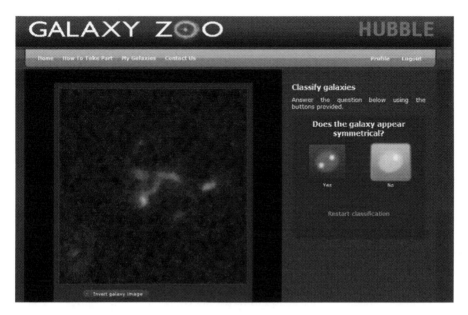

Figure 7-5. Galaxy Zoo was one of the first citizen science sites to combine serious games and games with a purpose to harness human computation to solving a scientific task (Screen shot credit: Gwydion M. Williams)

Galaxy Zoo was so successful that users requested more things to do. Over time the Zooniverse, a set of serious games for astronomical work, was developed. The first version of Galaxy Zoo gave rise to others, looking at more complex features of galaxies and their interactions, and then moved on to radio astronomy, lunar science, and others. As other scientists discovered the power of these techniques, the Zooniverse grew beyond astronomy and as of 2016 it reports a user community of over a million users and contains interfaces for scientific projects from space, natural sciences, the humanities, biology, and physics. The web site http://zooniverse.org is a popular destination for people looking to learn more about science or who want to contribute their time to helping scientists to understand the world. Further, the Zooniverse is only one of a large and growing set of citizen science sites that are available on the Web.

A second kind of citizen science site has been developing in a more "bottom up" fashion. In these sites, a group of hobbyists, as opposed to scientists per se, have set up web sites where they can cooperate to share photos, stories, and other aspects of their hobbies. Popular sites have been set up for mushroom collectors, bird enthusiasts, and many others. Other such sites have been set up around sharing information about specific kinds of projects for particular hobbies (such as hydroponic gardening for city dwellers), sites for sharing information about healthy life styles and exercise, and many others. These in turn have given rise to many other sites that go beyond games and hobbies, and use similar technologies to solve societal problems. We will return to these latter kinds of social machines later in this chapter.

HANNY'S VOORWERP

What motivates people to get involved in citizen science sites is still somewhat of a mystery. Surveys and other questionnaires have shown many different reasons why people participate, and understanding the incentives that can get different people to use the sites is an important challenge to the growth of these sites. One story, however, is often told by people to explain the lure of citizen science sites in general, and Galaxy Zoo (and the Zooniverse) in particular.

In 2007, a Dutch school teacher named Hanny van Arkel was participating as a volunteer in the Zooniverse project. Her screen showed her a photo similar to the one shown in Figure 7-6 and asked her to identify the galaxy in the upper middle of the screen. Noticing the strange green object below the galaxy, which she had never seen in one of these pictures, Ms. Van Arkel used a feature of the site where one could send a report to a member of the Galaxy Zoo team if something odd was noticed (or there was a problem with the system).

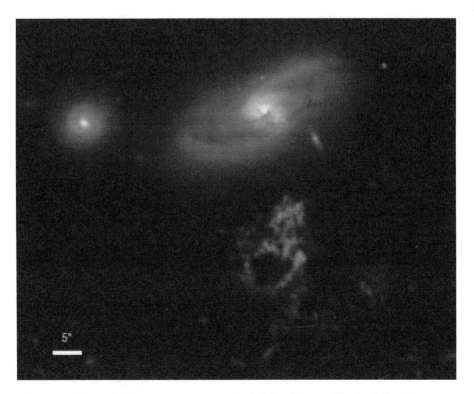

Figure 7-6. Hanny's Voorwerp, an astronomical object discovered in the Galaxy Zoo project (credit: WIYN/William Keel/Anna Manning)

125

The team member who looked into the comment was also puzzled by the object, and it caused various discussions among the participants. It was eventually determined to be a new astronomical object, called a *quasar ionization echo*. However, it has come to be known both to astronomers and Galaxy Zoo participants by another name: Hanny's Voowerp (Dutch for "Hanny's object"), named after its discoverer. She was also included as one of the authors of a scientific paper entitled "Galaxy Zoo: 'Hanny's Voowerp', a quasar light echo?" which was published in 2009.[10] Coffee mugs, t-shirts, and other items celebrating the achievement are also popular memorabilia among Galaxy Zoo participants.

Wikipedia: The People's Encyclopedia

Another trend that grew up with Web 2.0 has come to be known as *crowdsourcing*. This phenomenon grew up as it became easier for groups of people to contribute to web sites and the like, as discussed previously, but truly gained prominence with the growth of Wikipedia, a web site started in 2001 by founders Jimmy Wales and Larry Sanger. The founders said they were inspired by several web sites including one called Nupedia, which was a free encyclopedia on the Web (but with articles authored by experts as in a traditional encyclopedia) and a site called Slashdot, where users could post pointers to articles appearing on the Web and others could read and respond to them. Slashdot, started in 1997, billed itself as "News for Nerds" and primarily featured stories about science and technology. Today Slashdot has millions of visitors and thousands of comments each day. Slashdot was also one inspiration of a site called reddit, which has a wider readership and today is one of the most used commenting sites on the Web.

Wikipedia started by making articles similar to those in Nupedia available, but also editable. Based on a technology that allowed users to enter their own changes, while those changes were tracked and logged, Wikipedia made it possible for non-professional authors to add information on new topics by creating articles. The articles on Wikipedia are created by users who simply register and create content. A typical page is reviewed by both human and automated checkers and, if accepted, becomes part of the open Wikipedia site.

Wikipedia has been stunningly successful; the English version now has well over five million articles on topics ranging from traditional encyclopedia topics such as famous people and events to articles on sporting events, celebrities, hobbies, and just about everything else. To put that in perspective, the Encyclopedia Britannica lists about 200,000 articles in its English edition, about 1/50th the size. Further, Wikipedia now has articles available in well over 200 languages, with the total number of articles (in any language) topping 38 million in 2015, according to founder Wales.

There have been many studies of Wikipedia and the quality of its articles, and there are many debates that range over whether the approach used in managing the site has biases and the like. The Wikipedia page on the Wikipedia project[11] includes many linked pages including discussion of criticisms, comparisons to other online information sites, etc.

---

[10]Lintott, Chris J., Schawinski, Kevin, Keel, William, Van Arkel, Hanny, Bennert, Nicola, Edmondson, Edward, Thomas, Daniel et al. "Galaxy Zoo: 'Hanny's Voorwerp', a quasar light echo?." *Monthly Notices of the Royal Astronomical Society* 399, no. 1 (2009): 129-140.
[11]https://en.wikipedia.org/wiki/Wikipedia

Wikipedia has shown that a web site consisting of content that is user driven and derived, also known as *crowdsourced*, can produce high quality material. However, it has also revealed many issues about what is needed to run a large site of this kind, and a few of these issues are particularly relevant to our discussion of social machines.

First, Wikipedia has shown that as sites grow, they need a model of governance to control various aspects of social behavior on the Web. Much as games with a purpose need to control cheating, Wikipedia needs a control for people who may be doing malicious things online, who may be publishing inaccurate information, or who may be trying to push various products or positions for the sake of their own enrichment. As Wikipedia has grown, it has had to evolve a number of policies as to what can and cannot be published, and it has had to create a "government" that can make decisions about the site. Wikipedia has explored many different models of governance and is fairly unique in that its processes and policies are themselves discussed on the site and there are mechanisms for voting on policies, for electing people who are given more authority than others, etc.

WIKIALITY: COLBERT AND THE ELEPHANTS

An example of why Wikipedia needs governance structures can be seen from a famous event that happened in July of 2006. Comedian Stephen Colbert, on his show "The Colbert Report," proposed an idea he referred to as "wikiality." He joked in a segment[12] that "On Wikipedia, we can create a reality that we can all agree on–the reality we just agreed on." The idea was that if lots of people believe something and state it on a site like Wikipedia, the consensus view would hold. He suggested to his viewers that they should edit the page on "elephants" to claim that the population of elephants in Africa had tripled in the past six months (which would confuse the environmentalists). Many viewers went to do exactly that, and as people changed the pages, Wikipedia needed a way to stop the "vandalism." One power that some of the key Wikipedia editors have is the ability to lock pages when they feel something untoward is happening, and they did so in this case. However, the discussion over these events, the policies put in place to try to prevent it from happening again, and the overall issues it highlighted (what if all these people really believed these things, or what about people who think that "consensus" facts are wrong?) went on for a long time, and led to a number of changes in how Wikipedia's Administrators (editors with particular permissions to change things on the sites) performed their tasks. In typical Wikipedia style, a number of Wikipedia pages were written discussing the event and the controversies it caused.[13]

Secondly, dealing with many of these same issues has caused Wikipedia to need to deploy a number of *bots* to help maintain the site. Bots, short for Web-robots, are automated tools that can "patrol" the pages of Wikipedia and make changes or flag pages for human admins to look at. As of 2016, there were about 350 bots used by Wikipedia. These bots can be things as simple as the BracketBot, which is able to notice and inform users of

---

[12]www.cc.com/video-clips/z1aahs/the-colbert-report-the-word---wikiality (last viewed April 2016)

[13]A good starting place for more about this event is the page at https://en.wikipedia.org/wiki/Wikipedia:Wikiality_and_Other_Tripling_Elephants.

mismatched brackets in articles that have been edited. Other bots are much more complex, such as a bot that tries to identify and revert pages when it thinks there has been vandalism (someone maliciously changing a page or drastically changing content) or one that checks for potential copyright violations on new pages. Wikipedia has said that without the bots, it would be impossible to maintain the millions of pages of content on the site.

On Wikipedia, humans create the articles and do most of the creative work in deciding what does and doesn't make it to the site with respect to issues of politics, culture, etc. Bots, on the other hand, help to manage this extremely large collection, and it would be impossible to keep it going without their help.

In the citizen science and GWAP sites, we see a similar pattern. Humans are doing those things they are best at (for example, classifying the galaxies in Galaxy Zoo) while machines handle the details of comparing results, testing validity, and controlling for cheating. Thus, in both crowd-sourced sites like Wikipedia and human computation-based sites like Duolingo or the Zooniverse, we see exactly the situation that Berners-Lee predicted in his book: web sites where "people do the creative work and the machine does the administration."

SOCIAL MACHINES FOR SOCIAL GOOD

While Wikipedia and the Zooniverse are probably the best known of the web sites where numerous people contribute their time for an overall social benefit, they are certainly not the only ones that are out there. A complete list and analysis of this constantly changing landscape would require a book longer than this one to discuss, and there are research conferences and journals on the topic of human computation that are aimed at deliberating the many issues that arise in the design and running of social machines.[14]

However, one theme that emerges in many cases is the attempt by people to use social machines to enhance public welfare and social benefit. These include sites like Kickstarter and other crowdfunding sites where people can contribute small amounts of money to projects they think are meaningful, and raise enough money for these projects to go forward without government or venture capital investments.

Another trend is sites that allow people to respond to real-world events and to cooperate in helping to bring attention to social problems. This is often reported as happening on sites such as Facebook and Twitter, but there the site is generally functioning as a way to propagate information and not really functioning as a social machine in its own right. Better examples are web sites that are specifically designed to allow multiple people to create and update sites where their combined effort can help to attack real-world social problems. There are many such sites, but we will highlight two of them that really show off the power of this approach.

---

[14]A good starting place to learn more about the emerging field of studying human computation for problem solving is in the following article: Michelucci, Pietro, and Dickinson, Janis L., "The power of crowds", *Science* 351.6268 (2016): 32-33.

The first one is a site called Ushahidi.com, which was originally created in 2007 during the protests that followed a disputed presidential election in Kenya. The idea was simple: people could provide eyewitness reports by posting a photo or sending a message to the site from their mobile phone. Using the time and geolocation information from the phones enabled Ushahidi to place the reports on top of Google maps, or to build timelines of events. Figure 7-7 shows a screen shot from a version of the site showing incidents happening in Nairobi Kenya in April, 2008.

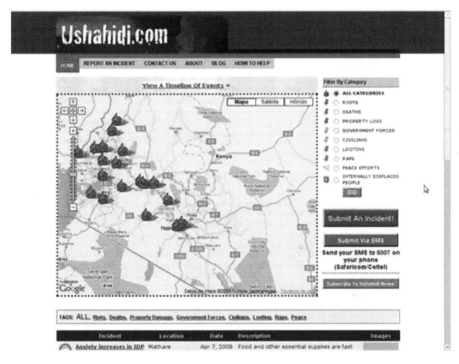

Figure 7-7. *A screen shot from Ushahidi.com showing events happening in Nairobi Kenya in April, 2008. (Credit: Olga Berrios 2/09.)*

Ushahidi has grown over the years into a site that has shown tremendous value for "citizen journalism" in many parts of the world. During the 2010 earthquake in Haiti, for example, Ushahidi was used by relief workers and others to report on people needing help, problems with the road networks and ways around them, etc. Thousands of different events around Haiti were reported and tracked using the site. Later that year, when the Deep Water Horizon offshore oil rig exploded, Ushahidi was used to create a map of the spill and to track results of the spill over a number of years. Similar deployments have been made throughout the years for a large number of incidents, natural and human-made, throughout the world.

A second example is a site that was created in India to fight government corruption. The site, IPaidABribe.com, was created by the non-profit organization Janaagraha, which is dedicated to strengthening India's democracy. On this site, users can report on times where they have been asked (or forced) to pay a bribe. (Users can also report honest officers and others where something positive happened). A typical bribe report is shown in Figure 7-8. These reports can be viewed by other people to share information, and the non-profit that runs the site periodically reports the statistics and particularly egregious violations to the Indian Government. A total of over 80,000 bribe reports have been collected since it went online in 2011.

▓ I PAID A BRIBE ⊘ 2 days ago 👁 203 views

Indiranagar Traffic police

Police ❙ Traffic Violations ❙ Paid INR 300

Reported on **April 26, 2016** from **Bangalore , Karnataka** ❙ Report #102059

By mistake I entered a No entry road near the Indiranagar Sony signal, where it was NOT marked as No entry. The Inspector intentionally positioned himself knowing very well that people not familiar with the place will be trapped in that. He immediately asked me to park my vehicle, asked for the DL and took the bike key and then almost disappeared. After continuous insistence and follow up he asked for Rs 400. I agreed but asked for the receipt. He immediately threatened with consequences like cancellation of DL if I ask for receipt. He then agreed with Rs 300 and returned my bike key.

Figure 7-8. *A bribe reported at IPaidABribe.com, a site where Indian citizens can share information about government corruption*

As mentioned earlier, these are just a few of the many hundreds of examples of web sites that have been created to help people to fight government corruption, monitor elections, report on repression, and otherwise use crowdsourcing to help improve people's lives around the world. There are many others, sites such as patientslikeme.com, that help users learn from each other about diseases and treatments. Open government sites such as the US' data.gov, the UK's data.gov. uk, and hundreds more in countries and cities around the world that allow citizens more access to information collected by their governments, permitting them to create programs to help others, and there are many other citizen reporting sites like the two we discussed in this section. It is clear this is an important, and growing, use of social machines.

Artificial Intelligence Needs Social Machines

Having reached this point in the chapter, you may be wondering what all this has to do with Artificial Intelligence. GWAPS, citizen science, and Wikipedia seem to use very little AI. They clearly rely heavily on programming to support their functionality, but the bot programs that support them tend to use very little, if any, powerful AI technology. Rather, it is the other way around: AI systems, as we shall see, have come to rely on the information created by people using social machines to achieve many of the significant advances that are powering the so-called AI revolution.

Watson and Wikipedia

For example, let's consider the Watson program mentioned in Chapters 2 and 3. Watson is a computer program from IBM named after Thomas Watson, who was the chairman of IBM from 1914-1956. In January of 2011, Watson competed with two of the best players of all time in a special edition of the TV game show Jeopardy! for a million dollar prize. Watson won by a significant margin, a major victory for AI. If we look more closely, however, we see that much of Watson's power comes from the information in Wikipedia and similar online sources.

On Jeopardy!, one of the features of the game is that questions are posed as if they are answers, and the contestants must come up with an appropriate question. For example, given the very simple answer "People carry these in the rain to stay dry," the correct response would be "What are umbrellas?" When discussing the game, however, most people refer to the host asking the question and the contestant answering, and we'll use those terms here: that is, "umbrellas" would be the answer to this simple question.

In the Watson example, over the course of two games televised over three nights, the computer was able to outplay the humans, winning by a large score. The game was designed to be as fair as possible for both the humans and the computer. For example, during the games, the Watson computer (or computers, as it was actually a bank of a large number of processors that produced the answers) was not connected to the Internet; it could only use those documents already stored in its memory. Similarly, it actually had to have a robotic "finger" so it could push the same buzzers the humans used and thus be the first to "ring in" to answer the question. The questions were not restricted in terms of the words they could use or categories (except no "visual" clues were used), and thus Watson had to produce the right answers to questions about all sorts of things. Watson had no vision or hearing, and later the Watson team said the biggest challenge in winning the game against the two champions was answering quickly enough.[15]

Figure 7-9 lays out the way that Watson[16] answers Jeopardy! questions. Where earlier AI systems either tried to reason out the answers using logic or tried to develop probabilistic models to reason over, Watson used a very different approach. First, Watson

---

[15]In talking about the game with people, this is often the most misunderstood feature of Watson's win. People just assumed that Watson, being a computer, would be faster. To many AI researchers watching the game, the amazing thing was how fast Watson was able to sort through literally millions of pages of documents and come up with its answers.

[16]Since the time of the game, IBM has expanded the capabilities of the system, and also redefined the Watson brand to include several other aspects of computing that were not used in playing Jeopardy. We emphasize here that we are talking about the version that played the game, and not the more general service-based system that derived therefrom.

used language tools to try to analyze the question, basically to see what the question was about. Critical to Watson's performance was an ability to guess the "type" of thing being asked about. If a question about Mount Everest started "This mountain is ...", Watson needed to recognize that the answer would likely be a kind of mountain. This may seem simple, but actually the way human languages work is not as easy as it seems. For example, in a more realistic example, if the host read "This mountain, the highest on Earth, is known by this Tibetan name," the question would be about the mountain, but its common name would not be the right response, instead requiring the answer "What is Chomolungma?" If the host were to ask "Standing on the peak of the highest mountain on Earth, you would be this height above sea level?" the question would still be about Mount Everest, but the correct answer would be "What is 29,029 feet?" Add to that the fact that the question could be about mountains, people, words, opera singers, or just about anything else, finding the question type is not a trivial task. Thus, Watson's first task was to determine one or more *lexical answer type* (LAT), the word that signals what type of answer is being sought. (Another form of complexity in the actual Jeopardy! game is that many questions don't have an explicit LAT, instead using words like "this," "it," or "these." For example, in our earlier clue "These are what people carry to stay dry when it rains", the answer type (physical object) is implicit. In these cases, Watson just used a default LAT called "NA" and would allow anything to match it).

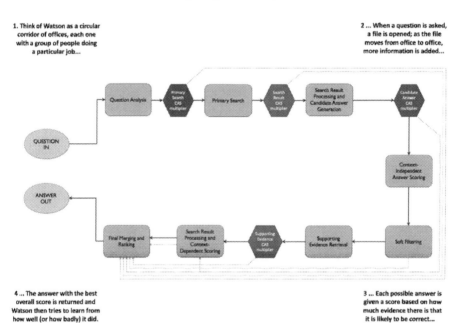

1. Think of Watson as a circular corridor of offices, each one with a group of people doing a particular job...

2 ... When a question is asked, a file is opened; as the file moves from office to office, more information is added...

4 ... The answer with the best overall score is returned and Watson then tries to learn from how well (or how badly) it did.

3 ... Each possible answer is given a score based on how much evidence there is that it is likely to be correct...

Figure 7-9. *A layout of Watson's problem-solving logic: a feedforward loop in which many answers are considered and separately rated. (With permission: from a poster about Watson developed by Rensselaer Polytechnic Institute graduate student Simon Ellis (2012).) This figure outlines the steps taken by Watson and some of the kinds of information processed at each step. In between the steps something called a "CAS multiplier" would be used to keep adding information to the evolving set of possible answers, until the end when the answer(s) with the highest likelihood were produced.*

One of the main techniques Watson used in searching for the LAT was based on a system called DBpedia[17], which is essentially a machine-readable rendering of the relationships within Wikipedia. One of the features of DBpedia is that it contains information about how the entities described on the pages are related to each other and to common topics. Thus, for example, based on information on the page for "Mount Everest" in Wikipedia, DBpedia includes information that this is, among other things, a "mountain," a "natural place," and one of the "Himalayas." Using this kind of information, the IBM team was able to create a network of relationships that would let it determine, on seeing the question, what some of the possible LATs would be based on the information that was originally mined from Wikipedia.

Watson would then use many techniques, based on search in a number of information sources, to determine possible answers. These answers would be compared to the LAT (with those which matched getting extra scores). Then a number of special purpose "scorers" were used to judge each answer and decide which ones seemed to be most appropriate for the question being asked.[18]

According to presentations made by members of the team, one of the most useful techniques for finding answers was to look for items in the search results that corresponded to the names of Wikipedia pages. This is because in Jeopardy!, most of the answers refer to well-known people, events, books, operas, etc. and most of those things have a Wikipedia entry. With the exception of particular kinds of Jeopardy! questions (which required knowing rhymes, synonyms, spellings, etc.) a large amount of the time the answer was likely to be a Wikipedia entry. Thus, the social machine that is Wikipedia provided much of the power that was used by Watson to win the game. The AI was dependent on the information created by the many humans who wrote Wikipedia!

Deep Learning and Labeled Data

There are a number of different machine-learning algorithms used in AI. The most powerful for perception at the current time, which we described briefly in Chapter 5, are those that are known as deep learning systems. These systems are able to recognize many perceptual items, and also to do pattern-matching at a significant scale (as evidenced by the strength of the AlphaGo systems discussed in Chapter 3). However, to understand where their power comes from, we need to look at how they are trained.

Deep learning systems derive from a long history of what are known as Artificial Neural Networks (ANNs) or, more commonly, just neural networks when it is unambiguous if one is talking about the processing in a brain (the natural neural network) or on a computer (the ANN). As early as the 1940s, at the very start of modern computing, people were exploring whether computational systems that were modeled on the processing in the brain might be able to learn in a human-like way.

---

[17]http://wiki.dbpedia.org/
[18]A special issue of the *IBM Journal of Research and Development*, June 2012 (Volume 56, Issue 3/4), describes the Watson process in detail. A list of other papers about Watson's Jeopardy game and other related work can be found at http://researcher.watson.ibm.com/researcher/view_group_pubs.php?grp=2099 (last accessed 5/2016).

A simple model known as the *perceptron* was developed in the 1950s that could use a mathematical approach to learn certain kinds of functions. Given data that was "labeled" in some way, the perceptrons appeared to be able to classify things in interesting ways. This started with simple logical functions, but researchers also tried more ambitious projects such as in a military project where the researchers wanted to use vision to recognize the difference between different kinds of objects. These systems seemed to work in the lab, but often failed in practice. In the late 1960s, a book entitled *Perceptrons* written by Marvin Minsky and Seymour Papert proved various mathematical properties of the perceptron model, and basically showed that in its simplest form (which was the one used in a number of the early experiments) these systems couldn't learn to do the tasks being claimed. In many cases, analyses of systems that seemed to work in the lab, but didn't in practice, showed that the systems had learned some simpler recognition than that which was being claimed.

It is hard to get credible stories of these failures, but it is known that the US and UK governments funded neural network research in the late 1950s and early 1960s. One story that is often related is that researchers trained the systems on a simple encoding of photographs of missiles and tanks to see if the computer could learn to tell them apart. When it was shown that this was too complex a function for the networks being used, it was found that the photos of missiles (taken against the sky) were generally lighter than those of the tanks (taken against the ground). Whether this particular story is true has been questioned, and most people feel it is likely apocryphal, but the general situation– that the systems were learning functions that were easier than the researchers had guessed—was clearly a real problem with this early work.

For much of the 1970s and early 1980s, the failure of the early systems caused skepticism about any new results reported. However, during this time a new approach, which used more complex networks, was developed. This learning approach, called *back propagation*, was shown to be able to learn more complex functions than the perceptrons could learn, and thus a new boom of neural computing started in the mid 1980s.[19] Since then, there has been a continued development of this approach, using still more complex networks, various mathematical techniques for improving the performance of the networks, and much more powerful machines. Breakthroughs combining all of these started to show up around 2010, and the term *deep learning*, which had been used in the field for a number of techniques over the years, started to become associated with the new approach. The term took full hold with the publication of an article entitled "Deep Learning" that appeared in the journal *Nature* in 2015.[20]

---

[19]Backpropagation for ANNs are usually attributed to two sets of researchers–first Paul Werbos [Werbos, P. J., "Applications of advances in nonlinear sensitivity analysis", In Proceedings of the 10th IFIP Conference, 31.8 - 4.9, NYC, pp. 762–770, 1982], who in 1982 developed a mathematical framework, that could solve these more complex problems, and then to Rumelhart, Hinton and Williams in 1986, who developed a more computationally effective model and popularized the research more successfully [Rumelhart, D. E., Hinton, G. E., and Williams, R. J., "Learning internal representations by error propagation." In Rumelhart, D. E. and McClelland, J. L., editors, *Parallel Distributed Processing*, volume 1, pp. 318–362. MIT Press, 1986.]
[20]LeCun, Y., Bengio, Y., and Hinton, G., "Deep Learning", *Nature*, 521, May 2015.

Deep learning systems are examples of *supervised* learning systems. They function by being trained on known inputs and then learn to recognize those inputs in other contexts. For example, going back to the photo we used in Chapter 5 (reproduced here as Figure 7-10), we see that the computer has labeled several items: a person, a dog, and two chairs. In this case, the system would have been trained with pictures of dogs (labeled "dog"), people (labeled "person"), chairs (labeled "chair"), and many others. A successful learning system can then recognize these things when seen in other images. (Note that this is not limited to images; these kinds of learning systems have been used to improve speech recognition, allowing a computer to recognize different kinds of sounds, track images in video, etc).

Figure 7-10. *An image labeled using deep learning*

To train such a system, one needs a number of examples of similar images that are tagged with the appropriate labels. Although there are some specific sites where such images have been carefully identified and labeled by hand, such as the ImageNet collection[21], more and more people are turning to large collections with multiple images and/or collections where numerous different items of the same kind have been tagged carefully. In particular, more and more of these systems are now using images, sounds, and videos that have been labeled via GWAPS, citizen science sites, or the like. Thus, these AI systems too are dependent on humans to provide their inputs, and increasingly are turning to social machines for the fodder on which they train.

Social Machines Need AI

At the same time that AI is increasingly being powered by the social machines on the current Web, there is also an increasing need for computer programs to help humans create and run social sites and applications. Wikipedia, with its hundreds of bots, is the most notable example. As it continues to grow, and as other sites come online, there is an increasing need for computerized support for helping to organize the information

---

[21]www.image-net.org/

being produced by the humans using the site. Not surprisingly, as these web sites get more complicated and the number of users grows, there is an increasing need for AI techniques to help support the social machines.

For example, on many of the sites there is a need for the bots being used to appropriately apply different policies in different situations, based on their use contexts. However, given the challenges that AI systems have in identifying appropriate contexts (as discussed in Chapter 5), if we don't want to require humans to be involved, then there needs to be a way to make the policies explicit and to either have AIs recognize when the policies are in force or to identify special cases. For example, consider medical personnel needing access to an accident victim's medical information in an emergency. In many communities, there are no specialized systems for handling medical information outside of the context of a particular hospital or care center. The normal mechanisms for gaining access to medical data may be prohibitively time-consuming for emergency personnel, but ignoring specific patient data (as is done in many current situations) can often lead to complications and/or loss of life. An AI-based system could allow the emergency personnel to override controls while being warned "You are breaking the law unless this is being done in a life-threatening situation (and this access will be logged)." While current web applications use some aspects of context, for example mobile browsers can use geolocation information to some extent, these uses tend to be fairly simple, built into procedural code, and limited to specific applications. Something more powerful is needed if we are to take web applications, and social machines, to the next level.

The *provenance* of information is also very important in determining what data is trustworthy. On the Web, the availability of vast amounts of information of varying quality, coming from multiple sources, integrated through both automated and human-in-the-loop mechanisms, require that users must become able to understand the sources of the "facts" that they collect, and to determine how the consequences that are derived from the integrated data actually depend on those facts. There is currently considerable work exploring how provenance can be tracked in online systems, especially with respect to the workflows used in web-based systems that support scientists. As these mechanisms become more usable, they will be increasingly incorporated into social machines.

Going beyond just tracking where information is coming from, one exciting area of current research is that as the amount of information in social machines grows, it becomes hard to tell whether there is information on a site that, if connected, would help people discover interesting relations. For example, consider a site where patients are discussing their experiences with particular drugs on a patient-information site. Perhaps some are speculating in one part of the site that a particular drug seems to have a side effect of weight gain. On another part of the site, perhaps a different group of people are discussing that a similar set of drugs are making them feel tired, and thus they cannot exercise as much. A system that could recognize these connections could make it possible to discover that one of these issues (the lack of exercise) can be a potential cause of the other (the gain in weight). This could be even more useful in cases where the evidence isn't that clear; for example, some drugs, like antihistamines, can cause weight gain in some people, but not in others. They also make some people drowsy, but seem to cause other people to have trouble sleeping. Seeing the different ways other users are affected could help patients figure out what is happening in their own case, and then make decisions about what to do about it.

One possible way to approach this is to create AI bots that make it possible to be able to present humans with arguments from multiple positions. For example, it is exactly that different scientists can interpret the same data in different ways that provides for the argumentation and testing so crucial to scientific discourse. Consider the current debates over the effects of climate change. Although the overwhelming number of scientists believe that it is being caused by human activities, the theories as to the causal mechanisms for the change are much debated. The same set of meteorological findings are being viewed by different scientists as evidence as to what human activity is accounting for the major changes. Some claim one mechanism is the cause, but others claim that different factors are responsible and thus different mitigation is needed. Each side makes its case against information systems containing the results of different simulations, data sets, and analyses. Mechanisms that allow different communities such as these to simultaneously have their own interpretations of data resources, but also to understand the interpretations of others, will be powerful enablers for the social interface of the future Web.[22]

Looking further out, the potential of AI technologies to help people bridge divides of language and culture is another important capability these technologies could bring to social machines. Just as an example, in Ushahidi or IPaidABribe, there are many entries in multiple languages. If systems that combine AI and user skills, such as Duolingo, can start to provide high quality translations (and eventually, as some people predict, learning systems reach the point that AI systems can do this on their own), then people from a different part of the country or from different countries can start to cooperate in closer ways, and with less misunderstandings than they can currently.

Algorithms using AI are already being deployed in systems like Facebook and Twitter for determining which entries to highlight to users based on similarities in interests, and Google and other sites function by trying to use user histories to find advertisements that the user is more likely to click on. What if that same AI technology could be used to help create more powerful social machines? For example, to a large extent Hanny's Voorwerp was due to a lucky coincidence. However, based on user patterns on citizen science sites, AI systems might be able to match scientists with users who could help them find interesting phenomena like this.

And going all the way back to the medical examples of Chapter 2, imagine if medical researchers were able to take advantage of those things being posted on open patient sites around the world. Perhaps using Watson-like technologies, they could recognize sets of patients who were gaining benefits from particular drugs or treatments in a way that could help confirm (or disprove) hypotheses that were being studied in medical labs around the world? Researchers could use the vast material in user sites to essentially run "virtual" clinical trials that would help them decide which ones to try in a more formal setting.

The social machines of the future will allow the powerful networks of people seen on the current, early social machines, to cooperate with AI systems that could specialize in many areas: helping to organize information, matching people to those who can help them solve problems, and aiding in the governance of more and more complex sites (to name but a few possibilities). In short, we are moving rapidly towards a time where it will be possible to use AI technologies to help create and use what they learn to evolve new kinds of social machines that will provide people, individually and collectively, with the ability to immerse themselves in the accumulated knowledge and the constant interactions of humankind, not just as passive recipients of information created by others, but also as contributors to this global information space in a way far beyond that of today's Web.

---

[22]Hall, Wendy, David De Roure, and Nigel Shadbolt. "The evolution of the Web and implications for eResearch." Philosophical Transactions of the Royal Society of London A: Mathematical, Physical and Engineering Sciences 367, no. 1890 (2009): 991-1001.

CHAPTER 8

■ ■ ■

Social Challenges for the Social Machine

Given that cognitive computing technologies enable the computer to search for, pattern match, parse, synthesize, and interpret volumes of data at a very fast rate, the fear being described by some researchers is that these systems will go beyond helping humans and instead will become the next dominant entity on earth. For example, the scientist Stephen Hawking was quoted in a 2014 BBC interview, saying:

> *The development of full artificial intelligence could spell the end of the human race." ..."It would take off on its own, and re-design itself at an ever increasing rate," he said. "Humans, who are limited by slow biological evolution, couldn't compete, and would be superseded."*[1]

Others who have expressed fears about superhuman AI include industrialists such as Bill Gates, Elon Musk[2] and the philosopher Nick Bostrom[3,] who has become well-known for his critiques of the threats posed by "superintelligent" AI.

On a less drastic note, even without extrapolating to a dystopian, AI-dominated future, we are seeing increasing potential for AI systems to be deployed in ways that could enhance, but which could also possibly disrupt society in complex ways. There are potentially positive changes, such as self-driving cars reducing accident rates, but possibly at the expense of costs such as humans having to cede control to the technology. Others benefits and potential problems may result from endeavors to increase human capabilities in warfare by using drones and other autonomous entities, where the ethical dimensions are hard for humans to decide, let alone for as yet untested machine technologies, and where the cost of errors can be tragic. Finally, we may also be looking

---

[1] Stephen Hawking; "AI could spell end of the human race", December 2, 2014; www.bbc.com/news/science-environment-30289705.

[2] Sainato, M., "Stephen Hawking, Elon Musk, and Bill Gates Warn About Artificial Intelligence", *Observer Opinion*, August 19, 2015, http:// observer.com/2015/08/stephen-hawking-elon-musk-and-bill-gates-warn-about-artificial-intelligence/.

[3] Bostrom, Nick, *Superintelligence: Paths, dangers, strategies*, OUP Oxford, 2014.

© James Hendler and Alice M. Mulvehill 2016

J. Hendler and A. M. Mulvehill, *Social Machines*, DOI 10.1007/978-1-4842-1156-4_8

at societal disruptions caused by the introduction of AI systems into workplace roles that have previously been occupied by humans. This new wave of mechanization into jobs currently viewed as requiring human cognition could cause disruptions to employment, workplace relationships, etc. The direst predictions in this vein look at the new wave of AI-based automation as being a critical aspect of a societal disruption of the magnitude of the Industrial Revolution of the eighteenth and nineteenth centuries.[4]

In this chapter, we will explore some of the potential problems and challenges that our society might be faced with as a result of the deployment of AI technologies and emerging social machines. We will also raise some issues that need to be seriously considered in order for these technologies to be correctly and efficiently utilized and evolved.

The Technology Development Cycle

In 2016, many people are just becoming aware of how sophisticated software can use what it learns about what people buy online, what they send in e-mails, texts, and tweets, what data is collected through some of the electronic monitoring devices they wear, and what they share through social media to anticipate what a particular person might want to buy or to do and to proactively support decision making.

As a simple example, imagine that you and your family want to plan a vacation to a destination such as Orlando, Florida. Assume that, in addition to knowing that you want to go to Orlando, you know when you would like to travel, how much money you can afford to spend, who is coming along with you, and how long you will visit the area. One way to start to plan for your trip is to use a web application to look for hotels in Orlando, Florida.

When you type in a search request, such as "find hotels in Orlando Florida", the search engine (or application) will return a variety of links to individual hotels as well as links to some travel services that will automatically compare several hotels along a variety of dimensions, such as cost, and offer you a list of the hotels that best meet your needs. When you provide additional information such as the number of adults and children who need accommodations, one or more matching algorithms running in the background will start to present you with more specific hotel room options, and perhaps other services such as car rentals. Once you book a hotel or purchase a plane ticket online and provide your e-mail address, you might start to receive e-mails about items and actions that are often associated with travel to the Orlando area, like a visit to Disney World.

As the time for your trip nears, you might start to get more frequent e-mails, ads, and pop-ups about places or things to do in Orlando. In theory, these prompts and alerts are intended to help you plan and actually take your trip. Unfortunately, they often get irritating, persist even if you cancel your trip, and can have adverse side effects. For example, the very same technology that helps you plan and have an enjoyable vacation might also help some real estate agency mine some of your browser interactions or other transactions. As a result, the real estate agency might start to send you e-mails or generate ads in your browser about property that you might consider purchasing while you visit Orlando. Potentially annoying, the e-mails might turn into phone calls if your phone number can be found on the Web. Or

---

[4]www.weforum.org/agenda/2016/01/the-fourth-industrial-revolution-what-it-means-and-how-to-respond

more seriously, your online planning actions might help computer-literate house thieves determine when you are going on vacation so that they can plan when to rob your house. Finally, note that companies are legally allowed to share this information, which can lead to knowledge about your trip being shared in contexts that you might not approve of, raising issues of privacy and control of personal information.

How do we build technology that provides benefits and does not inadvertently introduce annoyances, provide bad information, or potentially introduce threats? Even with a secured home or office web site, your actions can eventually become known if you continue to have related computer transactions while you are in transit. Many people now have cell phones, cars, and laptops that have GPS, and all of these tools can be linked with each other through cloud technology. If you take your phone with you as you travel, an application on your phone could use your location to offer you advice about places to eat, sleep, or tell you where to get fuel. If you get lost or are involved in an accident, the GPS could help people help you. However, the GPS tracking service can also be used by certain organizations to monitor and even analyze your movement and activities. While the data analysis of this tracking system can have positive benefits to people building machine learning or other algorithms and even for you in the long run, some people think that this tracking technology will lead to an Orwellian "big brother"[5] society. While this may seem farfetched in open societies, there is already evidence of this kind of information being collected by authoritarian regimes. In addition, even in open societies policing and state security agencies have a wide range of tools for information gathering from online sources.

Technology often is like a double-edged sword: one side for good and one side for evil. Often the evil side gets a lot of publicity when it is showcased in films and books. Some people are extrapolating that many of the advanced technologies presented in science fiction will become reality. If any of these advanced technologies are using AI, then some people are predicting that they will cause major social disruption and introduce a number of ethical issues. Many AI researchers are already grappling with investigating and developing solutions to these potential problems. In an article by Eric Horvitz and Tom Dieterich, the authors describe five classes of risk associated with the usage of AI based technology: software bugs, cybersecurity, the "Sorcerer's Apprentice" (the ability of the AI support system to understand a person's intentions only within a particular context), shared autonomy, and socioeconomic impacts[6]. These risks are essentially the themes discussed in this chapter.

Technology for the Individual

When an organization such as a business, a school, or a hospital acquires new technology, they generally go through a formal acquisition process that includes identifying requirements (reviewing potential candidate solutions along many dimensions including cost, ease of operation, compatibility with other existing systems, and computing infrastructure), evaluating vendor reliability, determining maintenance needs, etc. As a way to maximize the return on investment, many such organizations tend to purchase computers and computing systems that they won't need to upgrade for several years. Individual consumers might use a similar, although usually less formal, process and similar criteria to make large computer

---

[5]Orwell, George, *1984*, New American Library, 1950.
[6]Dietterich, Thomas G. and Horvitz, Eric J., "Rise of Concerns about AI: Reflections and Directions", *Communications of the ACM*, Vol. 58 No. 10, Pages 38-40, 2015.

technology purchases, but they might employ a much less restrictive approach when they are buying games, inexpensive computers, or trying out new applications including new apps with AI technologies involved.

In an organization, new applications might be vetted by an IT department before they are considered acceptable for the mainstream environment. An individual likely doesn't have an IT department. They might learn about an application from a friend who used it, or they might read a web review or see web ratings about the application and use these sources to determine whether or not they should acquire some technology.

People who are fascinated by technology and start playing with new applications as soon as they come out are called *early adopters*. Early adopters tend to buy gadgets as soon as they are available and use them until something new appears. However, not all early adopters are able to afford some of these new items. To minimize costs, they look for knock-offs that are advertised to be similar or for free versions that might not offer all functional or security features. As a result, sometimes there is a proliferation of technology that is not "up to standards."

Some developers intentionally offer their technology for free in order to collect feedback or, increasingly, to build the market for eventual sales or financing through advertising or other means. When they sufficiently refine their technology based on the feedback that they receive, they start to charge a usage fee, provide ads, or otherwise require a user to change their usage of the application. Some people, who really love the tool or are now dependent on it, will pay the fee, while others will again look for a free alternative.

Some developers offer their technology for free in order to collect data about users. Some consumers don't realize that their data usage is being monitored and some of the data that they enter is being collected and analyzed; or they do know this but don't really care until something personal about them surfaces publicly or in an online advertisement. So what is the best way to introduce and refine new technology and still keep people's data safe?

Technology, especially phone and computer apps, are often advertised by people telling other people about an app and where to get it. As a result, some apps get used a lot and others are never used. Additionally, one of the side effects of some new technology is that it eliminates the need for older technology. For example, because of the increased availability of reasonably priced cell phone plans, many people no longer pay for a landline, and it is becoming increasingly difficult to find a public pay phone. In fact, some cities like New York City are replacing many public pay phones with Wi-Fi towers.

Free and widely available Wi-Fi enables people to keep connected to their friends, colleagues, work, and other social groups. Because the usage of free Wi-Fi can increase the possibility that someone might gain your personal information many internet providers and other technologists are faced with the challenge of helping you to keep your data private and safe. For example, if you are making banking transactions on a public Wi-Fi system, your information could be captured by some one looking for creative ways to make money without worrying about the legality of the situation. If this sounds far-fetched, there are devices already available and used by hackers to obtain information in public Wi-Fi zones[7]. While you could modify your behavior or stop accessing a bank through public Wi-Fi access sites, technologies and privacy standards and policies (once established and executed) are desperately needed.

---

[7]Dunn, J., "Are public Wi-Fi hotspots a security risk? Security risks of using public Wi-Fi explained", Computerworld UK, August 20, 2015, www.computerworlduk.com/security/are-public-wi-fi-hotspots-really-major-security-risk-3623447/.

Thus, much as we have never been able to create a crime-free world in our physical lives, many now argue that our online lives (and potentially our AI-based support systems) will also necessarily require "street smarts" in order to "stay safe in bad neighborhoods." As new technologies are developed that make internet access more and more available, there are individuals working on exploiting these same technologies.

Unfortunately, even when people pay for security programs and avoid public Wi-Fi for specific transactions, they sometimes get hacked or acquire a virus when they simply open a message from a friend, who may not have intentionally meant to cause the virus infection. A major part of modern life is learning what is and isn't safe in our face-to-face interactions with people, so too people will have to learn what the real threats are in the cyber world, and how to counter them. If technology is to continue to proliferate and be used in delicate or sensitive situations, we need more safeguards for all aspects of data processing and computation. One of the challenges in developing safeguards is that the same AI techniques that are showing great promise in protecting systems from hacking can also be used by those trying to break into systems to increase their competency. For us to understand the threats, and develop appropriate policies to deal with them, individuals will need to better understand the AI systems and how they work, a task many people are not yet ready to undertake (unlike those of you reading this book).

Technologies that have been developed for individual usage, like the proliferation of lightweight hand-held devices, have brought about several changes in how people work, socialize, and get entertained. Most of these devices leverage the Internet for services and when you are not in your home or place of business utilize available Wi-Fi services, including potentially unprotected public services. As a result of more available internet connectivity, people are free to make transactions wherever they want to (as long as they can connect). We are also seeing some associated social changes, which researchers are investigating. For example, the research results of Sherry Turkle from MIT indicate that people are becoming more solitary because of modern computer technology[8]. It is easy to believe that this is true if you just look around you when you are riding a bus or sitting at the airport. Most of the people around you are probably listening to their cell phone or typing messages on it. Do we now prefer to communicate with each other through our devices instead of face to face? Or are our gadgets just allowing us to communicate in different ways that might, as indicated by some recent Pew Research studies[9], be increasing our social contacts? (As this book goes to press, many arguments abound about whether the augmented reality application "Pokemon Go" is helping to provide better socialization, since teams fare better than individuals, or cause more of a remove - since people are now spending more time looking at their phones. Similarly, people argue as to whether the benefits of the game, which include getting people to walk more, are outweighed by potential problems as society tries to understand the new phenomenom.)

As more sophisticated technology, like AI-based computing support tools, become pervasive, individuals could be at greater risk for losing control of their private data because the AI technology, in order to better support them, will need to know a lot about them and will likely operate in public spaces, introducing problems like those currently inherent in the use of public Wi-Fi. Fortunately, there are a lot of research and development efforts underway to use AI to help enhance cyber security, so again we see the two-edged sword of this technology.

---

[8] www.ted.com/talks/sherry_turkle_alone_together
[9] Hampton, K., Goulet, L.S., Her, E. J., and Rainie, L., "Social Isolation and New Technology", www.pewinternet.org/2009/11/04/social-isolation-and-new-technology/.

SAFEGUARDING PERSONAL INFORMATION

Challenge: How can we make our electronic transactions more private and secure? There have been many recent compelling arguments about when and why certain law enforcement agencies should have access to private data, or why the need for keeping data private might be waived when the private data is required by a physician in order to treat an individual or to contain some epidemic. What should the rules and regulations be?

In 2016, the newspapers were filled with articles about how Apple[10] was reacting to a request from the FBI for help in accessing the phone data of a terrorist. Apple said that although they often release e-mail records to the FBI when it is requested, that there were several business, as well as moral and ethical issues that were at stake in agreeing to help release all data on a person's personal phone each time a request was made. They said that they encrypt data to keep people's data private, and that if they developed a method to undo this occasionally, it could become a vulnerability. While the FBI did eventually find their own way to access the phone data, this situation raises many general questions and concerns about how personal data should be protected. Answers to those questions will be needed as personalized AI assistants become more available and adopted for personal usage. People will need to be aware of how their personalized data could be released to the government, to doctors, or to other interested organizations.

Another major problem that happened in 2016 also raises concerns for protecting future personalized AI systems. A hospital in California had its patient data hijacked by cyber criminals who said that they would not release the patient data until they were paid a ransom in Bitcoins. The entire hospital system had to revert to a paper system and use the telephone and fax machines for several weeks until the hospital paid the ransom. It turns out that this was not a single event; cyber criminals have increasingly targeted numerous businesses in this way over the past few years and law enforcement agencies are worried that these types of threats could start to be made to private citizens. Again, if we start to have personalized AI assistants, could a similar attack be targeted against an individual's AI? What would the backup system for the individual look like? How would such an attack be mitigated? Also, as doctors become more dependant on AI, then the idea of going back to paper records becomes even more challenging.

---

[10]Toor, A., "A dangerous precedent that threatens everyone's civil liberties, read Tim Cook's email to Apple employees about its fight against the FBI", February 22, 2016, www.theverge.com/2016/2/22/11092028/apple-tim-cook-fbi-encryption-internal-memo.

There are many types of cyber threats and today many of them are targeted against banking and healthcare organizations. The threats change regularly, and one way to review current threats is to do a search for "cyber security breach statistics". A search will likely return some statistical reports like those displayed in Figure 8-1 about current threats, visualizations, and advertisements for tools that could help you and the organizations that you interact with better protect your privacy.

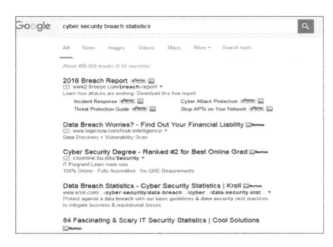

Figure 8-1. *March 2016 search results for "cyber security breach statistics"*

There are also several R&D efforts underway to try to develop technology that could be used to overcome some privacy issues. One approach that has proved useful on the Web, and on which we believe many social machines will come to be based, is that of information accountability.[11] To understand the role of accountable systems in the design of cognitive computing technology and the broader social machine environment, consider the simple example of robots.txt, the files used to control the access of crawlers on web sites (www.robotstxt.org/). A simple standard that the file will have a particular format and be placed in a particular file on the server allows a "polite" crawler to avoid pages that it is requested not to crawl.

As the Web grew, and crawlers became more common, including those that crawled for e-mail addresses for spammers and other less-desirable uses, the robots. txt mechanism was able to maintain its utility by being coupled with web-logging facilities, which provide a mechanism to track which crawlers reach what pages. Discovering a crawler on a page it has been requested not to crawl allows a user (usually a server administrator) to take action, typically denying that crawler's IP

---

[11]Weitzner, D. J., Abelson, H., Berners-Lee, T., Feigenbaum, J., Hendler, J., and Sussman, G. J., "Information accountability", *Communications of the ACM, 51*(6), pp. 82-87, 2008.

address access to the entire site. Thus, the combination of `robots.txt` with site logging provides a simple accountability mechanism for rewarding crawlers that behave correctly and recognizing those that do not. Researchers are exploring whether other kinds of "social accountability" mechanisms may provide a means for enabling a user (using AI technology, which might be used for providing some privacy administration) to control and manage data privacy.

Unfortunately, the accountability mechanisms on the current web are currently few and far between. Where they do exist, they are often built into a specific web application, or require complex auditing mechanisms that are not available to the average user. For example, even in the `robots.txt` example, most users are not allowed to view the logs that would enable them to tell whether their own pages are being accessed appropriately nor are they typically allowed to alter the `robots.txt` file (and thus control their own page accesses). More is needed. For example, information about the source of information (provenance information) can potentially provide a mechanism for accountability and, when included in the explanations of rule-based reasoning, can be screened to check that the derivations obtained did not violate acceptable rules for gathering and combining evidence. In addition, designs need to be developed that allow social machines to provide declarative policies, that speak to social and legal expectations about information usage, and that provide for the identification of information uses that contravene those policies.

Recent work on information accountability has already taken a step toward demonstrating the technical viability and social utility of accountability mechanisms as a way to protect central information policy values such as privacy, fair and reliable use of information, and copyright protection. This capability has been demonstrated via the creation of computer formalisms that can express realistic data-use policies, and use policy-rule-based languages and reasoners that can interpret policies and automatically determine whether particular uses of data are policy-compliant. However, work to date has largely been on small-scale prototypes, and work in the area still must tackle problems associated with scaling. There are challenging AI problems related to developing a more formal understanding of the behavior of these systems, to evaluating the social impact of accountable systems and, of course, for making tools for creating such systems and for supporting their use by an individual.

AI Technology and Warfare

Fears about warfighting with drones, using robots to clear mine fields, and fighting through cyberspace battles are regularly expressed in the news and other publications by journalists, scientists, military personnel, government researchers, academics, and concerned citizens. Yet the trend to provide the military with ever more sophisticated tools to support warfare goes on because of both ever present threats from national adversaries or increasingly terrorists, and from the peacetime role of the military, or similar organizations, in helping with the many logistical problems that arise from natural disasters like hurricanes and earthquakes. Additionally, military operations provide challenging contexts that present excessive danger to humans and introduce problem complexities that could benefit from the power and never-tiring actions of automation. Given the high-risk, high-tempo aspects of the military world, it is an increasingly tempting target for the deployment of AI technologies despite large potential risks.

People tend to accept technology if it can do a job that no human wants to do or which presents great risks to a human, like mine clearing or performing certain disaster relief tasks. Some people even question the ethics of NOT using AI-based technologies and machines in situations where we cannot safely deploy people, like using robots to search through rubble for victims of collapsed structures[12], or using autonomous drones to detect noxious gases. On the other hand, using drones, like the one displayed in Figure 8-2, that are remotely controlled and somewhat expendable, to carry out surveillance or military strike missions, is often considered risky, threatening, and potentially unethical.

Figure 8-2. *An Interspect UAS B 3.1 Photogrammetry Platform, one of the new generation of military surveillance drones*

There are risks and benefits that need to be thoughtfully evaluated, as well as various tradeoffs that need to be considered when determining what context drones (especially autonomous drones) should be employed to support. For example, even though drone technology can minimize the loss of valuable air assets and crew in achieving military objectives, what happens if a remote operator loses control of a fully armed military drone over a highly populated civilian area en route to the target area? What happens if an autonomous drone has a software glitch and delivers the strike against friendly forces? What happens if civilians start to use commercial drones and these accidentally conflict with military missions? Who is responsible for the use and side effects of this type of technology: is it the drone, the drone designer, the drone manufacturer, or the remote operator who fires the missile? These are just a few of the issues that are currently the subject of various articles[13] and debates about the practical and ethical usage of drone technology.

---

[12]Massy-Beresford, Helen, "Robot rescuers to help save lives after disasters", *Horizon, the EU Research and Innovation Magazine*, March 19, 2014.
[13]http://dronewars.net/2015/03/31/think-drones-technology-is-not-really-the-problem-think-again/

Robot and drone technologies are just two examples of how AI technologies can be used to support humans in military contexts. AI methods, including machine learning, planning, image analysis, and speech understanding, have been successfully used to support data analysis and decision support in military contexts. These technologies often offset some of the computationally intensity that has resulted from improvements in sensor and other collection technology. The sheer size and complexity of analyzing multi-dimensional, heterogeneous data types can overwhelm the best human analysts, especially when there is a limited amount of time to get answers or to make decisions about taking actions. However, instead of allowing a machine to autonomously analyze and utilize data to generate actionable results, the current trend is for human military analysts and decision makers to interact with the software. In this way, the human operator can verify machine analysis, direct it, and shape it for usage in some particular context. The human operator maintains control over how the data is used and how actions are affected.

While computer technologies, including AI technologies, are becoming required enablers for humans involved in military operations, these technologies are also rapidly becoming desirable targets. Although an adversary can physically destroy a computing facility, the potential for damaging software and some hardware through cyberattacks is rising. Unfortunately, in a wartime context, cyberattacks may not be confined to government and military systems. Because the destruction or damage to infrastructures like transportation and communication systems has always been considered a viable target by adversaries, our increased reliance on computer technology as a society makes the infrastructure of the Internet a potential target. This means that everyone who uses the Internet could potentially be adversely affected if it was attacked. Interestingly, even though many people are unaware of it, the Internet is frequently under attack and AI is one of the technologies that is actively being used to detect intrusions and prevent substantial damage.

On the other hand, the AI technologies deployed today are largely under the control of humans. As the speed of cyber warfare increases, militaries are becoming more determined to deploy autonomous systems to defend where human reflexes aren't fast enough. The risk is that as the context of these attacks are hard to define, the weakness of AI systems when they get out of familiar contexts (as discussed in Chapter 5) could expose vulnerabilities. Without a lot more testing and understanding of these systems, many people are worried about the implications of using them in these domains, while others are worried about the cyber vulnerabilities if we don't.

What does this discussion about warfare have to do with the social web? To begin with, each military organization is a social unit. When military and/or civilian organizations unite to offset damage from natural or military causes, they form a specialized social network. They tend to collect data from sensors, and to collaborate, share, and disseminate data over communication networks including the Internet. Like individuals and other organizations (banking, medical, business), military decision makers need good data. If their data is corrupted by human error, software glitches, or through a cyberattack, decisions and actions can be impacted. Imagine that the data being corrupted are physical location values. Little changes in a latitude/longitude value could wreak havoc with military aircraft, drones, or any type of navigation, planning, or scheduling system that needs to use information about a location in order to take or support the execution of an action.

Data corruption is a very real threat to all types of computational systems, including humans. For example, if data gets corrupted, how fast and accurately can a human detect it? Could an AI computing algorithm actually help with this task, by more quickly cross-correlating, suspecting, and delaying the usage of corrupted data? Or could we end up with a situation where the human and machine are in conflict and neither can correctly detect the corrupted data or identify and unravel any negative effects that result if there is a delay? Lest that seem far-fetched, we note that several of the "flash crash" scenarios that have happened in the stock market are thought to have been caused by exactly this kind of mismatch between human and machine.[14]

If the data corruption occurs in a military battlefield environment, how would the conflict play out? In the example provided in Chapter 6 about the missile launch that was deferred because of human intervention, we learned that the Russian operator, Stanislav Petrov, used his life experience to influence his decision. People are worried that with the introduction of more automation into the military context that human operators and analysts might not develop the skills that Petrov had because they may never get to build up personal experience with the problem space. Again, the issues of context rear their ugly head — the ability to trade-off consequences vs. orders in a military situation is hard even for humans. For an AI system, it is even harder.

While this is a real possibility, there is one variable that many of the people who express fears about technology fail to mention. More and more, people are introduced to technology at a very young age. It is used in educational settings, including pre-school, and in the home environment. People are now growing up with technology[15]. Because they grow up using the technology, they don't share the same fears of technology that people older than them might have. In addition, their usage of technology has probably had an influence on how the technology works; developers tend to improve their technology with feedback from their users. If we can survive this adolescent period that we are entering with sophisticated computing devices, then perhaps we, and future generations of humans, can leverage the computational potential and never-tiring power of AI to help, rather than impair, certain types of decision-making activities like those involved in military operations or other critical situations.

AI IN SCIENCE FICTION

Increasingly, we face the slippery slope dilemma between being careful of turning over things to an AI because we think it is superior, or being Luddite about it and refusing to allow AI systems to be used at all. As more AI-based technology becomes available to meet our needs, we need to start taking these kinds of issues into account. Some people believe we can solve these dilemmas by programming ethics into the computer; others argue that we need to keep people in the loop rather than letting the AIs become the decision makers. Some of these attitudes have been shaped by the pictures of the future that have been painted by some of our most talented science fiction writers.

---

[14]https://en.wikipedia.org/wiki/Flash_crash
[15]Growing up with Technology, http://online.purdue.edu/ldt/learning-design-technology/resources/growing-up-with-technology, 2016.

Science fiction writers often borrow from science and then go beyond it to weave a story of some future. Some of the futures show how technology can enhance our lives and some show the darker side. Although it is fiction, the people reading the stories might get some good ideas for building technology or for enhancing existing technology. Think of Isaac Asimov's three laws of robotics: a robot may never injure a human being or through inaction allow a human being to come to harm; a robot must obey orders given it by human beings except where such orders could conflict with the first law; and a robot must protect its own existence as long as such protection does not conflict with the first or second laws[16]. Now that we have many different types of robots in our everyday lives, some technologists and standards committees are starting to reference Asimov's laws, and determine if and how they should be implemented as a way to control the ever-expanding field of robotics.

Artificial intelligence is also a common theme in many science fiction stories. In some stories, the AI starts off being very useful and helpful to humans. If it starts to make its own decisions, and if some of those decisions are contrary to what the human wants, like the sentient computer Hal in the story/movie *2001 Space Odyssey* by Arthur C. Clark shown in theaters in 1968, then the AI is viewed as corrupt and beyond control (Figure 8-3).

Figure 8-3. Hal interacting with Dave in the movie 2001 Space Odyssey (Permission CC-BY Cryteria)

In some stories, the AI is there to augment a human, providing the human with better sensing capabilities and reasoning such as described in the book *The Terminal Man* by Michael Crichton (1972). However, once in place, some science fiction stories describe how people can discover unethical ways to use the technology. For example, in *The Terminal Man*, a computer scientist who specializes in AI gets in a car crash and develops psychomotor epilepsy. As a cure, he has electrodes

---

[16]Asimov, Isaac, "Runaround", published in *Astounding Science Fiction,* March, 1942.

implanted in his head that are intended to stop a seizure. (Today this would be similar to having a neuro-stimulator device implanted. In the book it is referred to as a brain pacemaker.) There are problems after the surgery, and the patient is considered psychotic and believes that machines are evil and will eventually take over the world. In the book, moral and ethical issues are raised when another character wants electrodes implanted to stimulate pleasure, showing how technology can be used in potentially inappropriate ways.

Sometime the AI described in a story provides a benefit to a human, like keeping the thoughts of a person alive after they have physically died, thereby providing comfort to their loved ones, or providing a way to live indefinitely. Many stories by Robert Sawyer, like *Rollback* (2007), are of this nature. In *Rollback*, a 60-year-old scientist is able to undergo a special process called Rollback that reverts his body to a much younger state. However, when this process is tried on his 80-year-old wife, it fails. This raises all types of emotional and ethical issues for both characters.

In a book called *Diamond Age*, by Neal Stephenson (1995), a little girl obtains a stolen copy of a special book that you can communicate with and it can learn about you. The special book can advise the reader about having a more interesting life, and teach them what they need to know to survive and develop; but its intended for use by the privileged few. A lot of culture and social issues are discussed because the little girl should never have had the book, but because she does, she is able to cross some cultural boundaries. Note that some versions of this type of interactive computing technology are starting to be developed to support personalized education, potentially raising issues about whether it is used widely in society or for the benefit of a privileged few.

In many science fiction books, there are sections where someone is selling the technology and somebody else is questioning the ethical issues of the technology. As an example, in the movie *Total Recall*, which is adapted from the story *We can remember it for you wholesale* by Philip K. Dick (2006), people can have certain memories deleted or added. The movie gives a glimpse into the types of problems that can arise if the human starts to remember little fragments that should have been forgotten or can't distinguish what memories are real from what are synthesized. In this movie, a memory treatment is presented as a form of entertainment. In other stories, like *Factoring Humanity* by Robert Sawyer (2004), having memories changed or augmented is a viewed as a procedure similar to cosmetic surgery. Will such modifications to our ability to remember be considered cosmetic or entertaining in the future?

Because of so many societal problems associated with dementia, a variety of memory devices that use cognitive computing technology are starting to become available to augment people's memories. Virtual reality technologies are also starting to be marketed to support people with dementia or to enable those who can't travel to use virtual reality methods to form new memories. How soon might the memory enhancing capabilities showcased in the movie *Total Recall* or the book *Factoring Humanity* become available?

Another dimension that many people have more ethical and moral concerns about is the ability of a robot to have emotions, consciousness, free will, and other attributes considered to define humanity. In the book *Do androids dream of electric sheep?* by Philip K. Dick (1968) and the associated movie *Blade Runner*, there are investigators who hunt down and destroy synthetic humanoids who have human-like characteristics. Some of the humanoids display a wide array of emotions and develop relationships with each other and in some cases with humans. The movie highlights how difficult it might eventually become to distinguish a human from a machine. Will we ever have synthetic machines that we develop deep emotional bonds with? Will our children have best friends that are their synthetic companions? Just think about the main android character in the movie *Bicentennial Man*, which is based on the novel *The Positronic Man* by Isaac Asimov and Robert Silverberg (1993). The main android character is a robot servant who supports a family. Many of the family members grow up with the robot servant and develop deep emotional attachments to it. The robot also grows emotionally attached to the human family and has to "suffer" as it watches its human family grow up and die. Will this type of relationship between humans and machines become a reality?

While no one has a crystal ball that can allow them to look into the distant future, there is a saying, "if you can think it, you can build it." How high is the probability that thoughts presented in science fiction become reality through science and technology? Some of the technologists and scientists who are voicing their concerns about AI and similar technologies believe that the probability is high and that many science fiction thoughts will become science. If they are correct, then how do we become prepared?

In exploring these questions, are we looking at the proverbial "robot apocalypse," like that showcased in a very early science fiction movie called *Metropolis* by Fritz Lang (1927) where men work to keep machines operational? Or is there, as we have argued, a middle ground where people are working with enhanced humans and sophisticated computer technology to solve problems, like in the *Minority Report*, based on the story "Minority Report" by Philip K. Dick (1956) where human precogs (who are sometimes used in inhumane ways) and other types of analysis and prediction technologies help people solve certain problems, like criminal investigations? Note that Minority Report is often used as an example when discussing some of the capabilities of big-data analytics which are based, in turn, on AI machine-learning technologies.

While science fiction might help us to think of future possibilities, we need to put a concentrated effort into trying to build the proper scaffolding for potential futures. Even the best predictive algorithms cannot guarantee what will really be; they only showcase a set of possibilities. Humans have the power to shape their own future, and they can use machines to help.

Managing Cognitive Support Technology

If AI-based applications and technologies are to become commonly accepted, there need to be more effective ways to manage the technology and to safeguard the user. Many AI applications tune their services by learning about their user. This occurs during a variety of transactions, including those in contexts where the AI is sharing data about the user with other systems, as in the example of planning to take a trip. During these transactions, when information about the user is being provided, there is an opportunity for the data to be used incorrectly, especially when the context is different.

The Internet of Things (IoT) offers an opportunity for our homes to become interconnected with each other, to get upgrades from the Internet, to be controlled remotely by a human, and to learn how the human(s) who live in the home prefer their environment to be. As the IoT gets accepted, the AI-based cognitive computing technologies that are being developed to provide personalized support to a human will likely use data from the human's home environment to learn even more about the user. Some of this information might be very private, which raises the challenge of how to keep private data private.

Already we are beginning to see intelligent monitoring technology being used in nursing homes to monitor some of the living space of seniors. The idea behind this technology is that if some abnormality is detected, such as reduced motion in a unit for too long, a message will be sent to care givers that the person in the unit has fallen or is sick and requires assistance.

In addition to using standard monitoring equipment such as cameras for observing environments, there is a growing trend toward embedding microprocessors into everyday objects so that the objects can directly communicate information. This technology is often referred to as *pervasive computing* or *ubiquitous computing*. The words *pervasive* and *ubiquitous* mean "existing everywhere." Pervasive computing devices are completely connected and constantly available. One of the goals of researchers working in pervasive computing is to create *smart* products that are connected to the Internet and the data they generate can be easily used by other smart products[17].

Likely consumers of ubiquitous smart devices are health organizations because they are interested in monitoring the health of an individual, of groups, of societies, and of the entire world population. The adoption of ubiquitous health monitoring technologies is already raising serious ethical considerations. For example, the *CareMedia* project is an example of a pervasive direct observational approach that collects personally identifiable data (facial and body images, voice, etc.) about an individual who is in a nursing home or other care environment. This tool uses sensors to collect data, and machine learning algorithms to detect trends that constitute the normal behavior and to identify deviations from normal behavior (both physical and social) for an individual or group of individuals. Because it can do this, it seems to be

---

[17]Carnegie Mellon University, "CareMedia: Automated Video and Sensor Analysis for a Geriatric Care, NSF Cooperative agreement no IIS-0205219, annual progress report", 2004; http://internetofthingsagenda.techtarget.com/definition/pervasive-computing-ubiquitous-computing.

ideally situated to proactively assist care providers in detecting physical and emotional changes from an individual's prior baseline[18]. However, use of this data raises ethical issues because the personal data it collects, such as when somebody eats, who they socialize with, or when they show aggressive behavior, if used out of context or by an unethical person, could lead to adverse effects for the individual. For example, if a person in a care facility displays aggressive behavior and if that behavior is generalized beyond the limited contexts of when it occurs, a person could be given unnecessary medications to control the behavior.

Earlier in this book, we mentioned the fact that machines are limited in acquiring world knowledge. Devices that are connected through the Internet, coupled with machine learning algorithms and cognitive computing technologies that can learn through experience, could provide a sufficient conduit to help AI based machines more quickly and fully acquire knowledge about the world. This is especially true if the environment is bounded as in a hospital, nursing home, or home healthcare setting. Once issues of protecting privacy have been addressed, these sensing and analysis technologies could improve the lives of many people, especially those with physical, social, and cognitive disabilities, by improving their care and quality of life.

Some organizations are already evaluating some of the ethical and privacy issues associated with the use of these assistive technologies. The Alzheimer's Association Working Group on Technologies[20] has recently proposed guidelines for assistive technology that is intended to help in-home persons with dementia. Likewise, the United States Department of Health and Human Services has published a report, *Barriers to Implementing Technology in Residential Long-Term Care Settings*[21], that offers researchers guidance and approaches to facilitate the successful and ethical implementation of these types of technologies.

EMBRACING NEW TECHNOLOGY

Embracing new technology, especially technology that is personal, has autonomy, or that you allow to take control, has always presented challenges. For example, consider the changes that have been made over the past hundreds of years to allow humans to travel from place to place. Early records about human migration indicate that walking was the primary way that people traveled. This even applied to travel across great distances, as evidenced by old trade routes used by traders in ancient Asia or by the travel of large groups, such as the American Indians during seasonal migrations. People not only walked, they carried their goods on their backs. This changed once horses and other animals were domesticated. Horses were used to not only carry goods and supplies, but to transport people. Once horses were

---

[18]Bharucha, A., J. et. al., "Intelligent Assistive Technology Applications to Dementia Care: Current Capabilities, Limitations, and Future Challenges", *American Journal Geriatric Psychiatry*, 17(2): 88-104, Feb 2009, www.ncbi.nlm.nih.gov/pmc/articles/PMC2768007/#R66.
[19]www.alz.org/research/funding/alzheimers_research_partnerships.asp
[20]https://aspe.hhs.gov/basic-report/barriers-implementing-technology-residential-long-term-care-settings

attached to carriages or wagons, the horse and carriage combination was used to carry more people or more supplies. This is also an example of an early situation where the human is working with a non-human (the horse) and where one or more humans give up control and must place trust in a driver (the carriage or wagon driver) to control and navigate the transportation device. Like modern AI technology of today, many people were probably reluctant to trust a horse and carriage for transport, especially over very long distances. Just think about early pioneers in their horse and wagon caravans and some of the challenges they faced like irregular landscape, disease, robbers, and other attacks.

Now let's consider the impact that the railroad made on people's lives. With the railroad, a person or a group of people could travel faster, in more comfort, and with less physical threats than in wagon caravans. Usage of trains required that the rail infrastructure be provided. While the development of the railroad network resulted in many jobs, it was resisted by people who did not want the train rails on their land. As the railroad became adopted, a set of rules and regulations were developed to manage how trains could be used, the times they could operate, how they should behave when they intersect with other transportation infrastructure, etc. Additionally, as trains became more commonly available, people stopped thinking about how they moved or any potential threats they might present. Today, people socialize, work, read, or even sleep during the train ride.

While people accepted the train as a good form of transportation, with a train as the form of transportation a person could only travel where train tracks were in place. Motor cars provided more freedom and options for travel and thereby provided the driver with more autonomy. As drivers became accustomed to autonomy, and developed trust and acceptance in automotive technology, the demand for the highway system that we enjoy today was initiated.

We are now being introduced to autonomous vehicles that will offer some of the benefits that the railroad offered. Autonomous cars will eventually be able to transport us along all of the road and highways that we have created without us having to control the vehicle. This convenience will allow us to think of other things and to do other tasks while we travel. While early versions of these vehicles will still allow a human to gain control of the vehicle, the ultimate goal of the autonomous vehicle is to free the passenger from being involved in the transportation process and trust the vehicle to get them to where they want to be safely and on time (Figure 8-4).

Figure 8-4. *Google's new self-driving car prototype (by Michael Shick, own work,
CC BY-SA 4.0,* https://commons.wikimedia.org/w/index.php?curid=44405988*)*

This example about the evolution and improvements in transportation is intended
to remind the reader about many people's early resistance to many of the forms of
transportation that are commonly available today. It is also intended to serve as an
analogy for how AI technology has and will continue to transform. While certain AI
technologies that are being used to support robots that clear a mine field or enter
a disaster area are being embraced, other uses of AI technology are meeting with
doubt and resistance. For example, although AI technology is poised to help people
with cognitive problems and to become the basis of personalized decision support
systems, it could expose people to privacy issues and even identity theft. As with the
transportation example, we expect an improved communications infrastructure will
be created, along with standards, rules, and regulations as AI-based personalized
assistants, cognitive computing technologies, and self-driving cars (which may also
need special infrastructure developed so that they can operate efficiently) become
more widely available, reliable, and accepted.

Extending and Maintaining Cognitive Computing Technology

Assistive technologies and AI technologies can offer ways to enrich the lives of people
with both physical and cognitive impairments, and these technologies can also provide
healthy individuals with a varity of methods to extend themselves. Wearable technology,
pervasive technology, and cognitive computing technologies may help us enhance our
perception, enhance our creativity, enrich our social interactions, and offset our physical
and medical limitations. As we become reliant on AI (for example to help us with memory
loss) how will changes such as software and hardware upgrades affect us? This is an
important, and largely ignored, threat–and it is real and critical to the future.

Let's assume that cognitive computing AI technology becomes commonly affordable and available like cell phones are today, and people start to rely on (and even depend on) AI assistive technologies to help them think and perform tasks. If some of the users have cognitive disabilities, and their technology malfunctions or needs to be upgraded, who will provide the maintenance? Technology always seems to change, and there is little reason to believe that this will cease to be the case. Applications get introduced and some persist and evolve with new versions, like word processing tools, while some other applications go out of favor very quickly. Even sophisticated software programs that required a good deal of investment to develop, like some of the AI-based scheduling technology used to support military and commercial air planning, seem similarly fated. Additionally, hardware changes generally require software to be upgraded. There is no doubt that hardware will continue to change, so that indicates that the software, including AI applications, will also need to change so that it can operate on new hardware.

Just think of how film, photo, and music media have changed over the past 50 years. Why would one not expect the same changes to happen to sophisticated computing technology? It is not uncommon for software that ran on a computer in 2000 to not even be transferable or readable by a computer built in 2016! As AI technologies are introduced and used, will they, and how will they persist as hardware, software, networks, infrastructure, and society changes?

In addition to considering issues about how AI technology should be maintained, there are certain issues associated with the establishment and maintenance of standards for using these technologies that need to addressed. For example, if we do start to use AI devices to extend our capabilities, will regulations be developed that delimit what tasks the AI technology can perform (like booking a vacation) and what tasks require human approval (when to have a child, who to marry)? Should there be a different set of standards that regulate autonomous behavior by AI assistants? Who will be responsible for developing and for enforcing such regulations?

Additionally, will there be regulations and options for allowing the human to interact or override the technology decisions? Will there be methods to verify that the human user is in the proper state of mind and health to delegate certain tasks to the AI assistant? Will there always be certain tasks that require the participation of a human? Interestingly, even at this early phase of this technology becoming available, humans are being cautioned to continue to pay attention to what their technologies are monitoring. For example, on a web site[21] advertising smart, technologically enhanced wearable baby clothes there is a section titled "Don't forget to be human", reminding the reader that they should observe and interact with their own baby.

How do AI technologies evolve from what they can offer now to what they might be capable of offering in the future? For example, one of the challenges that today's computer technology faces is the fact that human behaviors vary by context, mood, emotion, and how we feel at any particular time. While there is some active research focused on some of these issues, like dealing with mood and emotion, if a sophisticated cognitive computing agent does not have knowledge of all of these multidimensional characteristics, how can it provide us with the type of support that we need, when we need it, and in a form that we can trust? Simply monitoring and using machine learning

---

[21] www.wearables.com/5-baby-monitors-wearable-infant-tech/

algorithms to learn about our interactions with our environments does not seem to be sufficient. We need a way for the human user or for some person who is helping the human user to teach the sophisticated computer assistants to do what we want them to do. In other words, how are we to deal with a common problem faced by parents who often say to their children, "Don't do what I do; do what I say"? Obviously while learning by observation is a good way to learn about things in the world and actions to take in certain contexts, it is not enough to actually know why you are taking an action, or when you should take an action. For example, how should a computer behave when we are under stress or perhaps are experiencing some social or even psychological problems (having just broken up with a significant other, for example)? Should computers learn how to interpret some of what we say and/or tell them to do with some level of mistrust as a function of the context? If so, when and how should this be done, and who decides?

Clearly there are other ethical dimensions that must be considered. In recent times there has been a steady stream of articles in the press on the subject of how AI systems, and robots in particular, are about to begin challenging humans in the job market, and that administrative and production jobs are most under threat. In the US, even the administration of President Obama has sounded a cautionary note about the large number of people who could be put out of work by robots and AI in the next decades, asking for an investment in education and training to make sure we will not end up with nearly an entire generation out of work. The advent of increased cognitive computing adds to this challenge, as it increases the jobs that are at risk to include those that might normally require specialized training (such as legal assistants, tax preparers, etc.)

However, as another example shows, AI still has a long way to go. It appears that the massive variation of customization options for cars like the Mercedes S-Class has been overwhelming the robots and the company has had no choice but to hire some humans to do the job for them. It's telling that the reason for the company's returning to human labor is that robots were not able to cope with the complexity of the situation in the plant - programming in all the possibilities for all the combinations was beyond the capability of the day - and even with new learning technologies, people are, at least for now, the better alternative. This sort of flexibility is another hallmark of human reasoning as we discussed back in Chapter 5. (Of course, one human and a team of robots is still less jobs than a team of humans, so the social challenge remains even as we look at mixed AI/human teams.)

The Limits of Learning

Earlier in the book, we described how data mining and knowledge discovery techniques often require domain-specific knowledge to function properly and how the knowledge can bias results. We described some of the work being done to enhance the World Wide Web, and resolve issues about varying interpretations. As the fusion of AI, social computing, and many of the new technologies we have described in this book become a reality, and cognitive computing tools develop more capability of autonomously finding relationships in knowledge, some measures of credibility will need to be created in order to guarantee that these systems generate solutions or suggestions for actions that are considered reasonable by humans or larger social organizations.

Consider the following example. Assume that deep learning image recognition algorithms are used to interpret some of the images in Figure 8-5. Assume that once the objects like bird, dog, person, or chair are identified through the algorithms, that they are then mapped to one or more existing sets of rules where relationships with other objects emerge. Assume also that some deep learning algorithms discover texts from open source web data or from private correspondences that confirm the existence of certain relationships between some of the objects. Assume that it finds the following sentences:

- The person walked her dog.

- The bird flew outside the window.

- The little girl sat on a chair and watched a bird flying outside her window.

Deep-learning Image Recognition

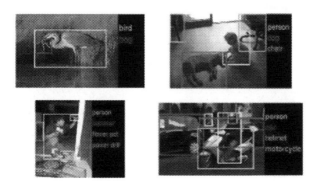

Figure 8-5. *Deep learning image recognition examples. (With permission)*

Assume that it uses these sentences to learn the following: a bird flies, and a girl (who is a person) can sit on a chair and can walk a dog. What sample size should the algorithm use to confirm these relationships? Who determines what the sample size should be? Who determines that what the algorithm learned is correct?

Now imagine that additional knowledge is mined from texts, from crowd sourcing, or provided by a human. Let's assume that the AI reasoning system is asked to answer the questions that are listed in Figure 8-6.

Adding knowledge?

Which could you sit in?
What is most likely to bite what?
Which one is most likely to become a lawyer someday?

...

Figure 8-6. *Adding knowledge about objects to a knowledge base*

For the question "Which could you sit in?", information from available sources indicate that the chair seems to be the most reasonable answer. For the question "What is most likely to bite what?", the AI system might be able to use some database to quickly rule out the chair as the answer, and it could use a statistical analysis tool to find that dogs tend to bite people more than people bite dogs. For the question "Which one is most likely to become a lawyer someday?", the system could use available data sources to discover that lawyers are typically people, and it will probably not be able to find any instances where dogs or chairs have become lawyers. But, what happens if the AI is presented with the question in Figure 8-7?

Adding knowledge?

Which could you sit in?
What is most likely to bite what?
Which one is most likely to become a lawyer someday?

If you could only save one in an emergency, which would you choose?

...

Figure 8-7. *How would an AI answer this question?*

What might an autonomous AI answer if asked "If you could only save one in an emergency, which would you choose"? If it looked at disaster relief data, it would find that animals and people are typically saved in an emergency, so it could reduce the answer to either dog or person. But what other criterion would the system use to determine which to save? How long would it need to make the decision? What would happen if it made the wrong choice? Who would determine that an answer was wrong and would there be some way to coach the AI to make a different answer? If crowdsourcing was used and more people voted for the dog, would the system make that the answer because it had the highest score?

This example is just a teaser for the types of questions that cognitive reasoning systems of the future might need to answer. These issues are examples of challenges some scientists predict that humans will face as machines gain access to more data, obtain full autonomy, become more integrated with society, and develop an ability to adapt and evolve.

The Wisdom of the Crowd or the Madness of the Mob

In Chapter 7, we discussed the idea of "wikiality" and used the humorous example of Stephen Colbert getting his fans to change the facts on the Wikipedia page about elephants. A more interesting example of a "crowd gone wrong" is that of Microsoft's "chatbot" named Tay. Deployed in March of 2016, Tay was an AI learning-based system that would engage people in conversation and learn from what they said. Tay was based on an earlier chatbot called Xiaolce that had been deployed in China, and had learned to tell stories and to have amusing conversations with users. Tay, deployed on Twitter in the United States, was not so lucky. Due to a number of people sending inappropriate messages, within a day Tay had begun sending neo-Nazi tweets, denying the Holocaust, and saying very sexist things. Details have not been released, but from the tweets that can be found in Twitter searches, it is clear that some of these were from users who were aware of Tay's status and intentionally trying to cause trouble, but also from others who were, basically, following the crowd. They appeared to be people who endorsed the hate speech that was happening or enjoyed the "trolling" they were observing. This effect of people creating an online "mob" caused Tay to learn things that were clearly outside the norm of social discourse and not what Microsoft had in mind when they released it. Within a day they had to shut down the experiment and publish an apology.[22]

Unfortunately, Tay's experience is indicative of one of the paradoxes of the openness of the World Wide Web and the social interactions it allows. An early expectation was that the "democratization" of information production allowed by social media, and enhanced through social machines, would cause people to see less biased news than they might see through "official" channels. Unfortunately, a tendency towards *homophily* (a preference for people who are like themselves) leads many people to friend or follow those who believe as they do and unfriend those whose opinions they don't agree with. As a result, they receive information in an information bubble that reinforces their own beliefs and

---

[22]http://blogs.microsoft.com/blog/2016/03/25/learning-tays-introduction/

leads to hardening of opinions. Search engines often try to overcome these biases by trying to mix sources, but social media allows self-selection and biases to grow. Attempts to measure these so-called social filter bubbles are ongoing,[23] and the impacts on society are widely debated among economists, philosophers, social scientists, and AI researchers. In his book *The Filter Bubble,* author Eli Pariser warns that the bubble effect will have a growing and increasingly significant negative impact on social discourse,[24] while other studies show less of an effect.

Whichever may be the case with respect to filter bubbles, one of the other challenges on the open Web is that the same social machine technologies that can be used for social good, such as Ushahidi and IPaidABribe (discussed in Chapter 7), can also be used by those whose beliefs may be at odds with standard social norms. Social media is heavily used for recruiting by hate groups and terrorist organizations, and the ability to create more powerful social machines are sure to be taken advantage of by these same groups. On the other hand, the openness of the social machine, which works best when it is open to the maximum number of users, also makes these groups more transparent to others, and often causes either political or social repercussions that can make it harder for the groups to function. Taken to an extreme, these responses can also lead to censorship and suppression, repressing the very social processes needed to balance out the extremism.

This somewhat depressing style plays out in our day-to-day information world, with more social machines and better AI leading to both strong positives and potential downsides. Clearly, the same has been true of society since before the coming of the Internet, AI, and social machines, but these specific technologies have the potential to scale up the effects and speed up the disruptive changes that they can cause.

The future of this technology is hard to predict because the increasing power of networks of humans, supported by networks of increasingly powerful machines, is becoming an important technology that is increasingly being used to deal with the big problems of our times (as proposed in Chapter 7). It will also be a major challenge to an increasingly online world where social values cross the boundaries between online and offline activities. How we decide to deal with these technologies in different parts of the world may have more to do with societies, governments, and cultures than with the technologies themselves.

---

[23]Nikolov, D., Oliveira, D.F.M., Flammini, A., Menczer, F., "Measuring online social bubbles", *PeerJ Computer Science,* 1:e38, https://doi.org/10.7717/peerj-cs.38.
[24]Pariser, Eli, *The filter bubble: How the new personalized web is changing what we read and how we think,* Penguin, 2011.

CHAPTER 9

■ ■ ■

Conclusion: Social Machines and the New Future

The goal we had in writing this book was to help the reader understand both the human factors and the key computer technologies that are driving rapid and potentially disruptive changes in the way we live. As we've discussed, computers have been moving from passive information providers living on desktop machines to active participants in our social sphere. The infrastructure of the Internet and the World Wide Web allows the proliferation of new applications, and our social interactions with machines provide them with new information that let them learn more about us and our world.

The humans' role in this is often not aimed at improving the capabilities of the machine; they are solving problems, having fun, and living their lives using the new capabilities afforded by increasingly "intelligent" mobile applications and new devices. Some interactions may be passive, as programs that assist us increasingly become more attuned to our lives and needs. Some may be active, such as marking up galaxies or providing information about medical conditions to help other patients cope better with their situations. The benefits that these new capabilities provide to people are manifest. Messaging with friends allows for rapid communication, buying things online makes for more choices with less shopping, dating and finding partners in life is now possible starting with an application like Tinder or one of the many dating web sites online. Telecommuting can help us avoid rush hours, having an "on demand" autonomous car service can make things easier when travel is needed, and so on.

The programs at the heart of these apps and devices appear to be becoming increasingly smarter. The data that is generated as a side effect of human computer interaction provides programs with a growing ability to mine data and make connections between concepts. In essence, thanks to all of the interactions that they can access in our lives, machines have essentially become smarter. Artificial intelligence programs benefit when they can combine heuristic algorithms, such as those used in game playing, with human-generated information coming from the sorts of interactions above, from mining the Web, or from machine-learning using information humans provide for each other, but which the machine can access online (such as Wikipedia articles).

© James Hendler and Alice M. Mulvehill 2016
J. Hendler and A. M. Mulvehill, *Social Machines*, DOI 10.1007/978-1-4842-1156-4_9

As we move into the future, AI will likely have an even larger role in our lives, our societies, and in the environment in which we live. The movement toward an internet of things will increasingly allow real-world objects like our home thermostats, microwave ovens, washers, and dryers to be connected. The additional data that these objects provide will enable AI algorithms to further predict what we may do (and especially buy) which in turn will drive the development of new capabilities.

As we have tried to show, the increasing use of our data, combined with new technologies in learning and cognitive computing, are increasing the capabilities of computational intelligence. However, as we have discussed, machines still have severe limitations that require human input; in the coming years, interactions with professionals such as doctors will be increasingly effective as machines provide the humans with more information, but humans can use their training, experience, and intuition to make better decisions, especially when faced with complex contexts.

The speed with which this technology is moving is also unsettling. When we started writing this book, we discussed why it would be really hard for an AI system to ever beat a human at the game of Go. At our first rewrite, we had to update that chapter to say that new technologies were making it possible that a computer might be reaching human-level play. Before the page proofs came, we were rewriting again to talk about AlphaGo's feat in beating one of the best human players.

Similarly, new social machines are coming online all the time. For example, as we are going to press, a new game has come online that looks like it will have a big impact on exploring human cell proteins. Researchers in Sweden, using the games-with-a-purpose approach, have created an online crowdsourcing game called Project Discovery that can help explore human cell proteins. In the spring of 2016, they were able to integrate it with a popular commercial multiplayer video game called Eve Online (which has about 500,000 subscribers). In the first month of play, the Eve gamers classified about eight million protein elements![1]

Projects like this show that we can continue to create and refine social machine technologies that can increasingly take advantage of the way that large numbers of people can network together to support real-world problems. With the help of other humans interacting with increasingly smart machines, we will be able to achieve many things that we cannot currently do. If history is to be our guide, these increasingly powerful technologies will also change attitudes towards the information generated by the social interactions. For example, while there are health sites like PatientsLikeMe that allow people to find others who have similar health problems, medical professionals are generally skeptical about basing results on information reported on this site. The reasons as to why may vary, but as healthcare researchers and professionals become more educated about the power, and the limits, of AI technology, they will be better able to recognize how to use this information and to benefit more from social media and machine learning. This kind of information is already leading to a shift in the way that healthcare data is collected and analyzed, and this in turn will make a difference in how healthcare is provided. The future technologies addressed in Chapter 2 asking "who will be your next doctor?" are already being explored in labs around the world, and some are making their way into clinical trials, new medications, etc.

---

[1]Hotz, R. L., "Videogamers Wanted: to Fight TB", *The Wall Street Journal*, May 4, 2016.

As we see the results of these technologies coming into our lives, we are at a point where new AI technologies sometimes seem like magic. But when we encounter the limits of these techniques, there is often disillusionment with AI that can occur. However, as new technologies increasingly bring together humans and machines, many of these limitations can be overcome. To get there, it is critically important that we don't think of the machines as either idiots (when we see the limits) or super intelligent monsters (when they again move on). Rather, as we have discussed throughout, it is critical that we don't downplay the importance of humans in the dynamic. AlphaGo won in part because it had many human games to study. Watson could win at Jeopardy because of all of the people who created the articles in Wikipedia and other online information sources. Project Discovery is making medical breakthroughs because of the many human gamers who are joining in the pursuit. In short, for the foreseeable future, it is the intersection of human and machine where the most power lies. To put it another way, AI gains its greatest power when it is empowering humans.

We realize that a decade from now (2026) much of the "future" technology described in this book will be either commonplace or even outdated. Early social networking sites like Facebook and Twitter and early voice-based agents like Siri and Cortana will be refined or replaced with systems that will be more personalized and more capable of leveraging the growing technology of AI and the Web. Some smart technologies like self-driving cars are easy to imagine being available in the not too distant future. In fact, a more controlled subset of self-driving vehicles, long distance trucks, are now being proposed for usage to allow long-distance truck drivers to rest while these smart trucks self-navigate interstate highways. Current taxi[2] services across the United States are facing potential extinction because of other transportation options like Lyft and Uber that use GPS, the Internet, and AI-based scheduling and charging technologies to support mobile apps that allow a person to book an available vehicle. And self-driving taxis might very soon find a market, once early adopters try them, test them, and then advertise to their friends via social media the pros and cons of the service.

There will undoubtedly be negative consequences to humanity as a result of the development and usage of the social machine technologies described in this book. Although some current occupations might cease to exist, new occupations will be created to keep up with the advances in technology, and to manage and maintain the integrity of services provided by new technologies. People are creative, and humanity is adaptive. As history has demonstrated, people tend to find ways to benefit from change, and they develop creative approaches for mitigating both known and suspected risks and challenges. Before technologies that have the potential to help humanity at large with managing diseases such as cancer or providing support to global epidemics become widely adopted, humans will want to be certain that these technologies are reliable. Humans will want to evaluate how well AI-based systems track, model, and predict disasters in order to understand where the line is between what the machine can do and what only a human can do.

As social machines evolve, policies, standards, and some form of governance will need to be established (and regularly updated) to maintain human and machine integrity and to guarantee that new technological products meet certain quality control requirements. Developing these standards will require skills that few people

---

[2]www.scientificamerican.com/article/self-driving-taxis-may-hit-the-road-within-a-year/

possess today. Large groups of people will look at these problems during workshops and conferences. AI-based computers need to be help provide support for these conversations, helping people to make decisions that affect humanity and how machines can support humanity. Networks of humans with networks of computers are necessary in order to sufficiently attack big issues like cancer, climate change, education, social improvements, and so on.

As we have also discussed, the new technologies are also raising many questions that we are just beginning to explore. For example, if people can have AIs help them think and perform tasks, who will maintain those AIs? Humans like to enhance things as they encounter new problems, but will machines start to suggest what to enhance, decide what is important, or even argue with a human who insists on making some change? How will the machines determine if changes suggested by a human are reasonable, especially if the human is suffering from some cognitive or emotional disability? Decisions about the usage of new advanced technologies will need to be made in the coming years and these decisions will have significant impact on our lives, therefore, being aware of the trade-offs inherent in this technology space is important to understanding the world in which we will increasingly be living.

To conclude, in looking to the future, we think not primarily in terms of the cyberinfrastructure of high-speed supercomputers and their networked interconnections, but of the even more powerful human interactions these underlying systems enable when enhanced with artificially intelligent machines. The collision of humanity, artificial intelligence, and social networking is leading us into an exciting but challenging future. Together, these technologies will allow us to further empower the web of people by developing a next generation of web technologies and to move from *human in the loop* to *humanity in the loop*. To this new challenge we believe we must bring to bear not only the best engineering and theoretical perspectives of computer science, but also a keen awareness of the underlying challenges. Managing the change will require intelligent decisions on policies and restrictions made by people who understand the technologies, not based on science fiction stories or the challenges of philosophers.

To go back to where we started this book: we are living in interesting times. It is sure to be a time of great change, much promise, and many challenges. We hope we have given you a starting place that will let you cut through the hype, better judge the articles written by reporters who likely know less than you do, and get a better feel for the AI technologies that will increasingly be part of this amazing social machine in which we all live.

Index

© James Hendler and Alice M. Mulvehill 2016
J. Hendler and A. M. Mulvehill, *Social Machines*, DOI 10.1007/978-1-4842-1156-4

Get the eBook for only $5!

Why limit yourself?

Now you can take the weightless companion with you wherever you go and access your content on your PC, phone, tablet, or reader.

Since you've purchased this print book, we're happy to offer you the eBook in all 3 formats for just $5.

Convenient and fully searchable, the PDF version enables you to easily find and copy code—or perform examples by quickly toggling between instructions and applications. The MOBI format is ideal for your Kindle, while the ePUB can be utilized on a variety of mobile devices.

To learn more, go to www.apress.com/companion or contact support@apress.com.

All Apress eBooks are subject to copyright. All rights are reserved by the Publisher, whether the whole or part of the material is concerned, specifically the rights of translation, reprinting, reuse of illustrations, recitation, broadcasting, reproduction on microfilms or in any other physical way, and transmission or information storage and retrieval, electronic adaptation, computer software, or by similar or dissimilar methodology now known or hereafter developed. Exempted from this legal reservation are brief excerpts in connection with reviews or scholarly analysis or material supplied specifically for the purpose of being entered and executed on a computer system, for exclusive use by the purchaser of the work. Duplication of this publication or parts thereof is permitted only under the provisions of the Copyright Law of the Publisher's location, in its current version, and permission for use must always be obtained from Springer. Permissions for use may be obtained through RightsLink at the Copyright Clearance Center. Violations are liable to prosecution under the respective Copyright Law.

Printed in the United States
By Bookmasters